D0225945

DATE			

DISCARD

© THE BAKER & TAYLOR CO.

NURTURING ADVANCED TECHNOLOGY ENTERPRISES

Nurturing Advanced Technology Enterprises

Emerging Issues in State and Local Economic Development Policy

David N. Allen and Victor Levine

New York
Westport, Connecticut
London

Library of Congress Cataloging-in-Publication Data

Allen, David N.
    Nurturing advanced technology enterprises.

    Bibliography: p.
    Includes index.

    1. High technology industries—Government policy—
Pennsylvania. 2. Industrial promotion—Pennsylvania.
3. Industry and state—Pennsylvania. 4. Pennsylvania—
Economic policy. I. Levine, Victor. II. Title
HC107.P43H533 1986   338.4'762'0009748   86-9411
ISBN 0-275-92136-0 (alk. paper)

Library of Congress Catalog Card Number: 86-9411
ISBN: 0-275-92136-0 (alk. paper)

First published in 1986

Praeger Publishers, 521 Fifth Avenue, New York, NY 10175
A division of Greenwood Press, Inc.

Printed in the United States of America

∞™

The paper used in this book complies with the Permanent
Paper Standard issued by the National Information Standards
Organization (Z39.48-1984).

10 9 8 7 6 5 4 3 2 1

This book is dedicated to our parents, who nurtured and motivated us to advance in a technological world.

Preface

Virtually every day new technological advances and enterprise opportunities come to the fore. Our greatest challenge and frustration has been to keep abreast with changing developments. Because the central theme of this book concerns the changing economy and public policy responses, we must embrace the very dynamic that frustrates us.

We undertook this endeavor to fill a perceived void in an emerging area of public policy. Everywhere we turned people were clamoring about advanced technology and the hype seemed to ring louder than the substance. Silicon Valley, Route 128-Boston, and other emerging advanced-technology centers were reputed to be on the cutting edge of U.S. technological development. Could these success stories be emulated in other areas and, if so, what was the emerging role of government? Indeed would government even have a role in promoting the pioneer spirit of entrepreneurship as new frontiers of technology seem to emerge limitless to the imagination?

Although one of us was trained as a political economist and the other as a human resources economist, we had to constantly diversify our interests and sources in order to do justice to topics that are truly interdisciplinary. We are indebted to a large number of individuals who have led us in the right direction during our research and writing.

Among the many individuals whose assistance was invaluable, two gave us the impetus, support, and insight to initiate and complete this work. Walter H. Plosila, Deputy Secretary of Technology and Policy Development, Pennsylvania Department of Commerce and Gregg E. Robertson, the previous Director of the Pennsylvania MILRITE Council and now working for a growing information services firm, are examples of a rare breed of entrepreneurially oriented public officials that devise and implement the kind of programs discussed in this book. Other individuals employed by the Commonwealth of Pennsylvania who assisted in this work are Robert Coy, Roger Tellefsen, and Roz Weiss.

Many students, employed in various capacities as work study, graduate assistants, and faculty aides deserve mention: Cindy Bailey, Judy Ginsberg, Susan Marx, Jeffrey King, Carlton Berger, Sherry Stringer, Dillard Mosley, Susan Pine-Olson, Deborah Belt, Joseph Marie, Robert Holste, Gary Strausser, and Mark Batdorf. Additionally, other individuals provided assistance as readers or sounding boards: Amy

Glasmeier, Greg Balbierz, Mark Weinberg, Terri MacBride, and Frederick Norling. Three people were patient and gracious with their time in helping prepare the manuscript: Judy Musser, Peggy Repasky, and Lynn Kaltreider at Penn State and Michael J. Esposito at Praeger. Support was also provided by the Institute for Policy Research and Evaluation and the School of Education at The Pennsylvania State University. Finally, this research would not have reached completion had it not been for the steadfast support of Robert LaPorte, Jr., Director of the Institute of Public Administration at The Pennsylvania State University.

Contents

Tables and Figure

TABLES

xv

FIGURE

1 Technological Change and Development: An Introduction

OVERVIEW AND PURPOSE

Technological change influences economic, social, and cultural change. As technology becomes more sophisticated, the rate of change increases. Since colonial days, the United States has witnessed a major shift in what is produced, how it is produced, where it is produced, and who is involved in production. Production has moved substantially from the home to the firm – in colonial days about 80 percent of all clothes were home-produced. Today, some suggest that with the advent of the "electronic cottage," work may be migrating from the firm back to the home (Business Week 1984a).

In general, the shifts induced by innovation and technological advances in the United States have resulted in substantial net social gain. For example, in the 1930s about one-quarter of those employed were engaged in farming (U.S. Bureau of the Census 1984, p. 631). Today less than 3 percent of the work force not only feeds the nation but also produces a substantial surplus that generates important export income (U.S. Bureau of the Census 1984, p. 631).

As the United States moved headlong into the industrial era, the government began to help guide and stimulate economic activity. Not only has the government's share of the gross national product increased during the past 50 years [from 8.4 percent in 1933 to 10.6 percent in 1983 (U.S. Bureau of the Census 1984, p. 431)], but the government's direct and indirect role in allocating resources in the economy has also become pervasive. To counter market failure and stimulate economic

1

activity, governments pursue strategies of antitrust enforcement, economic regulation, social regulation, and direct participation in economic matters. Adaptations of these strategies, in the form of new and revised economic development policies and programs, have been formed as a response to changing economic conditions.

The change in the U.S. economy during the past ten years has been awesome. A variety of forces has converged to produce major social and economic advances and dislocations. The combined impact of energy price fluctuations, worldwide stagflation, the U.S. trade imbalance, budget deficits, productivity changes, international competition, changes in basic social institutions, demographic shifts, and fundamental technological advances has been enormous. The way goods and services are produced is undergoing a major transformation.

If one term seems to capture the essence of this rapid, contemporary economic transition, it is "advanced technology."[1] Advanced technology is believed to spur economic growth. Recognizing this, policymakers have reoriented development initiatives to attract and nurture advanced technology enterprises. No universal agreement exists, however, concerning the efficacy or desirability of these initiatives. Some harbor enormous hope that advanced technology will transform our economy, generate new jobs, and yield an overall higher standard of living. Others fear that advanced technology will render traditional jobs, skills, and ways of life obsolete.

Relatively few facts are available to support or disprove these generalizations. Although substantial literature exists on regional, national, and international economic development, relatively few empirical studies analyze the firm. Furthermore, much of the development literature focuses on the experiences of developing nations moving toward industrialization; the dynamics of movement toward a "post-industrial" economy are not as well understood. In this climate of conjecture, the United States has adopted no single industrial policy; most activities promoting advanced technology industries occur at the state level.

The state of Pennsylvania has been chosen as the context in which technological and entrepreneurial development policy will be discussed. Data collected from various primary and secondary sources will be used to portray the new face of economic development. Pennsylvania is an ideal "laboratory" for examining these issues because it is currently changing from a manufacturing-dominated economy to a diversified economy. In addition, Pennsylvania has gained wide acclaim for its innovative technological development policies (Pierce and Hagstrom 1983).

A central focus of this book is the changing nature of the U.S. economy and governmental policies promoting economic development. Specifically, the book focuses on how public policy may affect the behavior of advanced-technology firms and how the behavior of these firms, in turn, may affect the nation's social and economic environment. Public policy is a way of engineering change purposefully, and advanced technology is an important agent in that change.

ECONOMIC CHANGE AND ADVANCED TECHNOLOGY

Economic Growth and Jobs

Many people believe the United States is losing its international competitiveness. As recently as 1983, a prominent social theorist characterized the United States as an "underdeveloping country," a country "whose economic development had slipped into reverse gear" (Etzioni 1983, p. 677). In that year use of productive capacity reached its lowest point since the Great Depression. Two factors contributed to this trend: investment in the national infrastructure had dropped substantially, and investment in basic research had also declined.

The industrial prominence of the United States has been characterized by the introduction of technological innovations into production processes. While the United States once had a competitive advantage in its ability to inject new processes and technological advances into routine, large-scale production, manufacturing technologies now are easily exported and replicated. The United States may have to move away from the high-volume, standardized production that was the basis of its great prosperity in the post-World-War-II era to smaller-scale flexible manufacturing processes that are able to respond quickly to new market opportunities (Reich 1983).

Technological change is typically associated with increases in productivity. During the 1970s, however, attention was focused on relative productivity decreases in the U.S. work force and the implications of this decline for employment levels. During the same period, labor productivity in advanced-technology firms grew at six times the rate of the general business community (Business-Higher Education Forum 1983).

One implication of technological change is a shift in the work force. The percentage of the total national labor force employed in manufacturing declined from 24 percent in 1963 to 18.5 percent in 1981 (Coy 1984). One analyst predicts that in the United States, as many as 30 million jobs – half in manufacturing and half in service – may disappear within 20 years (Ehrbar 1983).

As traditional jobs disappear, high growth rates are seen in advanced-technology occupations and industries. Although these high rates of job expansion are not capable of compensating entirely for decreased manufacturing employment, the introduction of greater production efficiency through advanced technology will help offset the downward trend in manufacturing. Advanced technology will have a detrimental effect in many labor markets, but without advanced technology, U.S. losses of market share and jobs will be exacerbated.

Since advanced-technology employment constitutes a relatively small share of total employment, even high growth rates do not, in themselves, assure the creation of large numbers of jobs. Although advanced-technology firms are expected to generate about 1 million new jobs during the 1980s, the largest number of new jobs will be created in service occupations such as office-clerical worker, nurses' aide, and janitor (Bureau of the Census 1982). Even within the advanced-technology sector, not all new jobs will require high skill levels. For example, Jackman (1983, p. 36) describes the process by which a breakthrough in advanced cardiac pacemaker technology ultimately results in employment gains mostly by semiskilled and unskilled workers engaged in assembly-line activities. In certain areas where specialized high-level skills are required, the growth of advanced-technology firms may be inhibited by shortages of skilled workers.

Advanced Technology: State and Local Perspectives

Economic growth and employment issues are attracting increased state and local attention. Substantial public debate has focused upon the social costs of underused plants, the costs of migration, and competition between localities and states to attract and retain advanced-technology firms. It is unclear to what extent technological advances will permanently displace workers, but it is evident that new technology has resulted in substantial employment shifts among states and regions. New technological applications frequently require new plants and equipment. The rate of technological change, therefore, increases relocation since technological change generates obsolescence. In addition, the advanced-technology sector is less reliant on access to established facilities and services such as ports, railyards, raw materials, and power sources. Firms in the advanced-technology industries have been characterized as "footloose" (Roniger 1983). This movement of industrial facilities across state and international boundaries implies worker dislocation (Feller 1974).

The growth of the advanced-technology sector allegedly increases regional disparities. Dislocations in response to technological and price changes, which shift regional competitive advantage, are not unique to the advanced-technology era. In fact, the metropolitan Boston area, now a mecca of advanced-technology activity, experienced a sustained period of economic depression following the decline of the textile industry in the 1920s (Bluestone and Harrison 1982). The combination of surplus labor, depressed wages, and unused space resulting from this decline provided some of the conditions conducive to growth in the Boston area – the so-called "Route 128 phenomenon." The success of advanced-technology centers such as Silicon Valley in Santa Clara County, California, and Route 128 near Boston may preclude continued growth in these areas because of the increase in land value, wages, housing costs, pollution, and congestion brought about by success itself.

In the long run, market forces seem to prevail, resulting in net social gain. In the short run, however, the impact of the economic transition can be problematic, and much time may be necessary to approach equilibrium. Once shifts have been initiated, they can be self-sustaining for long periods of time. For example, the precipitous rise in energy costs in the mid-1970s contributed to the migration of plants, jobs, and income from the Northeast to the South and Southwest, changing substantially the income and tax base of state and local governments. At the same time, these energy price changes directly affected the relative well-being of these regions. "Because the U.S. buys about half of its energy consumption domestically, interregional transfers (of income) . . . have rivaled the much publicized transfers to OPEC in magnitude" (Burgaff 1983, p. 670). Furthermore, the demand for energy complements, such as automobiles, was depressed, affecting steel, coal, and auto production in the disadvantaged regions.

Inner cities are some of the most economically depressed areas in the United States. Recent gentrification by young professionals, the revival of downtown commercial districts, and the increase in service-sector employment have only minimally offset the social and economic maladies experienced by unskilled or otherwise disadvantaged individuals. An exodus of younger workers and reduced incomes for many who have stayed, due largely to a shifting of the economic base from manufacturing to services, has left inner cities with a disproportionate number of older and lower-class people who are more dependent on social service relief. Metropolitan areas, as opposed to inner cities, have generally benefited from the economic transformation and offer some attractive inducements for advanced-technology firms. Clearly, location and expansion decisions of advanced-technology managers (Chapter 4) are critical to an area's economic development.

Education and Human Resource Perspectives

Regardless of the cause of displacement (shifts in job structure, jobs lost to automation, jobs moving to new locations), a fundamental issue is the ability of displaced workers to find new jobs. Systematic differences in workers' ability to make employment adjustments is central to this concern. Occupational change frequently requires retraining; jobs in advanced-technology industries often require special skills and knowledge to use equipment or undertake training. As the rate of technological change increases, the need for ongoing retraining and self-education becomes more important.

Technological change has always involved new work roles and worker dislocation. The extent of dislocation currently being induced by advanced technology is not well understood. To develop policies for the country's future work force, information is needed about advanced-technology managers' decisions concerning job creation, plant location, training of new workers, and the role of higher education. These issues are examined in this book.

A related issue is the impact of advanced technology on the composition of the labor force. The 1970s witnessed a substantial shift in the sex and age composition of the labor force. Today, more women are working outside the home than ever before. Technology-induced changes affect the productivity and job prospects of these new workers. Technological change has a direct impact on women's participation in the labor force. Mechanization, in the form of labor-saving devices, has paved the way for many women to escape the confines of the home and has reduced the role of physical strength as a qualifying requirement of employment.

Older workers in particular are left behind by technological change. As workers approach retirement, employees and their employers have less incentive to invest in training; less time remains to receive a return on their investment. Moreover, learning may become more difficult as a worker ages. This whole process is exacerbated by shorter job cycles, that is, the period of time between changes in the core technologies of jobs (Choate 1982). Changes in the composition of the labor force contributed to labor productivity declines during the 1970s (Burgaff 1983). By the end of the century, the proportion of the population in the labor force will decline, increasing capital/labor ratios and labor productivity.

Technological change has major implications for the obsolescence of knowledge and human capital. Recurrent or lifelong learning may be essential in an era of technological change. This represents a radical departure from current employment policy. Additionally, questions exist about the resolve and adequacy of educators preparing students for tomorrow's jobs. The popular press frequently calls for increased collaboration between industry and institutions of higher education to facilitate research and improve curricula. But little is known about the factors that foster collaboration or the incentives for either institution to enter into such relationships. Universities are important in the emergence of a high-technology economy, yet this assertion has not received extensive systematic review (Levin 1984).

This review of economic transition and technological change suggests that economic development activity occurs in a dynamic, complex environment. One way to sort out what should and can be done to promote advanced-technology enterprise is to start at the beginning. Who are the major actors in technological development, and what are their objectives?

ECONOMIC-DEVELOPMENT OBJECTIVES

If state and local authorities are to promote technological development, they must understand the objectives of various actors in the development arena. Representatives from the public, educational, and private sectors serve their clientele with different interests. In most cases, mutual interests can be determined and partnerships created to satisfy the interests of the parties concerned.

Public-Sector Objectives

The primary objectives of nearly all public-sector development organizations are to create jobs and reduce unemployment. Little policy attention focuses on the quality of work, its durability, or the income-generation ability of new employment; if high-quality, stable, well-paying jobs are created, so much the better.

A corollary objective of job creation is job retention. Virtually all economic development programs creating jobs also count retained jobs, that is, jobs that otherwise would have been lost. In the realm of job retention, a broad conceptualization of advanced technology is particularly important. Although worker displacement by advanced technology is generally acknowledged, the substitution of capital in the form of new technology for labor will likely increase productivity. Increased value for the same or reduced levels of input means reduced product cost, higher product reliability, and retained or expanded market shares. These are important considerations given the intensity of international competition in many industries. Many persons, including labor leaders, now realize that reduced employment in a more competitive firm or industry is better than no employment at all. Similarly, recent evidence indicates that employment growth is greatest in firms and industries that learn to apply advanced technology to improve existing products and to create new ones (Birch 1984).

A second major objective of public-development policy is economic diversification. Industrial-development-attraction policies are predicated on the assumption that the siting of a large-scale facility reduces local unemployment. Although such development may reduce unemployment, it can also serve to magnify problems associated with geographic concentration of firms in a particular industry. Problems become acute when the industry is in long-term decline or in a downward phase of a boom-and-bust cycle, and when the displaced workers do not have transferable skills.

An area's heavy reliance on a particular industry has important long-term implications for economic development. The termination of manufacturing jobs usually means a glut of workers with roughly similar skills and knowledge. Although individuals may be able to establish new businesses based on their prior skills, trade opportunities for ventures that link backward into declining industries are limited. Other choices for displaced workers involve considerable costs: leave the area, retrain for new employment, or filter down to lower skill and wage levels. An inability to generate viable enterprise ideas in these local economies can produce long-term stagnation (witness the number of depressed coal mining regions in the world). In such areas, economic diversification becomes paramount because a singular focus on creating jobs in existing industries tends to entrench workers in a moribund local economy.

Higher-Education Objectives

Although many institutions of higher education are supported heavily by public funds, the motives for their involvement in economic development are different from job creation and economic diversification. Universities play an important role in innovation: through the pursuit of basic research, scientific findings are interpreted into new technologies (Tornatzky et al. 1983). Traditionally, university researchers have not followed through the process of adapting innovations derived from basic research to commercial products (Hise et al. 1980). Recent emphasis on industry collaboration and entrepreneurship on behalf of faculty members has bred new economic development missions for universities (Brown 1985). Universities see enterprise development and assistance activities as ways to obtain financial return for research supported by the institution; to create business employment opportunities for students and faculty; to increase local demand for educated workers; and to demonstrate to taxpayers, alumni, and other financial sources that the institution is making a positive contribution to state and local economies. Tangible rewards, such as industry and government funding and better qualified students; and intangible rewards, such as enhanced reputation and prestige, are the payoffs sought by higher-education institutions.

Private-Sector Objectives

The primary objective of private-sector participants in economic development programs is economic return. These participants are primarily interested either in high rates of return to offset high risk, or in reduced risks to assure a greater certainty of economic return, that is, investment protection. Those interested in the first aspect of this objective see advanced-technology products and processes as capable of generating appreciable returns on investments. For example, seed capital and early-stage venture capital deals involve considerable uncertainty over a firm's success. To compensate for those risks, a projected return greater than 40 percent per year is not uncommon as a prerequisite for investment. Those interested in the second aspect of this economic return objective – reduced risk – may be more willing to continue through the uncertain early stages of the new venture knowing that the burden of failure will be cushioned by other parties. For example, an entrepreneur may want to share equity with a business partner who knows some aspect of the product, market, or management because this individual increases the venture's likelihood of success. Similarly, a bank loan officer would be more confident granting a loan if some portion of that loan was guaranteed by a government authority.

A second important objective for private sector involvement in economic development, if properly executed, enables a large firm to do something it cannot do on its own – innovate. Many large companies have considerable difficulty seeing a new idea through to a final commercial product. Sheer size, organizational complexity, risk aversion, emphasis on short-run efficiency, territorialism, and other factors inhibit the innovation and "intrapreneurship" of large corporations (Hill and Utterback 1980; Mendell and Ennis 1985). On the other hand, a large corporation may want to work with smaller firms and universities to keep abreast of emerging technologies hoping that some will occasionally meet the firm's needs. Large-firm participation in small-business incubators, joint research partnerships with other firms, collaborative research with universities, and cooperation with venture-capital organizations are some ways that "windows on technology" and technology-transfer objectives are institutionalized. Just as the environment and objectives of different kinds of organizations interested in development are varied, economic development policies also are varied.

ECONOMIC-DEVELOPMENT STRATEGIES

Advanced technology has gained prominence in public policy because its proponents contend that it will usher in a new era of economic activity. The transition to the new era will be facilitated by existing and emerging technological development policies and programs, primarily at the state level. At this level, responsibility for economic development typically resides with a single agency or department, often a commerce department or development agency (Urban Institute 1983). At the local level, chambers of commerce and urban-renewal agencies are no longer solely responsible for economic development; general governmental and local development groups have assumed a greater role (Knack, Bellus, and Adell 1984). But many of these offices and groups have narrowly defined economic development policies and programs, and many are not keeping pace with the growth forces in the national economy. The emphasis of both state and local economic development agencies on attracting large industrial facilities to their jurisdiction is gradually changing, and the functions of many agencies have broadened in recent years (Urban Institute 1983). Activity in areas as diverse as education, labor, transportation, health, environment, and welfare have important economic consequences at both state and local levels. The advent of diverse and sophisticated economies, characterized by rapid change and interdependence, places greater emphasis on multifaceted approaches to economic development.

The Traditional Economic-Development Approach

Economic development strategies have traditionally been segmented into three general categories: regulatory policy, fiscal/tax policy, and expenditure policy (Pierce, Hagstrom, and Steinbach 1979). Of the three, regulatory policy, that is, those decisions affecting markets, products, and procedures that firms may or may not encounter or undertake, is thought to be the least appropriate way to stimulate economic development. Fiscal/tax policies are extensively used but questions exist concerning their efficacy. Expenditure policy, or how a government spends its money purchasing goods and services, is generally considered an appropriate governmental tool for improving economic conditions. Goods and services purchased from the private sector, like set-aside programs, help the development of individual firms.

These three general policy approaches have been directed at creating a large number of industrial jobs within jurisdictions, or in some cases at excluding facilities thought undesirable. For example, regulatory policy can either induce or impede facility siting: strict land-use and environmental regulations affect manufacturing firms that pollute the environment.

In contrast to regulatory policy, low-interest financing, site-infrastructure development, and tax reductions and abatements (usually in the form of reduced property taxes) are used as bait to lure large facilities to areas. These expenditure and fiscal/tax policies, known as "smokestack chasing" or more recently "chip chasing," have had only limited impact on development.[2] At worst, these traditional economic-development approaches have cost state and local governments tax revenue with little or no impact on the long-term behavior of firms.[3]

The evidence suggests that state and local tax reductions are decisive in relatively few cases. This insight is not new (Campbell 1958; Bridges 1965; Spiegelman 1964; Fischel 1975), but it has had little effect on changing state and local policy (Kieschnick 1981). Different taxes at different levels of government have different development outcomes (Friedman 1981). The ineffectiveness of state busines tax reductions to promote industrial siting is due largely to the limited differential among tax rates. According to Vaughan (1979, p. 72) "contrary to popular belief, interstate variations in business income taxes have had little impact on the location and relocation of businesses." Vaughan sees differences between high central-city and low suburban property taxes and stable tax rates as more important to location decisions than interstate variations in business income taxes.

A similar argument about development incentives concerns the provision of financial assistance through low-interest loans and direct grants. A general consensus has evolved that financial subsidies do not meet their intended purposes. Based on an extensive literature review, Mulkey and Dillman (1976, p. 41) conclude that ". . . most subsidies to large firms are probably wasted when viewed from the standpoint of the subsidizing community." While tax abatements are common, direct financial assistance to business by states is universal. Today all states offer some form of tax-exempt industrial revenue bond financing for purchasing land or industrial buildings (Chapter 9).

Even expenditure policy, generally considered a good policy strategy, can go awry. The history of infrastructure subsidies for business is a good example. A U.S. General Accounting Office (1980) study of publicly funded industrial parks found that 46 percent of the businesses that settled in parks funded by the U.S. Department of Commerce, Economic Development Administration (EDA), simply relocated from a site within the local area. It is likely that most of the other businesses that located in EDA-funded parks would have located within the general area of the park even if the park had not been built. Similar charges are also made about enterprise-zone programs.

State and local governments have sought to bolster their employment base by offering large industrial facilities a variety of business subsidies. These subsidies are extensive, and of dubious value. Schmenner summarizes the problem: "Taxes and financial inducements seem to be, at best, tie breakers acting between otherwise equal towns or sites. These traditional linchpins of state and local industrial development efforts simply cannot be relied on, by themselves, to attract new plants that would otherwise locate somewhere else. The fact that the tax and financial results . . . are so weak suggests that the traditional tax and financial incentives – tax reductions, moratoriums, roll backs, assessment breaks, industrial revenue bonding et al. – may not be worth the cost" (1982, p. 51). Nonetheless, a state not offering a subsidy may be deemed less attractive for industrial development. This diminished attractiveness may not result from market proximity, resource proximity, or other business-related factors (Chapter 4). Rather, the unattractiveness may simply be a perception that the state or locality is not probusiness; hence the state is a poor place to conduct business. Tax abatements and other subsidies may be little more than an expensive form of public relations.

Traditional economic-development approaches, which expanded rapidly during the industrial growth period of the 1950s and 1960s, were predicated on the assumption that financial and site inducements would attract large facilities, and hence create new jobs and fortify an area's economic base. Although evidence has shown that some states are more successful than others in attracting industrial facilities and that some industries benefit disproportionately (U.S. General Accounting Office 1984), it is generally believed that these traditional approaches result in little national net employment gain and that the costs to jurisdictions frequently outweigh the benefits.

The Emergence of Small Business

Policy focus on large-scale-facility siting is being reconsidered as development officials realize the changing structure of the economy. Manufacturing and resource extraction industries, the traditional focus of development efforts, have come increasingly under the pressures of foreign competition, high labor costs, automation-induced displacement, short-term management perspectives, and increasing energy costs. At the same time, entrepreneurship and small businesses are emerging as economic growth factors.

A study by David Birch (1979) helped set in motion a major shift in state economic-development efforts. Birch's well-known findings concern the superior job generation performance of small businesses: between 1969 and 1976, two-thirds of net new jobs were created by businesses with fewer than 20 employees, and 81 percent of all jobs were created by firms with 100 or fewer employees. Other recent studies (Armington and Odle 1982; Teitz, Glasmeier and Svensson 1981) generally support Birch's findings. Even during the recession of 1980-82, the small-business share of net new jobs was greater than the sector's share of total employment. During this period, those firms with fewer than 100 employees created 2.7 million jobs, offset by a 1.7 million job loss by corporations employing more than 100 employees (U.S. Small Business Administration 1985).

Recognition of the importance of small business has created a new development clientele and has ushered in a redirection of economic development policy (Stanford Research Institute International 1984; Vaughan 1983). States no longer have to compete solely for the jobs offered by large industrial facilities. The redirection of development assistance is not a simple matter; as seen in Chapter 9, new activities are widely diversified. The promotion of technological and entrepreneurial development is a new and largely unfamiliar endeavor for local and state governments. To support entrepreneurs, governmental officials have to act like entrepreneurs, that is, assume risky positions, defer gratification, and learn new skills. Government's capacity to assist entrepreneurs, who themselves often lack a full range of business skills, is limited (Zupnick and Katz 1981). To overcome these limitations, new approaches have been devised. These include business incubator facilities (Chapter 8) and small business development centers (Chapter 9). Small "home-grown" businesses can be nurtured, and with a little luck, what starts out as a backyard or garage operation can develop into an industry giant in just a few years. Very few firms will develop into the Apples, Wangs, DECs, or Data Generals of the electronics industry, but these companies and their smaller counterparts are the wave of the future.

A New Development Approach

Although advanced technology can enhance productivity in traditional manufacturing industries, it also can forge a new economic-development approach appreciably different from development efforts oriented toward traditional manufacturing industries. The promotion of entrepreneurship and technological development entails broad, but integrated, public and private-sector activities. Three assumptions related to the characteristics of advanced technology have served as guideposts for these new development initiatives.

First, advanced-technology industries are characterized by a higher percentage of technical and professional labor compared to the large unskilled and semiskilled needs of traditional industries (Chapter 2).

The traditional economic-development approach was predicated on the supposition that workers followed jobs; unskilled workers were often left with few work alternatives so they had to migrate. In the new model, the opposite may occur: jobs may be following people (Steinnes 1982). Technical and professional workers have more employment opportunities, and firms presumably seek locations where a larger number of these desirable workers live (Premus 1982). These include places with favorable cultural and recreational amenities (Chapter 4). These amenities are either provided publicly (through taxation) or through the private sector (if sufficient local demand exists). Community amenities such as favorable climate, quality schools, recreational opportunities, moderately priced housing, and a strong civic culture are features that allegedly make areas attractive to such individuals and families. Although not all of these features can be controlled by state and local governments, they represent the trend toward a broader approach to economic-development incentives and opportunities.

A second assumption implicit in the new development approach is closely related to the first. Highly skilled analytic/scientific workers are predominately trained at postsecondary educational institutions. Colleges and universities are assumed to have a special relationship with advanced-technology firms and serve as a powerful location inducement. In addition to supplying trained graduates, universities perform critical services for advanced-technology firms. These include research and access to laboratories, libraries, and information systems (Chapter 6). The university was less important in the traditional approach because innovation in mature industries is minimal; product changes become more difficult as processes become more standardized (Moore and Tushman 1982).

A third assumption about advanced-technology industries concerns infrastructure. In addition to financial subsidies and tax abatements, manufacturing industries traditionally have relied on site improvements offered or subsidized by governments. Demands for water resources, transportation, or energy services are characteristic of heavy-manufacturing industries. Allegedly, advanced-technology firms typically do not need such "hard" infrastructure facility development; their products are more likely to be low-volume, high-value-added goods not subject to the production input constraints of heavy industry. Their development needs, characterized by the "technological development infrastructure," are presumed to be fundamentally different. Emphasis on small business has focused attention on the ability of governmental business assistance programs to meet the needs of new and growing advanced-technology businesses. Notions of competitive advantage have changed from natural resource endowments and hard infrastructure support, to technological support organizations. If local and state authorities are to promote advanced-technology enterprise, technological support organizations must encompass a wide range of needs. Compared to single-activity support organizations, a consortium of organizations can offer a greater pool of expertise and wider coverage of needs.

THE CONCEPTUAL BASIS OF TECHNOLOGICAL DEVELOPMENT POLICY

As economic-development approaches have broadened, organizational structures have evolved to reflect the expanded scope of concern. Organizational structures comprise one component of technological development; the other component is technical in nature. Technical aspects of development are predicated on innovations in the production of new and improved products that rely heavily on a growing knowledge base in natural sciences, engineering, and mathematics.[4] Organizational aspects of technological development are associated with changes in the behavior of institutions and individuals. The study of institutional arrangements and human behavior occurs primarily in the social and behavioral sciences.

Public-policy responses to technological development focus mainly on the organizational realm rather than the technical realm. Certainly public-policy mechanisms can be used to support technical work, but that support occurs through organizational or social interventions. Adequate financial support and a noninterventionist approach to basic research will assure freely interacting professionals who seek consensus to establish knowledge (Ganz 1981). This noninterventionist approach promotes the social process of science, the creation of technical knowledge, and organizational change necessary for economic development.

Organizational Innovation Processes

One objective of management in advanced-technology firms is to guide and promote technical innovation. Management occurs in intra- and interorganizational contexts. Intrafirm activity is geared toward the technical development and commercialization of a product or service. Most firms, except perhaps for large companies operating in vertically structured markets, interact extensively with other firms to achieve mutual business interests or "trade relations" such as subcontracting, coproduction, marketing, and other joint ventures. Public-policy interventions are little concerned with intrafirm organizational arrangements. Interfirm interventions, however, have received considerable public-policy attention and a new trend has emerged in the past decade. Many interfirm (industry) regulations thought to inhibit market efficiency have been legislated out of existence. Market deregulation, or in the parlance of Washington, D.C., "a level playing field," is the order of the day.

In the current era of nurturing the development of business, new organizational issues are evolving. Groups that comprise the technological support infrastructure are reorganizing internal and external relations to bolster technical innovation. Many public and nonprofit organizations such as colleges and universities, other educational and training providers (community colleges, vocational-technical schools, and proprietary schools), and local development forces have restructured incentives and formed networks to support private sector enterprise (Chapter 9). Interorganizational arrangements discussed in this book include university-industry partnerships such as the Pennsylvania Ben Franklin Partnership Program (Chapter 9) and the Ohio Thomas Alva Edison program, interstate consortia to promote technology transfer such as the Midwest Technology Research Institute, and networks that seek to match venture capitalists with local entrepreneurs such as the one operated by the private sector's Business and Industry Association in cooperation with the University of New Hampshire. A common characteristic of these interorganizational agreements is that they build upon members' interests and strengths to create a competitive advantage for the particular partnership.

Interorganizational linkages occur because the complexities of advanced-technology environments dictate sophisticated responses that cannot be handled by small, medium, or even many large organizations.

Integrationist strategies are now called for in a world that has traditionally rewarded specialization and scholarship in single or narrowly defined disciplines. Advanced technology, or the sophisticated use of tools, conveys a notion of interdiscipline; certainly this is reflected in systems-based management approaches such as strategic planning and matrix organization, and in emerging areas such as biotechnology and artificial intelligence. Rapid environmental changes that necessitate interorganizational adaption also call attention to the need for intraorganizational change.

If linkage networks between firms and technological support organizations are to flourish, intraorganizational change must also flourish. In the literature on intraorganizational implementation of innovation, two issues appear paramount (Tornatzky et al. 1983, p. 145). First, strategies and tactics typically interpreted as incentives, rewards, and inducements (either positive or negative) are important because they reflect an organization's potential for linkage development. Organizations in which institutional goals and objectives are not congruent with the self-interests of individuals (for example, recognition, autonomy, economic reward, and so forth) do not function effectively (Downs 1967). Inducements for individuals to cooperate with other organizations are not easily and universally applied to workers with different self-interests. Flexible, experimental management approaches (Landau and Stout 1979) are not common in hierarchically structured organizations replete with layers of bureaucracy and output (not outcome) performance orientations (Wholey 1983). Fundamental incentive changes must occur if public-sector organizations are going to transform into environmentally sensitive, flexibly responding components in business support networks.

The second issue pertaining to intraorganizational innovation involves organizational characteristics that promote the fit between the organization and the technology or linkage being considered. These characteristics can be divided into three areas: organizational structure, cognitive factors, and core activities. Organizational structure presents opportunities and constraints for linkage. Decision rules, size, and boundary arrangements are a few of the organizational variables that affect linkage development. The more congruent the organizational "cultures," the greater the likelihood of success. For example, organizations that have centralized decision making may not easily fit with decentralized organizations. Small organizations may have difficulty retaining autonomy in partnerships involving large organizations. Organizations that do not have boundary-spanning units to facilitate and govern interaction may develop haphazard linkages that are unable to expand or endure.

Cognitive factors, generally thought of as perceptions and intentions, also play an important role in linkage development. Beliefs about rational self-interests determine if, and to what extent, linkage activity should be pursued. Even with positive attitudes and intentions, linkage activity may be stymied if individual rewards do not exist.

Core activities are mainstay tasks or work duties performed by the organization. To the extent that the core activities of different organizations fit or augment one another, a linkage is more likely to form. The converse is also true. For example, entrepreneurial development support activities would not fit well with an organization that has little outreach or that has little experience in business assistance.

The Development/Knowledge Connection

Economies develop by adding value to land, labor, and capital resources. Because of differences in natural endowments, the productive capacity of labor, and the local investment potential of capital, some areas have been able to develop competitive advantages to produce certain goods and services at low costs. Even today, the mix of these three factors – resources, labor, and capital – explains the competitive advantage of some advanced-technology centers. Some contend, for example, that Silicon Valley's development was due primarily to available land, skilled and flexible workers, and abundant capital (Rogers and Larsen 1984).

One influential element in Silicon Valley's success was technology in the form of improved knowledge and technique embodied in the land, capital, and labor forces used to fuel the area's economic growth. As suggested, technology is not an independent factor of production; rather, it is a mechanism or means of improving the productive capacity of the three primary factors. Technology is undeniably an important aspect of economic growth, but perhaps more fundamentally, it has become the basis of modern economic development.

Improvements in technical and organizational components of production are the result of new knowledge applied to practical purposes. Knowledge is embodied in technology, and the more advanced the technology, the more the knowledge is based on science. Science, in and of itself, however, is insufficient for technological development (Roy and Shapley 1985). Technological development requires that scientific knowledge be translated into practical, commercial application. Advanced-technology industries rely on knowledge of production forces to such a degree that knowledge seemingly becomes a production component itself. Applying knowledge for practical use is a technology-based innovation: the production of new goods and services, and the creation of new ways to produce old goods and services.

The role of technical knowledge in commercial application has had an increasing role in the development of economies. In the early industrial era (1760-1830), economic development was thought of primarily as the ability to exploit fixed natural resources. A competitive advantage was evident in certain favorable locations associated with coal mining, iron making, and textiles (Ayres 1984). A much later phase of the Industrial Revolution (1860-1930) also witnessed a competitive advantage because of favorable locations for steel production and other manufacturing innovations such as electricity, the internal-combustion engine, and mass-produced consumer goods (Ayres 1984). Important for the industrialization of the U.S. economy was a growing number of mobile workers, and the availability of investment capital and inexpensive raw materials. A competitive advantage during the beginning of the Industrial Revolution resulted from land and labor forces. Increasingly, however, manufacturing characterized by value-added, knowledge-based processes emerged as a driving force of modern economies. Knowledge translated into organizational learning and adaption (for example, scientific management), greater worker education and skills, and engineering advancement transformed the industrial landscape after the Second World War.

Silicon Valley is striking contemporary evidence for regional competitive advantage in knowledge-based industry. This area was transformed from an agricultural area to the world's most intensive concentration of innovative business activity in less than three decades. In 1950, Santa Clara County had 800 manufacturing employees; today over 6,000 Ph.Ds work in the area and over 3,000 advanced-technology firms are located there (Rogers and Larsen 1984).

This chapter has argued that economic-development activities in the era of advanced technology and entrepreneurship are fundamentally different from the economic-development activities that occurred in the industrial location-dominated era from the 1950s to the mid-1970s. By examining data collected from advanced-technology industries and individual firms, this book can provide the reader with an understanding of current development policy and what may lie ahead.

WHY PENNSYLVANIA?

State economic growth has traditionally been constrained by factors beyond the state's control. These factors include prevailing wages, land availability, access to markets, and natural resources (Dye 1980; Vaughan 1979). States do, however, have control over many factors that affect technological development. This book examines advanced-technology industry and policy primarily in one state, Pennsylvania. Pennsylvania is a good choice for a study of advanced technology for several reasons. The state's economy has relied heavily on traditional, basic industries such as mining, production of primary metals, and steel-related manufacturing (Coy 1984). These major industries are also characterized by declining employment, international competition, and slow productivity growth (Lawrence and Dyer 1983, pp. 55-85). Although Pennsylvania has experienced many of the difficulties associated with the broader economic transition, such as high unemployment and an exodus of young workers, it has made substantial adjustments. This section briefly examines Pennsylvania's position, public posture, and prospects for economic development. Considering the problems associated with economic transition and the process of technological and entrepreneurial development, Pennsylvania is an excellent research setting.

Economic Transition

Pennsylvania is simultaneously displaying the problems of an older industrial economy while showing significant activity in several advanced-technology sectors. Until 1975, Pennsylvania's unemployment rate was below the national average. After the 1974-75 recession, its unemployment rate exceeded the national average. In fact, since 1975 the spread has continued to widen and did not start to converge until 1984 (Chase Econometrics 1984; and Economic Report to the President 1983). One study of the state's economy conducted in 1982 stressed the magnitude of the unemployment hardship. "Of the 600,000 to 800,000 unemployed workers approximately half are either ineligible for unemployment compensation or have been unemployed for so long they have exhausted their unemployment benefits. This means that there are an estimated 300,000 formerly employed people in the Commonwealth who have no source of income other than what they may earn from investments and what they may be given by friends and relatives" (Schwartz 1983, p. 2).

The manufacturing sector of the state's economy is more severely depressed than the service sector. In 1970, about one in three Pennsylvania workers (34.1 percent) was employed in manufacturing. By 1980 the percentage of workers employed in manufacturing had declined to 28.6 (DeJong 1983, p. 50). These structural changes in Pennsylvania's economy closely parallel national trends; manufacturing employment has decreased as nonmanufacturing employment has increased.[5]

Pennsylvania's Advanced-Technology Resources

If Pennsylvania is going to prosper in the advanced-technology area, it will have to take advantage of opportunities and resources that can increase its competitive position. The list of human, and research and development (R&D) resources judged superior in Pennsylvania fall into three areas: a large number of quality research universities, a good supply of scientists and engineers, and a skilled labor force (Coy 1982). Some pertinent indicators of the state's favorable position are the following:

- In 1977, Pennsylvania ranked fifth in percentage (25 percent) of total state manufacturing labor force employed in advanced-technology firms (U.S. Department of Commerce 1981).
- In 1980, Pennsylvania had the fourth largest number of scientists and engineers among states (National Science Foundation 1980a).
- In 1979, Pennsylvania ranked fifth among states for corporate research and development expenditures (National Science Foundation 1980b).
- In 1980, Pennsylvania's university and college expenditures in science and engineering R&D ranked sixth nationally (National Science Foundation 1982). The corporate contributions to science and engineering R&D at Pennsylvania's colleges and universities during 1980 was the third largest in the country (National Science Foundation 1982).

- In 1980, Pennsylvania had nine universities ranked among the top 200 R&D universities (National Science Foundation 1982).
- In 1980, 9 percent of all R&D expenditures in math and computer sciences were made in Pennsylvania (National Science Foundation 1982).

Clearly, these indicators of human and R&D resources are important to a state pursuing technological development strategies. According to business-climate studies, however, these factors are not typically the ones entrepreneurs examine when they consider locating their businesses.

Business-climate studies (Chapter 4) illustrate differences in costs and location inducements between traditional manufacturing industries and advanced-technology industries. Generally, manufacturing-oriented business-climate studies have placed Pennsylvania below the median while entrepreneurial-oriented studies have placed the state above the median. These findings suggest that Pennsylvania is responding to the challenge posed by the transition from a heavy reliance on traditional manufacturing to entrepreneurial-based advanced-technology enterprises.

Demographic and Geographic Considerations

Pennsylvania offers an interesting contrast in demographics and settlement patterns. Although it was the fourth most populous state in 1980, the state's population base is slowly eroding. The estimated loss of residents from 1980 to 1990 is 1.2 percent, and from 1980 to 2000, 5.5 percent (U.S. Bureau of the Census 1983). This projected transition means not only a decline in total population, but also a shift in the composition of the population. DeJong (1983, p. 43) sees a "... coming labor shortage of young, highly educated, highly trained workers who will be needed to fill the high technology jobs of the late 1980s and 1990s."

About three-quarters of Pennsylvania's population live in urban areas, but the state also has more citizens living in rural areas than any other state in the country. Suburban and rural areas continue to grow while larger cities remain stable or slightly decline. At present, these demographic and geographic patterns make for a relatively balanced situation among rural, suburban, and central-city interests. But central-city and rural areas are considered most in need of economic-development opportunities.

PURPOSE OF THE BOOK

This book was written for a number of reasons. Foremost among them is the need for quantitative data obtained directly from advanced-technology firms. With few exceptions (examined in the book), little academic work on advanced technology uses the firm as the level of analysis. Academic studies tend to rely on aggregate data, and popular accounts report on only a few select firms. This book is not a definitive statement on advanced-technology development. The subject is too extensive for a single, cross-sectional examination. Rather, this research is an initial attempt to examine some of the suppositions, public-policy logic, and emerging trends in this dynamic field of study. This book is an exploratory work that will help set the stage for future research.

ORGANIZATION OF THE BOOK

The remainder of the book covers topics related to the changing nature of economic development. Whenever appropriate, data from the survey of Pennsylvania firms and other sources have been analyzed to provide an empirical perspective on the topics.

Because the book examines advanced technology, it is important to define the concept early on. Various operational definitions of the concept are presented in Chapter 2. This chapter also discusses the kinds of data analyzed and the constraints on analysis those data pose.

Chapter 3 focuses on job creation. It begins with an overview of national employment shifts and employment prospects. The chapter then considers the relative importance of advanced-technology jobs by examining the distribution of jobs in the national economy and in the advanced-technology sector. Employment data collected two years after the 1982 Pennsylvania survey are used to estimate the potential of the advanced-technology sector to create jobs in the Pennsylvania economy and the differences by characteristics of the firms. For example, how do small firms compare to larger firms in job creation? The chapter concludes with a discussion of the role of advanced technology in job creation.

Chapter 4 examines factors affecting the location and expansion of advanced-technology firms. Why do new firms locate in a particular area, and what are the factors affecting site choice as firms expand? Geographic characteristics and issues associated with "critical mass" are examined. Particular attention is focused on small, single-plant firms, and the unique characteristics of their location priorities. Implications of the findings on state and local policy are presented.

Chapter 5 considers the interaction of advanced-technology firms and the labor force. A number of critical human-resource issues are addressed. For example, how difficult is it for firms to recruit new employees at different skill levels? What kinds of training are provided for new employees? How important is the availability of skilled labor in site-location decisions? The chapter concludes by considering the appropriateness of alternative public-training approaches.

Chapter 6 explores the relationship between higher education and advanced technology from the perspective of firms in the Pennsylvania sample. Respondents were asked to provide information on the importance of universities in a range of activities related to their daily operations. Is the university actually seen as important to advanced-technology executives? What are the most important aspects of university service? Is the higher education sector perceived as being responsive? Here too, policy implications are discussed in the chapter's conclusions.

The important issue of financing small, growing enterprises is examined in Chapter 7. The problems associated with undercapitalized small firms and the array of financial arrangements for small firms are reviewed. Considerable attention is given to the venture-capital industry, and new, intermediary roles assumed by state and local organizations.

Although small firms are extensively discussed throughout the book, Chapter 8 specifically examines the role of entrepreneurship in economic development. One tool for promoting entrepreneurship, the small-business-incubator facility, is examined. Data from a 1984 survey of 12 incubators and 56 tenant firms are presented. Public policy responses for promoting incubators are discussed.

Chapter 9 presents an overview of state economic-development policies. A wide range of technological development strategies are reviewed. Other areas covered correspond to chapters in the book: labor and training, the educational sector, financing, and business assistance. The second half of the chapter is an in-depth case study of Pennsylvania's technological development program – the Ben Franklin Partnership.

The final chapter integrates the findings by discussing their effect on emerging development policy. The chapter examines a strategic planning perspective for state and local development policy and obstacles to improving technological development policy.

NOTES

1. Many use the terms "high technology," "technology intensive," "new technology," and "advanced technology" interchangeably. Virtually every researcher or author defines the terms to meet their own needs. An elaboration of our definition of advanced technology is presented in Chapter 2.

2. Large-scale facility siting does not necessarily mean that indigenous residents will be employed. As plants move, many workers move with the plant and additional workers are attracted from other areas.

3. An interesting contemporary example of a company's seeking a location for a large-facility siting is General Motors' new Saturn division. Company officials stated that because virtually all states offer identical fiscal inducements, such considerations had very little bearing on the final choice of a site.

4. There is extensive literature on technical innovation. See Mansfield (1968); Kennedy and Thirlwall (1972); Mansfield et al. (1977); Hill and Utterback (1979); Rothwell and Zegveld (1981); and Sahal (1981).

5. Pennsylvania's manufacturing work force has declined from 46 percent in 1963 to 33 percent in 1981, greater than the national average. The concentration of heavy industry in Pennsylvania also differentiates the state from the nation on another important point. Nationally, manufacturing's contribution to constant-dollar gross national product has remained fairly constant while manufacturing contribution to gross Pennsylvania product declined about 5 percent during the 1963-81 period (Coy 1984).

2 Identifying Advanced-Technology Firms: Data Sources and Analyses

INTRODUCTION: WHAT IS ADVANCED TECHNOLOGY?

A nearly universal perception exists that advanced technology is ubiquitous, pervading virtually every aspect of daily life. Increasingly, Americans encounter computers and computer-augmented devices in the workplace and even at supermarket checkouts. Another prevalent perception is that the fundamental nature of work is changing and that many traditional occupations will become obsolete. In many circles there exists a sense of the inevitability of change along with a concern that U.S. values and culture may fall prey to technology. The term "advanced technology" captures this zeitgeist; to suggest that we cannot readily identify the essence of this change seems absurd.

It is extremely difficult to develop an agreed-upon operational definition of what constitutes an advanced-technology enterprise. The Departments of Defense and Commerce, the U.S. Securities and Exchange Commission, and a number of state agencies each use different definitions (Office of Technology Assessment 1984b; Riche et al. 1983). Definitions are sometimes established to serve the objectives of local economic-development officials and promoters (Malecki 1984). Agreement exists, in general, that advanced technology is important and pervasive; in specific instances, however, a standardized rule is lacking to differentiate "advanced" technology from "conventional" technology.

Perhaps the only universal consensus among advanced-technology experts is that no agreement exists (Buck et al. 1984; Glasmeier, Hall, and Markusen 1984; Doeringer and Parnell 1982; Riche et al. 1983;

Office of Technology Assessment 1984b). The need for empirical studies of the impact of technology on the economy and society is clear, but the lack of definition is an obstacle to synthesizing knowledge. A study by the Congressional Office of Technology Assessment (1984b, p. 9) notes that "the lack of a single, generally accepted definition of 'high technology' constrains analysis."

The terms "high technology," "advanced technology," and "new technology" are often used interchangeably in referring to technological change. Brooks (1983, p. 116) describes two principal functions of technology: "to improve efficiency in the production of existing products and services, and to produce new products and services." To the extent that these terms can be distinguished, "high technology" is associated with producing new products, "advanced technology" with producing both products and services, and "new technology" with applications of products recently introduced to the workplace and the marketplace.

In this book, the term "advanced technology" is used because it best describes the activities of the firms included in our study (manufacturing and service firms). Advanced technology is also the term officially adopted by Pennsylvania, the location of the survey sample. Unfortunately, all three expressions heavily emphasize products rather than processes. For example, "the use of robots by the automobile industry does not classify this firm as high-technology. The high technology firm is the producer of the robot" (Conway Data 1983, p. 532). The product-versus-process distinction presents a limited view of advanced technology. The whole area of technological process innovation in manufacturing would not be classified as advanced technology if a commonplace product were the end result. As Malecki (1984, p. 262) notes, "The most useful definition of 'high technology' is based on the activities of local firms, not on the products or services they ultimately produce." Such a definition of advanced technology would include both sophisticated services producers and intensive new-technology users. This approach, however, increases the difficulty in identifying advanced-technology firms, but is more consistent with the concept of technology as tools that improve performance and interact with their larger environment.

Unfortunately, data on firms' activities are difficult to obtain while data on products and services are readily available. Operational definitions inevitably depend upon primary firms, products, or services and not on how they are produced.

Operationalizing a Definition of Advanced Technology

In trying to operationally differentiate firms that exemplify advanced technology from those that do not, analysts have generally focused upon quantifiable characteristics of the firm. The following list identifies some of the most frequently cited characteristics used in classifying firms:

- a high percentage of technical and professional workers (Premus 1982; Battelle Memorial Institute 1982; Riche et al. 1983; Office of Technology Assessment 1984b; Brennan 1983)
- intensive research and development (R&D) (Premus 1982; Doody and Munzer 1981; Battelle Memorial Institute 1982; Riche et al. 1983; Malecki 1984; Congressional Budget Office 1985)
- high value-added nature of products (Doody and Munzer 1981)
- high growth rates (Doody and Munzer 1981; Stengel and Plosila 1982; Congressional Budget Office 1985)
- product competition in national and international markets, not simply regional or local ones (Doody and Munzer 1981; Battelle Memorial Institute 1982a)
- technological intensity – high levels of R&D embodied in inputs used to make the firm's final product (Riche et al. 1983)
- high levels of continuing innovation (Brennan 1983)
- science-based products and processes based on state-of-the-art knowledge (Malecki 1984)

Generally, these characteristics involve science-based, sophisticated products that have wide market appeal. Perhaps, even more fundamentally, advanced technology can be characterized as "technology with a high rate of change" (Conway Data 1983, p. 532), although this definition certainly is not easy to operationalize.

Ultimately, all the different definitions are based on standard industrial codes (SICs). This somewhat arbitrary method yields a set of industry groups that are mainly product oriented, that is, interest is focused on what is produced, not on how it is produced.

The SIC-based operational definitions have a number of basic weaknesses. First, as noted, SICs focus on product rather than process. Many advanced-technology products are extremely labor intensive, involving traditional assembly-line production processes (Premus 1982). Much of the advanced-technology growth in the southeastern United States has consisted of standardized production and assembly of advanced-technology products. Although the region has experienced substantial advanced-technology growth when advanced technology is defined in terms of product, its growth would prove illusory if process-based definitions were available (Malecki 1984).

A second problem is that the SIC-based definitions place little emphasis on services. Definitions derived from fundamental characteristics often ignore a group of rapidly growing, research-and-development-based, high-skill, high-value-added products. In particular, the entire area of business services such as data processing and management consulting is ignored. Browne (1983) argues that the growth in these business service industries is due primarily to growth in the advanced-technology manufacturing sector. For example, computers (hardware) are not useful in and of themselves; they need instructions and tasks to perform (software).

Another problem is that, by construction, SIC definitions are based on industry averages rather than the characteristics of individual firms. If firms within an industry are very heterogeneous, the industry may be classified as advanced technology, but relatively few individual firms will actually match the criteria used to develop the definition (Office of Technology Assessment 1984b). Moreover, firms frequently engage in activities outside the primary SIC category in which they are classified, further decreasing the utility of the SIC as a basis for identifying process (Armington, Harris, and Odle 1984).

Finally, advanced technology, by nature, involves rapid change; no system of categorization can remain current in a changing environment. Newly emerging industries tend to be placed in indistinct subclassifications within the SIC system (such as "Not Elsewhere Classified") until industries become mature. Armington, Harris, and Odle (1984, p. 139) observe that in 1984 the two largest robotics manufacturers in the country were assigned different four-digit SIC groupings. Virtually all industries have some advanced-technology activities (Malecki 1984). It is generally conceded, however, that no single definition captures the essence of technological innovation and it is self-evident that "there can be no temporally static list of high technology industries" (Glasmeier et al. 1984, p. 146).

The Definition of Advanced Technology Used in This Book

Despite the obstacles to SIC-based definitions of advanced technology, any empirical analysis requires some working definition that differentiates technology-intensive firms from others. Virtually all operationalizations of the concept rely on SICs. The definition of advanced-technology firms used to generate the survey population for this book is borrowed from the Pennsylvania Department of Commerce and underlies the state plan for advanced-technology growth. The discussion that follows draws upon the report, *Advanced Technology Policies for the Commonwealth of Pennsylvania* (Stengel and Plosila 1982).

According to the Pennsylvania standard, advanced-technology enterprises do at least one of the following three things:

(1) conceive of and develop new technology; for example, altering the genetic material of plants and livestock to produce new strains;
(2) improve on existing technology by incorporating innovations; for example, applying cellular radio technology to the development of sophisticated mobile telephones; and
(3) apply technology to the manufacture of what is generally considered a non-technical product; for example, using computers to measure feed for livestock.

Advanced-technology firms also have one or more of the following six characteristics:

(1) rely on skilled and creative people requiring some technical training even for entry-level positions;
(2) conduct research to improve products or services;
(3) employ a high percentage of engineers and other scientific and technical personnel;
(4) incorporate newer technology in their manufacturing processes;
(5) have faster than average growth of employment opportunities; and
(6) tend to be highly competitive in the international marketplace.

Based on this definition of activities and characteristics, 42 four-digit SICs were selected as constituting the advanced-technology sector in Pennsylvania. (A list of SICs, with data on employment and establishments in the state and nationally, is presented in Chapter 3.)

DATA USED IN THIS BOOK

Analyses presented in this book use data drawn from six sources. Three of the data bases (County Business Patterns, Dun Market

Identifiers, and Higher Education General Institutional Survey) are widely used national data sources and are described here very briefly. Three additional surveys (a 1982 mail survey of advanced-technology firms in Pennsylvania, a 1984 telephone survey of advanced-technology firms' employment in Pennsylvania, and a 1984 telephone survey of Pennsylvania small-business incubators) are described in greater detail.

County Business Patterns (CBP)

County Business Patterns (an annual series provided by the U.S. Department of Commerce, Bureau of the Census) provides data on mid-March employment, first-quarter payroll, and number of establishments in the United States broken down by four-digit SICs and county. Data are available both in tabular form and on machine-readable tape. The data series is available (irregularly) back to 1946 and has been available on an annual basis since 1964. (See Bureau of the Census 1982 for details.)

This book uses published data on total employment, payroll, and number of establishments nationally and in Pennsylvania in 1972 and 1982 and contrasts these aggregate figures with employment in 42 advanced-technology industries. These data provide a framework for examining the relative size of the advanced-technology sector, Pennsylvania's share of national employment, and patterns of growth during the decade immediately prior to administration of the survey of firms (Chapter 3).

The Dun Market Identifier (DMI) Files

Dun and Bradstreet, Inc., collects data continuously on the commercial credit rating, employment, sales, and principal activities of firms in the United States. Using the definition of advanced technology described above (operationalized to identify 42 SICs), the 1982 DMI files for Pennsylvania were used to identify advanced-technology firms and generate a list of addresses and chief executive officers. The 2,432 identified firms formed the sample for the 1982 mail survey and the 1984 telephone surveys. Because the DMI is used primarily to verify commercial credit, new firms and those not seeking credit may be significantly underrepresented in the DMI files (Reynolds and West 1985; Birley 1984). Advanced technology tends to have a high proportion of very small firms. To the extent that these firms were systematically excluded from the 1982 DMI files for Pennsylvania, the size of the advanced-technology sector is underrepresented in this book.

The DMI data were used in this study for two principal purposes. First, as noted, the 1982 Pennsylvania file was used to define the universe of advanced-technology firms in Pennsylvania. Subsequent survey research was directed to this universe of 2,432 firms. In addition, DMI data on sales, employment, and manufacturing status were used to check for systematic nonresponse bias in the follow-up studies.

Higher Education General Institutional Survey (HEGIS)

The National Center for Educational Statistics, U.S. Department of Education, collects data annually on a wide range of institutional characteristics and activities from all postsecondary institutions in the United States. Using data on degrees granted in 1982, a set of three indexes of higher-educational activity in areas related to the advanced-technology sector were constructed for each of Pennsylvania's 67 counties. Five general areas of study were believed strongly related to advanced technology; indexes were constructed for baccalaureate, master's and doctorate degrees granted in each area (Table 2.1).

For each of Pennsylvania's 67 counties, three sets of dichotomous variables were constructed from these data reflecting whether the local higher-education establishments in the county combined issued: over 300 advanced-technology baccalaureate degrees, over 10 master's degrees, or any doctorates.

The 1982 Mail Survey of Advanced-Technology Firms in Pennsylvania

In late December 1982, a four-page survey (see Appendix A) was sent to the chief executive officers of the 2,432 advanced-technology firms (identified by SIC) from the DMI files. The study was conducted jointly by the Institution of Public Administration at The Pennsylvania State University and the Pennsylvania MILRITE Council (Allen and Robertson 1983). Data were collected on firm characteristics, employment history, plans for expansion, factors affecting initial location and expansion decisions, perceptions of the local labor market, training

TABLE 2.1 Advanced-Technology Degrees Granted in Pennsylvania, 1981-1982

Degrees Granted	State Total
Business Administration	
Baccalaureate	12,678
Master's	3,167
Doctorate	59
Computer Science	
Baccalaureate	1,489
Master's	339
Doctorate	32
Engineering	
Baccalaureate	4,986
Master's	956
Doctorate	166
Mathematics	
Baccalaureate	622
Master's	99
Doctorate	22
Physical Sciences	
Baccalaureate	1,874
Master's	265
Doctorate	172

Source: "Degrees and Other Formal Awards Conferred" by Pennsylvania Department of Education, 1983, *Education Today*.

policies, perceived role of the university, access to finance, ratings of the state's business climate, and other related concerns.

In mid-January 1983, follow-up postcards were sent requesting responses to the survey. In mid-February, a second wave of surveys was sent to nonresponding firms in electronics, instruments, and business service areas (about half of the initial universe of firms). Useable responses were received from 459 firms (19 percent of the sample). Although this is a low response rate according to general social-science standards, it is respectable for mainly small advanced-technology firms for several reasons. Private firms are oriented toward protecting rather than sharing information; firms in this sample are less likely to respond than other firms both because they tend to operate in more competitive arenas and because they are smaller (decreasing the likelihood of an individual or department involved in external dissemination of information). The response rate was consistent with other studies of advanced-technology firms. For example, a National Science Foundation survey of 13,000 small research and development firms conducted in 1977 yielded a response rate of 14 percent, with useable data for less than 7 percent of the sampled firms (NSF 1981). In a mail survey of 1,700 rural technology-based entrepreneurs located near universities, Buck and her colleagues (1984) received 300 responses, for a response rate of 19 percent. Response rates tend to be somewhat higher when directed to university research centers (Hise et al. 1980 had a 24 percent response rate in a survey of university-affiliated centers) or when the survey is sent by a trade association to its members (39 percent response from members of the American Electronics Association in 1983).

Data from the DMI files were used to test for systematic differences between the 459 responding firms and the 1,973 nonrespondents. The mean characteristics of the two groups of firms were compared for the following factors: age, sales, number of employees, ownership, and organization. No statistically significant differences were found using a t-test and a significance criterion of .10.[1] The responding firms appear representative of the advanced-technology sector in Pennsylvania as operationally defined in this study.

1984 Telephone Survey of Advanced-Technology Employment in Pennsylvania

In December 1984 (two years after the mail survey), attempts were made to contact the 459 firms participating in the study to obtain information on number of employees. Firms for which telephone numbers could be obtained in 1984 were contacted by phone. Letters were sent to those firms with no telephone listing and firms that refused to provide information over the phone. In the 1984 study, 67 firms could not be located and were assumed to have failed; 22 other firms provided no data.

Study of Pennsylvania Business Incubators

In early 1984, the Pennsylvania Department of Commerce and the Institute of Public Administration at The Pennsylvania State University collaborated on a study of small-business incubators in the state. Twelve incubators with 126 tenant firms were identified. Surveys were sent to all tenants in February 1984, with follow-up letters and phone calls to nonrespondents. Forty-four percent of the surveyed tenant firms participated in the study. Survey data were augmented with telephone interviews and site visits to selected incubators (see Allen, Ginsberg, and Marx 1984).

DATA ANALYSIS

The analysis reported in this book is basically descriptive. It attempts to draw a preliminary portrait of the advanced-technology sector in one state, and examine the fit between new economic-development initiatives and the self-reported priorities of advanced-technology executive managers. The book is also intended for a nontechnical audience of policymakers and economic-development officials. Thus, the data are presented as simply as possible.

The most common form of data presentation involves univariate descriptive statistics – the mean and standard deviation of characteristics of firms in the sample, or the proportion of responding firms having a particular characteristic. Bivariate relationships are presented, where appropriate, to describe patterns of relationship. No causal inferences can or should be drawn from these relationships. Generally these relationships are explored through contingency tables or correlations. In Chapter 6, factor analysis and stepwise multiple regression are used to identify the underlying dimensions of the relationship between advanced-technology firms and universities.

SUMMARY

This chapter reviewed some of the conceptual issues related to defining advanced technology and provided an operational definition of the advanced-technology sector used in selecting Pennsylvania firms for inclusion in the study. Six data bases (three national and three developed specifically for this book) are described. The analytic chapters in this book focus on 459 advanced-technology firms in Pennsylvania that appear representative of the state's advanced-technology sector.

NOTE

1. The t-test is an appropriate test statistic for assessing the difference between sample firms' means and means from the remainder of the population, that is, non-responding firms. The test concludes that it is unlikely the means of the two groups are unequal. The significance criterion is set at the .10 level because of the nonserious consequences of rejecting a true null hypothesis, that is, that the means from the two groups are equal.

3 Advanced Technology and Jobs

INTRODUCTION

The main impetus for the development of state and local advanced-technology initiatives came during the recession of the late 1970s and early 1980s. Without question, the single most important issue behind interest in advanced technology was job creation. High levels of unemployment resulting from the economic stagnation combined with job losses because of structural changes in the economy placed many localities' long-term economic prospects at considerable risk. The mystique of sophisticated technology, and the promise of high economic growth and job creation made technological development initiatives politically attractive. Initiatives were based on popular beliefs about the efficacy of advanced technology as a source of jobs. In general, these beliefs lacked a solid empirical base. This chapter examines some important advanced-technology employment issues, such as firm failures, job creation, and the relationship between firms' characteristics and employment growth. Findings are based on national data and on data obtained from the survey of 459 firms in Pennsylvania during the period 1982-84.

STRUCTURAL CHANGES AND JOB LOSSES

From about the mid-1970s on high unemployment in "smokestack" industries made many local and state officials concerned about long-term employment prospects. Advanced-technology issues surfaced on state and local agendas for several reasons. One, it seemed that little could be done about workers laid off in declining industries; causes were beyond local control although consequences were felt locally. Two, high unemployment levels undermined the fiscal capacity of local governments; those areas most in need of increased services experienced reductions in resources. Three, given the dynamics of economic change, it became increasingly evident that even when the general economy improved, many of the workers in basic industries would not return to their old jobs. A national report by the Business-Higher Education Forum (1983, p. 13) noted that "to many Americans, technological change today seems a dark and threatening force, rather than a bright confirmation of our national genius."

Advanced technology was a double-edged sword. While one side promised economic renewal, the other side eliminated inefficient jobs, firms, and entire industries. By 1981, more U.S. workers were unemployed than at any time since the Great Depression of the 1930s.

The most adverse employment effects were experienced in the manufacturing sector. Even before the recession of the late 1970s, manufacturing in the United States was declining. For example, while the manufacturing sector added 4 million jobs between 1958 and 1968, fewer than 1 million new jobs were added in the following decade (1968 to 1978). During the four-year period between 1978 and 1982, U.S. manufacturing employment declined by almost 3 million jobs (Kuttner 1983). It is difficult to isolate the effects of the shift from manufacturing to service employment, which is characteristic of a maturing economy, and job losses due to economic recession from the effects of specific advanced-technology innovations. Choate (1982) has observed that current changes in the manufacturing sector parallel the dramatic changes associated with mechanization in agriculture – substantial increases in productivity and reductions in the number of jobs.

Predicting the exact number of manufacturing jobs that will be lost because of automation is difficult, but agreement exists that the overall job decline in manufacturing will be substantial. During the next decade, automation may reduce manufacturing jobs by 25 percent (O'Toole 1983); by the end of the century more than half of existing manufacturing jobs may have disappeared (Choate 1982; Office of Technology Assessment 1982). This translates into a loss of some 10 to 15 million manufacturing jobs by the year 2000 (Ehrbar 1983).

Employment within the service sector also may be adversely affected by technological change even though, in comparison to manufacturing, opportunities for substituting capital for labor are far more limited. Nonetheless, examples of dramatic automation-related changes in service employment exist. The introduction of computers into the telephone and telecommunications industries is estimated to have eliminated 100,000 service jobs (O'Toole 1983). Wells Fargo Bank was able to close 30 California branches and eliminate 700 jobs in a two-year period by installing automated teller machines (Business Week 1984d). Technological advances in the area of voice recognition and voice synthesis may have profound impacts on clerical and secretarial occupations in which 18 million people are currently employed (U.S. General Accounting Office 1982). Choate (1982) predicts that the number of service-sector jobs rendered obsolete by automation will ultimately rival that of the manufacturing sector; combined job losses in manufacturing and services would total between 20 and 30 million by the end of the century.

Concerns are also voiced about the quality of jobs lost and the distribution of losses between industries, occupations, and geographic regions. As automation becomes more sophisticated, workers in more advanced jobs can be replaced. While past technological innovations were limited largely to substituting machines for physical labor, advanced-technology innovations are beginning to replace mental labor (Rumberger 1984). Wage differentials between highly skilled and low-skill workers provide an economic incentive to invest in replacing more costly labor.

Employment decline is concentrated in specific industries and occupations. Only about 20 percent of U.S. industries are experiencing a long-term decline in total employment (Bendick 1983). Overall employment increased during the period 1972-80, but employment in 50 out of 235 occupations (over 20 percent) declined by more than 2 million jobs. Moreover, three-quarters of these job losses (1.5 million jobs) was concentrated in only ten occupations (Rumberger 1984).

Economic decline is also concentrated geographically within regions and within states. In the long run, localized economic decline is assumed to create investment opportunities in new industries; underused facilities and high levels of unemployment place downward pressure on rentals and wages, making economically depressed areas more attractive. The "long run," however, may leave generations of workers underemployed. The advanced-technology renaissance in Massachusetts, which was built upon the moribund textile industry, was 40 years in the making (Ehrbar 1983). Moreover, the advanced-technology sector differs fundamentally from traditional manufacturing – physical infrastructure and surplus low skill labor appear to be relatively unimportant (Chapter 4). This implies the possibility of pockets of sustained unemployment within states and regions experiencing rapid advanced-technology employment growth. In fact, the so-called "rust bowl" phenomenon, in which central metropolitan areas remain depressed as suburban areas expand, is not uncommon.

ADVANCED MANUFACTURING AND JOB LOSSES

Of general concern is the extent to which advanced-technology applications in manufacturing, especially the use of robots, may result in permanent job displacement. During the last two decades of this century, an estimated 36 million new workers will enter the world labor force each year (Reich 1983). Technology-induced gains in manufacturing productivity abroad require a substantial increase in the use of robots in U.S. manufacturing; the impact of this trend on employment is largely uncertain. The gains in overseas manufacturing resulting from lower labor costs, foreign government subsidies, and other factors require that labor productivity in U.S. manufacturing must increase. Robotics is only one element in advanced manufacturing techniques, but it has gained wide popular attention.

Currently, about 18,000 to 20,000 robots are in use in the United States. These have limited ability in sensing and interpreting information and are used primarily in repetitive tasks such as welding and painting and in jobs hazardous to humans (Business-Higher Education Forum 1983; Markusen 1983; Ayres 1985; Brooks 1983). An emerging new generation of intelligent robots will be far more versatile. By 1990, approximately 100,000 robots will be in use in the U.S. workplace (Markusen 1983; Rumberger 1984). Industries in transition, such as the automobile industry, which have been particularly hard hit by foreign competition, are investing heavily in this technology.

The extent to which robots can be substituted for human workers is limited by a number of factors. Manufacturing operatives constitute only about 10 percent of today's work force (Business-Higher Education Forum 1983). Current production processes favor robots only in large-scale repetitive manufacturing, although as intelligent robots are perfected, a shift toward flexible automated systems will emerge. No more than 4 percent of U.S. employment will likely be eliminated by the direct substitution of robots by the end of the century (Bendick 1983).

Losses are likely to be concentrated in specific occupations and industries, and in specific geographic regions (Business-Higher Education Forum 1983).

The robotics industry itself requires workers and creates jobs in production and maintenance. But growth in this industry will be insufficient to offset decreases in employment associated with robotics (Wiewel et al. 1984). An estimated three to six jobs will be lost to robots for each new job created in this industry (Rumberger 1984). Also, the United States may not be able to match Japan in the production of robots. In 1982, American robot production grew at less than one-third than that of the Japanese (Wall Street Journal 1983).

DISPLACED WORKERS

The long-term employment prospects of workers displaced by technological change is a pressing, intractable problem. Despite projections of long-term displacement in manufacturing as high as 15 million jobs (Choate 1982), little is known about what happens to workers displaced by automation (Ehrbar 1983). Expectations are that millions of workers not only will be displaced from current jobs but also will be unable to find new employment in their old industry (Gottlieb 1983; Business-Higher Education Forum 1983). The impact of plant closings is believed particularly traumatic with many workers taking years to recover lost earnings and some never finding comparable employment (Bluestone and Harrison 1982). At least one study on permanent job loss suggests, however, that the problems in aggregate may not be as bad as many suggest. Seventy-two percent of the participants in an assistance program for workers who had permanently lost their jobs ultimately returned to similar jobs (Ehrbar 1983).

A corollary concern is the impact of long-term displacement on the size distribution of incomes. If advanced technology is particularly detrimental to the job prospects at the lower skills levels, the poor will become further disadvantaged (O'Toole 1983). A large and growing number of individuals may be slipping into a permanent underclass; without the hope or promise of upward mobility the foundation of U.S. democracy may be at risk. The rapid pace of technological development, and in particular, the "thoughtware" economy (Birch 1984) has implications for the economic prospects of the educationally disadvantaged. A study by the Office of Technology Assessment expressed concern that "a significant social, economic, and political gap could develop between those who do and those who do not have access to, and the ability to use, information systems. People who cannot make effective use of information technology may find themselves unable to . . . obtain and hold a job" (1982, p. 10). The same OTA study also projected that by the end of the decade as many as half of all U.S. families will have home computers. Within the advanced-technology sector, some suggest a movement toward a bimodal skills and income distribution (Kuttner 1983; Malecki 1984; Markusen 1983), although this position is not universally supported (Grubb 1984). The topic of income distribution is treated in detail in Chapter 5.

ADVANCED TECHNOLOGY AND JOB CREATION

Although optimism about the job-creating potential of advanced-technology industries motivates many state and local initiatives, it is extremely difficult to make accurate projections of future employment in advanced-technology industries, or of the impact of technological change on employment in traditional industries. Given the range of definitions of advanced technology in use, one cannot specify the exact size of the current advanced-technology work force.

A Perspective on National Change

Estimating advanced technology's impact on jobs is complex. As noted in Chapter 2, definitions of the advanced-technology sector are invariably operationalized in terms of Standard Industrial Codes (SICs). Major impacts of advanced-technology innovations may occur in industries that are nominally traditional – robotics affects employment in manufacturing, word processing and voice recognition affect secretarial jobs, and so forth. In addition, advanced-technology products can alter traditional production processes enabling the continued operation of traditional industries that might otherwise have failed (Browne 1983). Depending upon the definition used, estimates of advanced-technology employment can vary by more than four to one, ranging from 2.5 to 12.3 million workers in 1982 (Office of Technology Assessment 1984b).

Much of the emphasis on advanced-technology job potential has focused on historically higher growth rates in this sector than in traditional industries. By one estimate, during the past 25 years advanced-technology employment grew at nine times the rate of "low technology" industries (Buck et al. 1984). These estimates of growth are also sensitive to the definition of advanced-technology industries selected. Growth estimates for the period 1972-82 varied by a factor of almost two to one, depending upon the definition used (Office of Technology Assessment 1984b). Even very high growth rates translate into relatively few jobs given the absolute size of advanced-technology employment. Moreover, growth rates differ very dramatically with firm size; small firms grow much more quickly than larger firms but, building on a smaller base, they translate into fewer jobs. In a study of advanced-technology employment growth during the period 1976-80, Armington, Harris, and Odle (1984, p. 128) found that employment in the smallest firms (fewer than 20 employees) increased by 70 percent, mid-size firms (20-99 employees) grew by 35 percent, while large firms (over 100 employees) increased employment by only 16 percent on average. The same study also found that growth rates also differed substantially among geographic regions. The concept of advanced technology defined as product and process applications may be too broad a concept to allow meaningful employment projections based upon historical growth rates.

Difficulties also exist in determining the appropriate starting point for basing growth projections, given the lack of a consistent definition of advanced technology. Projecting future economic activity is difficult and frequently inaccurate. This is particularly true of the advanced technology sector where innovation, rapid change, and volatility are commonplace.

As technology and the economy change, the nature of industries and occupations change as well. Between 1977 and 1983, the Department of Labor added over 275 new occupations to the *Dictionary of Occupational Titles*. A study by the Office of Technology Assessment (1984b, p. 23) observes that "an overriding difficulty comes from a basic inability to foresee job types and industries that simply do not exist yet. Complicating this is uncertainty about the impact of automation on employment in basic industries."

State and Local Policy and Jobs

The United States has no national industrial policy per se, but some argue that the nation has always had the effective equivalent (Business Week 1983). In an era of "new federalism," this policy manifests itself increasingly through state and local initiatives. These initiatives tend to be of two types. The first type are financed and regulated (at least in part) by the federal government and administered by states and localities. These are ostensibly designed to serve national interests by creating common or uniform outcomes across the country. The second type of initiative is undertaken directly by lower levels of government. Historically these job creation programs were in direct competition with other localities and intended to maximize parochial interests. With the new emphasis on home-grown economies in the past five years, the "war between jurisdictions" mentality is minimized. Increasingly, economic-development activities at all levels of government have focused upon advanced-technology industries (Chapter 9).

A study conducted by the Urban Institute (Rassmussen et al. 1982) identified over 500 incentive programs administered by states and another 350 programs administered by the federal government. Policy initiatives intended to promote industrial development are frequently criticized as being uncoordinated, ad hoc, economically inefficient, and generally ineffective. The acknowledged ineffectiveness and lack of widespread impact from the programs makes them easy and suitable targets for elimination. State and local programs, based on tax abatements and financial inducements that are explicitly intended to serve more parochial needs by creating or attracting jobs, may be similarly ineffective. A study by the Council of State Planning Agencies (1980, p. 1) notes that these programs have tended to evolve without "clear analysis of either the basic goals of economic policy . . . or the effectiveness of alternative development programs." Moreover, the net impact of such activities may be "zero-sum" having no impact on employment overall, merely moving jobs from place to place. Reich (1983, p. 16) argues that the "net effects of these programs cancel one another out, burdening taxpayers and granting companies pure windfalls that fail to influence location decisions." These criticisms are partially responsible for ushering in the new types of economic-development policies discussed in this book.

At the national level, concerns about economic-development policy parallel state and local issues. If the industrial policies of competing nations target advanced-technology industries, the United States must undertake similar national initiatives. Advanced-technology exports have long been a major surplus contributor in the U.S. balance of trade (Business-Higher Education Forum 1983); however, during the 1970s the U.S. share of world exports in this area declined from 25 to 20 percent (Choate 1983; Business-Higher Education Forum 1983). As the United States emerged from the recession of the early 1980s, the strength of the U.S. dollar further weakened the international competitiveness of

U.S. advanced-technology products. Today, the United States is a net importer of advanced-technology products: more of the advanced-technology products purchased by U.S. businesses and consumers are made abroad than in this country (Business Week 1985).

A point of general agreement is that growth within the advanced-technology sector (however defined) will proceed at a higher rate than in the economy generally, but given the relatively small number of jobs upon which growth projections are based, most new employment will be in traditional occupations. The Bureau of Labor Statistics (BLS) projects that to 1990, "no job within high technology fields even makes the 'top 20' in terms of total numbers of jobs added to the U.S. economy" (Institute for Research on Educational Finance and Governance 1983, p. 6). In fact, in terms of total job openings projected till 1990, over two-thirds are expected to involve filling existing positions, or replacing workers who withdraw from the labor force (Levin and Rumberger 1983).

This is not to say, however, that the advanced-technology sector is unimportant in terms of job generation. During the 1980s projections indicate the creation of approximately 1 million new advanced-technology jobs nationwide; by 1995, this may grow to as many as 4.6 million (Riche et al. 1983). Clearly, capturing a share of these new jobs represents an appropriate objective for state and local economic-development officials. While advanced technology may represent only a small share of total employment for the foreseeable future, advanced-technology employment can represent a substantial share of net changes in an area's total employment. For example, in early 1985, 22 state governors visited the General Motors headquarters in a bid to attract the 6,000 jobs associated with the planned Saturn project to their states. Moreover, these new jobs, like most advanced-technology jobs, are expected to occur in well-paid and stable occupations (Markusen 1983), making them particularly desirable.

ADVANCED-TECHNOLOGY EMPLOYMENT IN PENNSYLVANIA

Background

Although Pennsylvania has made an effort to attract advanced-technology firms, its primary focus has been on nurturing the creation and growth of existing firms in an attempt to create employment. The rationale for selecting Pennsylvania for this study was described in Chapter 1. Pennsylvania's advanced-technology policies (Chapter 9) have received national attention and have served as the prototype for similar advanced-technology initiatives in other states.

In large part, Pennsylvania's initiatives in the advanced-technology sector were driven by the failure of other sectors of the state economy. Recent regional shifts in employment have not favored Pennsylvania and midwestern states; southern and western states have added new jobs at two and one-half times the rate of these regions (Phillips and Vidal 1983). Pennsylvania's employment experience has been particularly problematic. Since 1976, the unemployment rate in Pennsylvania has been above the national average and until very recently the gap has been widening (Coy 1984). Between 1971 and 1981, employment in the nation grew by about 30 percent; the comparable rate in Pennsylvania was only 10 percent. And during the 1970s, Pennsylvania increased the number of business establishments at less than half the average rate of the rest of the nation (Erickson et al. 1983). The state economy, measured in gross state product (GSP), grew at less than half the national rate from the mid-1970s through the early 1980s (Schwartz 1983).

To a large degree, Pennsylvania's problems are traceable to its heavy reliance on extractive and transformative industries such as coal and steel. During the 1920s, Pennsylvania produced half the steel in the nation. Between 1979 and 1982, Pennsylvania's steel production dropped by 61 percent (Pierce and Hagstom 1983), leaving the state's principal industry operating at about 30 percent of capacity (Thornburg 1982). Between 1980 and 1982, Pennsylvania coal production dropped by over 15 million tons, leaving about one-third of the state's members of the United Mine Workers of America unemployed (Pierce and Hagstrom 1983). Pennsylvania has been more reliant on manufacturing than most states, and the state's manufacturing sector has been declining steadily since the early 1960s. Nationally, during the period 1963-81, employment in manufacturing grew by almost 25 percent. During this same period manufacturing employment in Pennsylvania declined (Coy 1984). Despite this decline, Pennsylvania is still more dependent on manufacturing employment than most states.

Manufacturing productivity in Pennsylvania decreased because the process technologies used by many older facilities could not be easily transformed or upgraded. When competitiveness could not be improved by new plant investment, entire plants were shut down. The recent Pennsylvania picture of new capital investment per worker has improved only slightly from 1978 to 1982 (from $4,060 to $4,432), and this reflects a lower rate of increase than most other states (Pennsylvania Business Council 1985). Even some of the state's advanced technology industries are not immune from the forces of obsolescence. For example, electronic computing equipment (SIC 3573) and radio and television communication equipment (SIC 3662) have decreased by 2,700 employees from 1972 to 1982.

The condition of Pennsylvania's economy has also had an adverse impact on the state's demography. During the 1970s the nation's population grew by 11.4 percent while Pennsylvania's population grew by less than 1 percent (Erickson et al. 1983). During the 1980s a similar pattern is projected (DeJong 1983). A central factor in Pennsylvania's demographics has been net out-migration, particularly among younger members of the work force. In 1980, the median age of Pennsylvania. residents was 32.1 years, the third highest in the nation (Erickson et al. 1983). Because of its economic problems, Pennsylvania was not particularly attractive to job seekers from other states. Recent evidence suggests that the state has turned the corner. In 1985, Pennsylvania's two largest cities, Philadelphia and Pittsburgh, were cited as the fifth and first best place to live in the United States by Rand McNally.

When population decline is precipitated by job loss, out-migrants tend to be young adults with above-average education and income (Levy 1981). Despite Pennsylvania's extensive educational system, with over 200 colleges and universities, the state ranks below the national average both in the percentage of the population aged 20-64 with a high-school education and in the percentage with college and/or graduate education. The state ranks fourth in the nation in production of engineers from its educational system, yet it is equal only to the national average in number of engineers per capita (Erickson et al. 1983). The state's overall demographic pattern adversely affects future employment prospects in two ways: 1) The out-migration of highly educated young workers makes the area less attractive to advanced-technology industries, and 2) the pattern increases the dependency ratio in the state, requiring higher public-service costs.

Pennsylvania's Advanced-Technology Employment Prospects

The long-term decline of the state's traditional economic base makes attracting and nurturing new advanced-technology industries particularly appropriate for Pennsylvania. To attain "full" employment by 1988, the state will have to create 350,000 to 500,000 new jobs (Schwartz 1983). The state already has a substantial advanced-technology base: it ranks among the top five states nationally in terms of advanced-technology manufacturing employment (Coy 1982; Glasmeier 1984), it is third in the nation in terms of advanced-technology industries represented (Glasmeier 1984), and it ranks among the top ten states in terms of employment under all three BLS definitions of the sector (Office of Technology Assessment 1984b).

The state has the fifth largest work force in the nation and it ranks fourth in the number of scientists and engineers (Stengel and Plosila 1982). Pennsylvania is third in the nation in its number of colleges and universities; however, per-student appropriations in public colleges are below the national average, and the participation rate of the population aged 18-24 is lower than that of comparable states (Pennsylvania Business Council 1985). The state ranks high on quality-of-life indexes and spends a higher than average share of public funds on primary and secondary education (Pennsylvania Business Council 1985).

The state urgently needs to create additional advanced-technology jobs and is apparently in a reasonable position to do so. One of the most important factors in Pennsylvania's favor is the strong commitment of the state government to act as a catalyst to promote local economic development. Although Pennsylvania is an acknowledged national leader in entrepreneurial and technological development programs, its ability to translate programmatic activity into jobs and economic growth over the next 10 to 20 years remains to be seen.

A DESCRIPTION OF THE ADVANCED-TECHNOLOGY SECTOR

An operational definition of the advanced-technology sector, which included 42 four-digit Standard Industrial Classification (SIC) codes, was developed in Chapter 2. In December 1982, 2,432 Pennsylvania firms were identified (from the Dun Market Identifier Files) that listed one of these 42 SICs as their principal focus.

This chapter provides an overview of the advanced-technology sector (defined by these 42 SICs) for the United States and for Pennsylvania using data collected annually by the U.S. Department of Commerce and called County Business Patterns (CBP). Data for two periods (March

1972 and March 1982) are presented on employment, payroll, and number of advanced-technology establishments (Table 3.1). The data provide an estimate of the overall size of the sector, the relative importance of Pennsylvania's advanced-technology base, and patterns of growth over the decade.

The available data have some limitations. For some industries, the four-digit code provided a finer level of specificity than was available in the CBP tabular data. In counties where total employment in an industry totaled fewer than 50 employees, data were withheld to protect employers in accordance with federal regulations insuring confidentiality. In a number of cells, ranges rather than point estimates were provided. These have been presented as the midpoint of each range in Table 3.1 and in the analyses. Finally, as might be expected in the advanced-technology sector, a number of industries appearing in the 1982 data did not exist in 1972.

Where data were unreported or withheld, a value of zero was assigned in the analysis. This procedure provides a conservative estimate of the size of the advanced-technology sector although it is impossible to know the exact magnitude of downward bias. One point of comparison is the Dun and Bradstreet file used to identify the survey sample. Based upon the 42 SICs identified as advanced-technology firms, the Dun and Bradstreet file identified 2,432 firms operating in Pennsylvania in December 1982. The comparable figure from the analysis of published CBP data was 2,038 firms (Table 3.1), about 20 percent fewer firms than identified by Dun and Bradstreet. Since the Dun and Bradstreet file is likely to exclude extremely small and new firms and those not seeking credit, the data presented in Table 3.1 probably understate the true size of the advanced-technology sector by more than 20 percent. Despite these limitations, the data are very useful in tracing patterns in advanced technology over time.

A strong general trend of employment growth is apparent in these 42 advanced-technology industries during the decade examined (Table 3.1). National employment data were not available in the CBP files for two four-digit SICs (3873 and 8922) in either 1978 or 1982. Thirty-four of the 40 industries for which national data were available experienced growth. In fact, 16 of those appearing in the 1982 data were not listed in 1972. Six advanced-technology industries experienced a decline in employment during this same period.

Table 3.2 contrasts total employment, payroll, and establishments for the overall U.S. and Pennsylvania economies with the advanced-technology sector in 1972 and 1982. Total employment in the United

States grew by 28 percent during the decade; advanced-technology employment grew by 112 percent, four times the national rate. In Pennsylvania, employment growth was much lower. Total employment grew by less than 10 percent over the decade, while advanced-technology employment in the state grew by 100 percent. Thus, although Pennsylvania's rate of employment growth was lower than the national rate, employment in the advanced technology sector in Pennsylvania grew at over ten times the rate of state employment.

Nationally, the number of businesses increased by 32 percent over the decade. The number of advanced-technology establishments increased by 228 percent, more than seven times the national rate. In Pennsylvania, new firms were established at a lower rate in all sectors. The total number of establishments increased by only 16 percent. Advanced-technology firms increased by 109 percent, almost seven times the overall rate for the state.

Both nationally and in Pennsylvania, advanced-technology employment grew substantially faster than the economy in general. In Pennsylvania, the relative growth rate of the advanced-technology sector (measured in number of jobs) was higher than in the national economy. This difference was because Pennsylvania's economy performed substantially less well than other state economies. In absolute terms, Pennsylvania's advanced-technology sector did not grow as quickly as the sector did nationally. The portrait that emerges over the decade preceding the survey of 459 firms is one in which advanced technology created jobs at a much higher rate than the economy in general both nationally and in Pennsylvania. In terms of jobs, advanced technology was particularly important in Pennsylvania during this period because of the extremely low rate of overall employment growth.

EMPLOYMENT GROWTH 1982-84

In the December 1982 survey of advanced-technology firms in Pennsylvania, executive managers were asked to provide data on current employment in Pennsylvania and plans for expansion of employment. Only one firm failed to provide the requested data, and four firms could not be identified for follow-up data collection. The average firm employed about 81 workers at the time of the survey; 273 firms (about 60 percent of all respondents) reported plans to increase employment over the next two years.

TABLE 3.1 The National Economy and Advanced-Technology Sector 1972 and 1982

Description of Industry	Code	U.S. 1972			U.S. 1982			PA 1972			PA 1982		
		Employ	Payrol	Est	Employ	Payrol	Est	Employ	Payrol	Est	Employ	Payrol	Est
Drugs: Biological Products	2831	6126	16326	133	21898	101751	328	191	539	8	750	0	16
Drugs: Medicinls & Botanicls	2833	6754	18236	113	18221	118634	205	748	2077	10	750	0	5
Drugs: Pharm. Preparations	2834	117738	326025	768	129665	778841	666	12463	33482	57	13338	82026	37
Computing Mach.: Electronic	3573	138729	406781	518	327503	1889723	1543	8107	24170	23	6522	35447	42
Calc. and Account Machines	3574	35710	72239	106	20218	99799	66	0	0	3	60	0	1
Radio and T.V. Sets	3651	100845	191975	387	57921	240099	417	4868	8896	13	1673	5621	9
Telephone and Telegraph	3661	136486	329356	167	134789	717426	305	209	432	6	1371	5561	9
Radio-T.V. Comm. Equip.	3662	291086	802033	1410	472253	2681804	2059	8450	21650	77	7401	33824	70
Electron Tubes-Receiving	3671	13175	28660	29	30814	157024	89	0	0	6	4976	26825	9
Cathode Ray Picture Tubes	3672	17899	37253	66	14	47	5	0	0	7	0	0	0
Electron Tubes-Transmiting	3673	15162	39805	54	474	2370	9	454	1427	3	0	0	0
Semiconductors	3674	74608	173365	330	177963	959899	76	10386	25216	24	9775	58964	38
Electronic Capacitors	3675	0	0	0	26937	8988	115	0	0	0	750	0	0
Electronic Resistors	3676	0	0	0	18431	65575	88	0	0	0	1125	5682	6
Electronic Coils-Transformers	3677	0	0	0	21912	64225	320	0	0	0	1750	0	0
Electronic Connectors	3678	0	0	0	34665	142590	150	0	0	0	4408	19347	15
Electronic Comp.-N.E.C.	3679	201396	403402	212	5215292	919514	3373	12299	20548	126	10156	38743	128
X-ray Apparatus & Tubes	3693	11745	29232	100	43515	235211	212	0	0	0	1633	7619	5
Aircraft	3721	260951	775608	135	270443	1880313	158	0	0	5	7500	0	2
Aircraft Engines & Parts	3724	0	0	0	134527	891669	304	0	0	0	3680	17900	10
Aircraft Equipment-nec.	3728	0	0	0	136041	831149	849	0	0	0	0	0	0
Guided Missiles & Space Veh.	3761	0	0	0	117335	859502	29	0	0	0	1750	0	1

SIC	Industry												
3764	Space Propulsion-Units & Parts	0	0	0	27620	182953	29	0	0	0	0	0	0
381	Engineering & Scient. Instr	41900	102816	633	53160	255266	851	1358	2824	47	3073	13531	45
3822	Automatic Temp. Controls	30032	62730	141	30517	135136	251	0	0	11	1372	6422	10
3823	Process Control Instr.	0	0	0	56614	287672	605	0	0	0	10495	60186	32
3824	Fluid Meters & Counting Dev.	0	0	0	11002	49517	118	0	0	0	3058	13972	9
3825	Instr. to Measure Electricity	0	0	0	95458	474629	718	0	0	0	1534	4812	35
3829	Meas. & Contr. Devices	0	0	0	39129	196148	668	0	0	0	2548	13030	32
383	Optical Instruments & Lenses	30032	62730	141	223333	893893	544	658	1585	27	3252	15373	29
3841	Surgical & Medical Instr.	31852	65274	415	58943	255287	816	1182	2033	20	2740	11073	41
386	Photo Equipment & Supplies	93579	298775	553	111331	835277	729	767	1647	21	1534	8960	31
3873	Watches, Watchcases & Clocks	0	0	0	0	0	0	0	0	0	0	0	0
3944	Games, Toys & Childrens Veh.	0	0	0	42405	144451	666	0	0	0	1449	4159	30
482	Telegraphic Communication	22648	64184	609	13320	72740	761	1070	2813	34	425	0	40
489	Other Communication Services	25011	52276	1609	100640	429391	4080	1459	2332	143	3455	13040	235
7372	Comp. Programming & Soft.	0	0	0	114912	706595	6631	0	0	0	3750	0	186
7374	Data Processing Services	0	0	0	193481	891496	7939	0	0	0	8688	39491	309
7379	Computer Related Services	0	0	0	46076	268295	3999	0	0	0	2049	11573	137
8071	Medical Laboratories	34549	64632	2988	65838	266473	4880	1005	1672	102	3589	12320	188
8072	Dental Laboratories	25735	46640	4396	39032	130044	6803	1211	2081	198	1599	4943	246
8922	Noncommercial Research	0	0	0	0	0	0	0	0	0	0	0	0

Note: Payroll figures represent first quarter payroll in thousands of dollars in current year.

Source: County Business Patterns, 1972 and 1982. Compilation of data assembled by the Bureau of the Census, U.S. Department of Commerce, for the United States and Pennsylvania.

TABLE 3.2 Growth in Advanced Technology and Total Economy – U.S. and Pennsylvania, 1972-1982

| | Total Economy | | | Advanced Tech Sector | | | Ad Tech's Share of Total | | Ratio Ad Tech Growth/ Total Growth |
	1972 [1]	1982 [2]	Growth [3]	1972 [4]	1982 [5]	Growth [6]	1972 [7]	1982 [8]	Growth [9]
United States									
Employment	58,015,901	74,297,252	28%	1,763,748	3,733,442	112%	3.0%	5.0%	4.0
Payroll*	432,340	561,288	30%	17,874	38,811	117%	4.1%	6.9%	3.9
Establishments	3,540,846	4,633,960	32%	16,013	52,454	228%	0.5%	1.1%	7.1
Pennsylvania									
Employment	3,579,128	3,919,201	9.5%	66,885	133,978	100%	1.9%	3.4%	10.5
Payroll	26,858	29,159	10.9%	622	1,1100	77%	2.3%	3.8%	7.0
Establishments	186,009	216,476	16.0%	971	2,038	10.9%	0.5%	0.9%	6.8

*Payroll in millions of 1972 (CPI deflated) dollars.

Source: County Business Patterns, 1972 and 1982. Compilation of data assembled by the Bureau of the Census, U.S. Department of Commerce, for the United States and Pennsylvania.

Two years after the initial survey, firms were resurveyed to obtain information on the current number of Pennsylvania employees. Initial contacts were made by phone. Firm representatives were reminded of the first survey, thanked for their participation, and asked to report the number of current Pennsylvania employees. Firms that either could not be reached by phone or refused to provide requested information on the telephone were sent a follow-up letter.

Of the 459 firms responding to the first survey, 67 (14.6 percent) were no longer in business two years later, 18 firms (3.9 percent) refused to provide the requested information, and 5 firms (0.9 percent) either could not be matched to original surveys or lacked 1982 employment data.

In the analysis that follows, the 67 firms that could not be located in 1984 are treated as having failed. In all likelihood this assumption overstates the actual failure rate in the sample, since mergers and take-overs among advanced-technology firms are common (Glasmeier, Hall & Markusen 1984). The actual merger and takeover experiences of these "failed" firms could not be tracked. The 22 firms (18 nonrespondents and four with incomplete data from the first survey) were excluded from the analysis of job creation presented in this chapter. The 22 firms for which data were missing were not statistically significantly different from the 437 firms for which data were available.

FIRM FAILURES AND EMPLOYMENT GROWTH

While overall the advanced-technology sector has outperformed the economy in general during the past decade, equivalent growth has not occurred across all firms. From a state and local development perspective it is important to identify the types of firms that are more and less successful within this sector. Table 3.3 provides data on firm failure and employment growth rates for all firms, and the employment experience of surviving advanced-technology firms in Pennsylvania during the period 1980-84.

Data on employment at three points over a four-year interval (1980, 1982, and 1984) allow estimation of rates of job growth. Data on both 1982 and 1984 employment are available for 436 firms in the sample. Data on all three periods are available for 390 firms. (Firms in existence fewer than two years at the time of the 1982 survey could not provide

1980 employment data). Similarly, firms that came into existence after December 1982 are not included in the study.

The first column of Table 3.3 shows the failure rate of different types of firms between 1982 and 1984. Columns 2-4 show rates of employment growth for 1980-82 using retrospective data, for 1982-84 using data collected in both periods, and for 1980-84, respectively. The last three columns of the table (columns 5-7) show employment growth for the same three periods, limiting the analysis to firms that were still in business in December 1984. Of the firms surviving in 1984, data were available for 369 firms in both 1982 and 1984 and for 337 firms in all three periods.

Firm Size and Age

Overall, 15 percent of the firms sampled in 1982 failed within the next two years (column 1, Table 3.3). The probability of failure is always highest during the first few years of a firm's existence and small firms are more vulnerable to failure than larger firms. The failure rate in this sample dropped consistently with both size and age. Over one-quarter of the smallest firms (five employees or fewer) failed during this two-year period. Small firms (6-24 employees) had a 13 percent failure rate while only 6 percent of the larger firms (50 or more employees) experienced failure. Similarly, failure rates dropped with the age of the firm. Over a quarter of the very young firms (less than five years in Pennsylvania) and over a fifth of the young firms (5-10 years) failed, compared to fewer than 10 percent of those firms in operation for ten years or longer.

High failure rates caused the smallest firms to experience negative job growth between 1982 and 1984. The 1980-82 interval is not affected by failures because the sample, drawn in 1982, excluded any firms that had existed in 1980 and failed during the following two years. Growth rates increase with firm size up to 50 employees and then decline. Over the four-year interval 1980-84, firms that had 20-25 employees in 1982 almost doubled their employment.

Despite high failure rates, young firms also experienced high growth rates during the same period. Between 1980 and 1984, employment in the youngest firms grew by 124 percent. During the same interval, employment in the oldest firms increased by only 4 percent.

When the analysis is restricted to firms still in existence in 1984 (columns 5-7), patterns become even more pronounced. Even when the

TABLE 3.3 Firm Failure and Employment Growth 1980-1984

	Percent Firms Surviving in 1982				Percent Firms Surviving in 1984		
			Growth		Growth		
	82-84	80-82	82-84	80-84	80-82	82-84	80-84
	(1)	(2)	(3)	(4)	(5)	(6)	(7)
AVERAGE	15	28	13	49	25	34	72
SIZE – Employees in PA							
up to 5	27	25	-14	-3	15	18	27
6-24	13	42	19	80	42	37	104
25-49	7	23	46	95	24	58	112
50+	6	9	27	41	11	35	48
	***	*	*	**	*	(ns)	(ns)
AGE – Years in PA							
1-4	26	77	34	124	80	80	194
5-9	22	41	0	54	38	29	94
10-14	7	5	20	29	6	18	36
15+	9	0	4	4	0	14	13
	***	***	(ns)	**	***	*	***
SECTOR							
Manufacturing	9	28	17	49	27	29	62
Service	21	28	10	49	24	39	82
	***	(ns)	(ns)	(ns)	(ns)	(ns)	(ns)

continued

TABLE 3.3, Continued

	Percent Firms Surviving in 1982				Percent Firms Surviving in 1984		
		Growth				Growth	
	82-84	80-82	82-84	80-84	80-82	82-84	80-84
	(1)	(2)	(3)	(4)	(5)	(6)	(7)
ANTICIPATES GROWTH							
No	20	8	-6	3	7	18	24
Yes	12	40	27	78	37	45	101
	*	***	*	**	***	(ns)	**
WORKFORCE COMPOSITION							
Percent Workforce Low-skill							
0	32	36	-13	31	35	28	80
1-20	11	53	16	91	47	31	117
21-50	9	17	33	59	15	47	76
Over 50	11	24	12	33	22	25	46
	***	*	(ns)	(ns)	(ns)	(ns)	(ns)
Percent Workforce High-skill							
0	20	7	-32	-21	3	-15	-15
1-20	8	22	10	37	24	19	49
21-50	10	18	27	52	17	41	66
Over 50	19	37	10	56	34	35	89
	(ns)	(ns)	(ns)	(ns)	(ns)	(ns)	(ns)
LOCAL LABOR MARKET							
Difficulty Recruiting Low-skill							
Little	20	33	14	53	29	42	88
Moderate	5	20	21	57	20	28	63
Considerable	18	27	-8	13	27	12	35
	***	(ns)	(ns)	(ns)	(ns)	(ns)	(ns)

Difficulty Recruiting High-skill							
Little	22	30	21	63	31	54	101
Moderate	9	24	19	54	24	32	68
Considerable	14	29	4	37	23	21	56
	*	(ns)	(ns)	(ns)	(ns)	(ns)	(ns)
TRAINING POLICY							
Train Low-skill Outside							
No	15	34	4	55	32	24	77
Yes	14	19	34	43	15	57	68
	(ns)	(ns)	(ns)	(ns)	(ns)	(ns)	(ns)
Train High-skill Outside							
No	24	19	−14	10	18	14	38
Yes	12	32	23	63	29	40	85
	**	(ns)	*	(ns)	(ns)	(ns)	(ns)
RESEARCH INTENSITY							
0%	18	19	−1	17	10	20	36
1-5%	10	16	21	35	15	34	50
6-13%	13	28	5	47	30	21	65
14%+	22	52	30	105	57	68	159
	(ns)	*	(ns)	(ns)	**	(ns)	**

***Significant at .001
**Significant at .01
*Significant at .05
(ns) = not significant at .05

Source: Compiled by authors from survey of advanced-technology firms.

59

effects of firm failure are excluded, the extremely small firms experienced the lowest growth rates of any group. Employment in surviving firms employing 6-24 employees more than doubled between 1980 and 1984, while the smallest firms (five or fewer employees) increased by less than 30 percent. The youngest firms, on the other hand, experienced very rapid growth. Employment among surviving firms that had been in existence for fewer than five years almost tripled compared to an overall growth rate of 72 percent. Employment growth rates decreased in a linear pattern with firm age, with the oldest firms experiencing only a 13 percent increase in employment over the same four-year period.

Sector and Expansion Plans

The failure rate in the advanced-technology service sector was twice as high as that of manufacturing. Despite differences in the probability of failure, overall employment growth was about equal in both sectors. Examining only firms that survived in 1984, service-sector firms experienced somewhat higher growth over the four-year period, but the differences were not statistically significant.

In 1982, the firms' executives were asked whether they anticipated expanding employment during the next two years. The failure rate was significantly lower among firms with expansion plans; however, 12 percent of those firms with plans to expand apparently failed during the following two-year period. Expectations are clearly influenced strongly by recent experience; firms anticipating expansion in 1982 had increased employment during the previous two years at five times the rate of those that did not (column 2). Executives' projections of growth also were reasonably accurate. During the two years following the survey, employment increased by 27 percent, on average, among firms anticipating growth and declined by 6 percent among those with no expansion plans. Over the four-year interval, firms that planned to continue growing in 1982 grew by 78 percent compared to only 3 percent for firms that did not project growth.

Composition of the Work Force

Another way in which firms differ is in the skills of their work force. Firms were organized into four categories depending upon the proportion of workers in low-skill (unskilled and semiskilled) and high-skill (technical and professional) occupations. These categories are examined in detail in Chapter 5. In general, failure rates were lower among firms that reported a heterogeneous mix of employees. For example, firms that reported using no low-skill workers were twice as likely to fail as the average firm in the sample. Similarly, firms that reported using no high-skill workers or those that employed primarily high-skill employees tended to have about twice the incidence of failure as those with a more balanced work force.

The proportion of high-skill workers tended to be strongly related to growth in employment in the full sample and among surviving firms. Between 1980 and 1984, employment growth rates increased with the proportion of high-skill workers both for the full sample (column 4) and for the subsample of surviving firms (column 7).

Recruiting Difficulty and Training Policy

The firms' managers were asked to indicate the degree of difficulty encountered in recruiting workers in their local area for the two skills categories just described. A U-shaped pattern emerges between recruiting difficulty and failure rates. Firms that reported either considerable difficulty or little difficulty recruiting were more likely to fail than those that reported only moderate difficulty. This pattern applied to both high-skill and low-skill workers. The pattern suggests that two fundamentally different mechanisms may be at work. Firms reporting little recruiting difficulty may not have been seeking new workers because of poor growth prospects. Among the remaining firms, those reporting considerable difficulty may have experienced a higher failure rate because worker shortages genuinely limited their ability to compete.

Of the surviving firms, growth rates tend to be highest for those firms reporting little recruiting difficulty, and growth appears to be inversely related to recruiting difficulty although differences are not statistically significant. For example, during the period 1980-84, surviving firms that reported little difficulty recruiting high-skill workers increased employment by 101 percent compared to a 56 percent increase for firms reporting considerable difficulty.

Managers were asked to describe their firms' training of new employees. Those firms that used outside training facilities for high-skill employees failed half as often as those that did not. Training policy regarding low-skill workers, however, was unrelated to firms' failure rates. Although differences were not statistically significant, firms that provided outside training to high-skill workers also had higher rates of employment growth. For example, employment increased by 63 percent between 1980 and 1984 among firms using outside training. This compared to 10 percent for nontraining firms (column 4). Even among surviving firms where the effect of differential failure rates is removed, training firms increased employment by 85 percent compared to 38 percent for nontraining firms.

Firms were organized into four categories based upon the proportion of gross sales devoted to research and development (R&D). A weak, statistically insignificant pattern emerged between the likelihood of failure and research intensity, with firms heavily committed to research and those conducting no research having the higher probability of failure. Controlling for differences in failure rate, research intensity was positively related to job growth – firms that devoted more of their resources to R&D increased their employment more rapidly. For example, during the period 1980-84, employment in surviving firms grew by 159 percent among the most research-intensive firms, compared to a 36 percent growth rate among firms conducting no R&D.

SUMMARY OF FINDINGS AND POLICY IMPLICATIONS

Concern about structural unemployment related to the decline of smokestack industries has been the principal factor motivating state and local advanced-technology initiatives. Little empirical work has examined the characteristics of advanced-technology firms that create jobs. Many policy initiatives have been designed and implemented on the basis of popular perceptions.

Over the decade immediately preceding this study, advanced-technology firms were found to have substantially higher employment growth than the economy in general both in the nation and in Pennsylvania. Given the relatively small size of the sector, however, high growth rates translate into a relatively small share of overall employment. This does not, in itself, suggest that advanced-technology initiatives are misdirected. In terms of state and local economic development, incremental changes in employment can be very significant.

During the two-year period 1982-84, advanced-technology firms in Pennsylvania increased employment by almost 22 percent even though almost one of every six firms in this sector no longer was constituted in 1984 as it was in 1982 (many failed during this period). Growth rates among surviving firms were high: 72 percent on average over four years, or about 15 percent per year.

Failure rates differed systematically with the characteristics of the firms. Consistent with other studies, small and young firms failed at a much higher rate, and failure rates declined consistently with age. The pattern suggests that initiatives such as new enterprise support networks, business incubators, managerial and financial support, and better ties to existing industry may be particularly important. Firms that used outside facilities for training professional and technical employees were only half as likely to fail as those that did not. This pattern suggests that development initiatives directed at fostering linkages and partnerships between firms and the higher-education sector may be critically important. A strong relationship also appeared between failure rates and difficulty in recruiting in the local labor market. Firms that reported considerable difficulty recruiting new employees had substantially higher failure rates than those reporting only moderate difficulty. The pattern suggests that training programs may be an important factor in a firm's survival.

Contrary to popular belief, extremely small firms did not exhibit high rates of job growth. Small to midsized firms grew at a much higher rate than did large firms, but given their smaller employment base these firms did not generate as many new jobs. In terms of forming policy, a danger lies in analyzing different-sized firms as discrete entities; with growth, small firms become midsized, and so forth. Development agencies may require sophisticated simulation models to project employment growth based upon data on firm size.

4 Initial Location and Expansion of Single Plant Advanced-Technology Firms

INTRODUCTION

The location of firms has concerned development officials, business executives, and scholars for years. The factors affecting a company's choice of location are multifaceted and dynamic. As development trends change, for example, from large facility siting to entrepreneurship and small business, the forces affecting a firm's locational behavior also change. The advanced-technology sector provides an excellent contemporary example of how changing economic activity at state and local levels influences locational and developmental outcomes.

This chapter examines the factors that influence executive decisions to locate and expand advanced-technology firms. A brief review of regional development and industrial location theories provides a backdrop for this analysis. Recent studies of advanced-technology locations are also reviewed. In addition to examining firms' initial location and expansion decisions, this chapter discusses an issue important to advanced-technology development: the agglomeration or "critical mass," which many claim is important for building and sustaining technology-intensive activity. Implications of the chapter's findings for economic-development policy are reviewed in the conclusion.

REGIONAL GROWTH AND INDUSTRIAL LOCATION THEORIES

Research on advanced-technology development has centered upon two traditions (Rees and Stafford 1983): regional economic-development theories with special attention on the role of technology in economic growth (Malecki 1983), and factors and decisions associated with the selection of a site. The first body of literature explicitly addresses technology issues, while the second addresses technology as embedded in factors relevant to the siting of advanced-technology firms.

Regional-Development Theories

No single theory of regional development sufficiently explains the growth of regions or provides useful public-policy insight (Lloyd and Dicken 1977). The widely accepted theories are partial, with only occasional convergence at certain points. Not all regional-development theories explicitly recognize the importance of technology.[1] Three that do are discussed here: innovation and diffusion, growth pole or growth center, and product life cycle.

Innovation and Diffusion Theories

Innovation is the application of technology in a new organizational setting (Tornatzky et al. 1983). Innovation is not a discrete event; it occurs as a process and involves different social groups at different times during the process. No clear articulation of innovation's role in economic development exists because the many different perspectives on innovation have not been integrated into a single theoretical approach (Rees and Stafford 1983). The difficulty in integrating the varying perspectives arises primarily because innovation is influenced by a wide range of environmental factors, from macroeconomic forces to discrete firm-level linkages and transfers. Although various units of analysis are examined in innovation research, the process is easiest to grasp at the firm level.

Competitive pressure is likely to be the greatest motivation for innovation for a particular firm (Malecki 1983). From an organizational perspective, firms that exhibit flexible, risk-inadverse management characteristics and information-sharing networks (characteristics of fast-growing firms) are more likely to be early adopters of an innovation (Abernathy and Rosenbloom 1982; Hall 1980; Quinn 1978). More rigid, conservative organizations adopt the same innovation somewhat later. These imitator firms are able to reap the benefits of others' early adoptions after continued improvements are made to previous stages of the innovation.

The diffusion of innovation, whether by imitation or some other process, is a pattern of new technology spreading through a group of potential adopters. The starting point of diffusion is the innovation itself, which occurs in an organizational and industrial context. The innovation moves within or outside the organization and/or industry based on a flow of information and the use of innovations by other organizations (Ganz 1981). For a group disposed toward adopting new technology, communication about the innovation raises awareness and provides choice criteria, two elements that precede user adoption (Tornatzky et al. 1983). Communication and adoption conditions can be facilitated by agents of industry and government that realize the mutual benefits of technological development.

Studies of the process of innovation that aggregate from the firm level to the regional level have gained wide acceptance, although they are perceived by some as less precise and realistic than firm-and-industry-level analysis (Gold 1981; Nelson 1981). The regional models of diffusion consider space a major constraint to the flow of information: ". . . when the space economy is not fully integrated, space prevents the various regions from having access to the same blueprint of technology" (McCombie 1982, p. 337). Epidemic or contagion models (Davies 1980) suggest that proximate adoptions are most likely, with a decay of adoption as distance increases.

Researchers disagree about whether or not a general, integrated theory of diffusion ever will evolve (Feller 1981). Widely differing perspectives are largely a result of technological innovation being an emerging field which addresses explanatory objectives compounding the situation in different perspectives drawn from different social and behavioral-science disciplines. An imperative for diffusion theory, however, exists: for the conceptual approach to be relevant for economic development, it must incorporate elements of varying locational environments (Ewers and Wettman 1980).

Growth-Pole Theory

The economic-development theory of growth poles, or its translation into growth centers, incorporates spatial environments and technology as central concepts. Agglomeration economies and concentrated economic activity create initial growth-center conditions that spread from central points to outlying areas. Early concentration of innovation is associated with fast-growing industries. Development in an area causes supply-demand relationships, competition, and induced demand with growth implications for firms and industries in proximate areas (Erickson 1972; Nelson, Peck, and Kalachek 1967; Perroux 1973). Multiplier effects and entrepreneurial development activities help promote growth away from central areas. Interfirm and interindustry linkages in the form of technological support organizations and other infrastructure arrangements promote growth beyond the initial concentration area.

The linkages formed as a response to new technological develop-ments spawn new enterprises or spinoffs. As discussed in Chapter 8, new enterprise linkages are diverse, and include forward and/or backward linkages with parent companies. Different forms of linkages are being developed in publicly supported technological and entrepreneurial development programs (Chapter 9). One reason why growth poles do not typically produce widespread benefits concerns poor linkages (Malecki 1983, p. 95). As technology spreads during its nascent stage, communication and support channels are narrow and closely shared. As the diffusion process multiplies, information diffuses, increasing access by others, but weakening the earlier closely established linkages. This process suggests that one role of public policy is to promote linkages by maintaining close communication and support in the technological infrastructure.

Life Cycle and Specialization Theories

Theories of product life cycle and regional specialization are offshoots of the growth-pole theory. The life-cycle theory refines the growth-pole theory, which emphasizes technology's role in growth and development, by emphasizing stages of technological development (Norton and Rees 1979).

In the initial innovation stage of a product's life cycle, R&D capacity, technically skilled workers, and local entrepreneurial support networks are important. Activities at this stage are typically carried out in high-cost areas where access to skilled personnel, facilities, local markets, and support networks is maximized. The second stage, the growth stage, is less skill intensive due to the increasing conformity of product and process. This stage is also characterized by increased external markets and production movement away from locations necessary during the growth stage. Production costs are lowest in the final or standardization stage, when low labor costs and transferable technology, which are the result of relocation away from high-cost centers, produce net benefits.

The concept of specialization in life-cycle theory is different from conventional specialization notions. Traditionally, specialization occurred in specific manufacturing industries, but with the advent of rapid technological change and international competition, many manufacturing areas experienced deindustrialization and decline. Diversification of an area's economic base, the process of becoming less reliant on one industry or employer, became a goal of economic development. Specialization in the first stage, for example, creating the conditions for high-growth startups and innovation, rather than in the standardization stage of the product life cycle, has become the optimal regional structure (Malecki 1983). Life-cycle theory emphasizes support mechanisms such as agglomeration effects and the technological infrastructure. Regions can grow and diversify if they promote entrepreneurship and ". . . change their roles from recipients of innovation via branch plants to generators of innovation through indigenous growth" (Rees and Stafford 1983, p. 101).

Industrial Location Theory

A second tradition in economic development uses a microeconomic framework: the works of Hoover (1948), Losch (1954), and Greenhut (1965) are examples of the "classical" approach to industrial location. This approach focuses on the individual executive or firm as the unit of analysis. In regional development theories, attention focused mainly on a macro (regional) pattern of industrial activity. In the industrial-location theory, attention is focused primarily on the specific characteristics of a particular location. These area characteristics are of two types: those concerning the friction of distance (costs of overcoming space), and the attributes of areas (Stafford and Rees 1983). The characteristics of various locations are compared in order to arrive at some judgment concerning a favorable business site.[2] A firm's top executives, using a profit-maximization criterion, arrive at a final choice predicated on the characteristics of the location. The relative importance of characteristics changes, however, as the geographic scale of the search is incrementally narrowed. Contemporary examples of these mainly survey-based location studies typically deal with large manufacturing firms (Ady 1981; Epping 1982; Schmenner 1983; Lund 1984).

A variation of industrial-location studies is the business-climate study. While Schmenner (1983, p. 53) acknowledges that a business climate means different things, he characterizes it as a ". . . metric of a location's expected ability to maintain a productive environment over the foreseeable future." Essentially this is another way factor costs can be compared across jurisdictions. A good business climate for manufacturing usually is associated with low state and local taxes, little union activity (right-to-work laws), and cooperative governments. The methodology of a business-climate study is relatively simple. Descriptive analysis is conducted on a set of factors thought relevant to business operations. Geographic areas, usually states, are ranked by their aggregate scores, that is, climates. The validity of the indicators, typically a result of the normative bias of the sponsoring association, and the results they generate lend themselves to wide disagreement, especially from states that do not rank highly.

An example of the traditional manufacturing business-climate study is the well-known Alexander Grant and Company (1984) study "General Manufacturing Business Climates," prepared annually in cooperation with the Conference of State Manufacturers Associations. In this study 22 factors are aggregated into five categories: state and local government fiscal policies, labor costs, state-regulated employment costs, availability and productivity of labor force, and "other factors," such as energy costs, environment control, and population. State manufacturing associations are asked to weight each of the five categories for their state and also the factors within each of the five categories. Weighting is subjective, based on their own perceptions of important factors. The weighted data yield a rank for each state.

In contrast to the Grant study, which serves a large-corporation and manufacturing clientele, *Inc.* magazine, which serves an entrepreneurial clientele, also conducts an annual study of state business climates. *Inc.* ranks the 50 states according to five major factors: capital resources, labor, taxes, state support, and business activity (Posner 1984). *Inc.*, also using a subjective weighting scheme, has deemed capital and state support two and a half times more important than taxes, and labor and business activity twice as important as taxes.

These two frequently cited business-climate studies highlight the differences between the clientele they seek to serve. For example, executives of large manufacturing firms consider energy costs, right-to-work laws, and pollution control important components in their consideration of business locations. State development officials trying to induce these large manufacturing facilities to locate in their state emphasize their state's business-climate advantage. Conversely, capital availability, state support, and business activity, highlighted by the *Inc.* survey, are important to the growth of new and small businesses.

The distinctions between regional-development theories, industrial-location theories, and business-climate studies are also evident in studies that address the location characteristics of advanced-technology firms. One reason for these various approaches and methodologies is confusion about advanced technology (Chapter 2). Given the complex, dynamic nature of advanced technology, this confusion is not likely to disappear anytime soon.

ADVANCED-TECHNOLOGY LOCATION STUDIES

As the topic of advanced technology has gained the attention of researchers, location studies have begun to emerge. These studies are frequently conducted by state agencies to aid in planning economic development strategies. Colorado (Allen 1984) and North Carolina (N.C. Board of Science and Technology 1984) provide two of many examples of this type of research. Much of this research is not published for national audiences, however, and is not readily available.

Other studies are national both in scope and in audience. One widely disseminated study conducted in the regional macroeconomic tradition, examined SMSA (Standard Metropolitan Statistical Area) level employment data for 29 three-digit SIC technology-intensive industries (Glasmeier, Hall, and Markusen 1984). The authors note that their model has relatively low explanatory power given their extensive data base. An aggregate set of industries was considered and five factors were significantly associated with advanced-technology employment: defense spending, percent Hispanic, percent black, industrial utility rates, and unemployment. Together these five factors explained less than one-fifth of the total variation in advanced-technology percentage change of employment. Analysis of each three-digit SIC industry group did not produce appreciably better results. The authors conclude that ". . . a whole host of factors – generally thought to be important and even critical in attracting high-technology industry do not appear from this analysis to have much, if any, significance. . . . Our most important conclusion is that the location and growth of high-technology industry is a varied and disparate process. . . ." (Glasmeier, Hall, and Markusen 1984, p. 166).

Another highly regarded study of advanced-technology regional-location characteristics was conducted using the U.S. Establishment and Enterprise Microdata files developed at the Brookings Institution (Armington, Harris, and Odle 1984). As one part of this study, the authors examined the relationship between spatial characteristics, business formations, and employment growth. They found business factors, such as electricity costs, labor considerations, previous population growth, the proportion of the labor force in technical occupations, city population, and density important predictors of the formation of advanced-technology companies. Results of their analysis of advanced-technology employment growth are similar to the results of their analysis of business formations. But, metropolitan characteristics generally explained less variability in employment growth than in company formation. The formation of small firms (less than 20 employees) depended more on previous population growth, technical employees ratio, and business costs than did the formation of large firms (more than 100 employees). The authors conclude that smaller firms are likely to form in growing areas that have a good supply of technical labor and relatively low business costs. Although these findings are relevant only for the period 1976-80, the authors emphasize the dynamic location aspects of advanced-technology growth: "Communities should prepare their institutions and residents to respond to the ever new social and economic contexts produced by rapid technological change" (Armington, Harris, and Odle 1984, p. 143).

Economic-development studies based upon location traits are also represented in advanced-technology location research. Perhaps the most notable study in this category was conducted for the Joint Economic Committee of the U.S. Congress (Premus 1982). Data for this study were obtained from a survey of 691 companies selected from the membership of the American Electronics Association and the Route 128 area around Boston. The sample was not stratified by state or region. Slightly over 30 percent of the firms employed 50 people or less while 25 percent employed over 500 workers. Forty percent of the firms were single-plant locations.

The data-collection instrument, a mailed survey, was designed with a two-stage view of location; it distinguishes interregional from intraregional location factors. The most important interregional influences were (in descending order): labor and skills availability, labor costs, tax climate, academic institutions, cost of living, transportation, access to markets, regional regulatory practices, energy cost and availability, cultural amenities, climate, and access to raw materials. Labor's importance is consistent with most other studies of industrial location, for both traditional and advanced-technology industries (Schmenner 1981; Wingate and LeRoy 1981). That amenities and living conditions were ranked low is interesting given the importance the popular media has placed on these characteristics as inducements for the location of advanced-technology firms.

The factors that influence the intraregional locational choices of advanced-technology companies are roughly similar to the interregional factors even though slightly different items were presented to respondents. The most significant intraregional influences were (in descending order): availability of workers, state and/or local tax structure, community business attitude, cost of property and construction, transportation for people, room for expansion, quality of schools, recreational and cultural opportunities, transportation for goods, proximity to customers, availability of energy, proximity to raw materials, water supply, and adequate waste treatment.

As with the interregional factors, labor and taxes were viewed as most important, but executives placed relatively higher value on intraregional amenity factors such as transportation, schools, and recreational and cultural opportunities. The interregional amenity factors were deemed more important than intraregional business-factor costs such as goods, transportation, energy, and raw materials. This finding can be interpreted in one of two ways; either many business-factor costs within a region vary only marginally across the region, or these business-factor costs are less important for an advanced-technology company than attracting technically skilled employees through local amenity inducements.

Although the Premus study was based on locational predispositions of advanced-technology company executives, the firms surveyed were generally large and only 40 percent had one plant. Large firms contribute significantly to regional employment and economic activity but they are typically in advanced stages of development. State and local governments no longer focus solely on attracting these larger companies to their areas, although they are easiest to target. The new focus of state and local economic-development policy, as elucidated in this book, is to nurture the growth of local companies that may eventually be significant regional employers.

SMALL FIRM LOCATION AND EXPANSION DECISIONS

Research on the location decisions of entrepreneurs who start advanced-technology companies is sparse because of the relative newness of the phenomenon. Many difficulties are encountered in finding young, small firms similar to those enterprises that state and local advanced-technology policies are trying to develop. A few studies (Jarobe 1984; Buck et al. 1984; Oakey 1981) have been made on these types of firms, but small sample sizes preclude a generalization of other geographic areas or segments of the advanced-technology industry.

The sample of firms used as the primary source of data for this book permits examination of location issues from the perspective of executives in small, young enterprises. In the following analysis only independent, single-plant firms are analyzed. The deletion of multiplant facilities and subsidiaries ensures that executives were not averaging or in some other way weighting their location dispositions among two or more sites. The number of cases in the single-plant sample is 380. Many advanced-technology firms are entrepreneurial. The medians for employment and age of these firms are ten employees and ten years.

From various sources, such as previous location studies, government reports, consultant studies, and knowledgeable officials, a group of items thought to influence business-location decisions was developed. A list of 31 items was presented to a top-level executive of each firm asking the executive to rate each item in terms of its attractiveness at the firm's present location. From that list of 31 items, respondents were asked to "rank in descending order the top five items that influenced the decision to locate at the present site." Using the same list, respondents were also asked to "rank in descending order the top five items that would affect a future decision to expand at the present site or another nearby site." Of the 380 firms, 310 completed the initial location ranking and 246 completed the expansion ranking. Fewer small firms responded to the expansion question, probably because they had no plans to relocate in the foreseeable future.

The 31 items were then ranked according to the number of times they were mentioned by respondents (Table 4.1).[3] How favorable an influence any one item is on initial location decisions can be assessed by the number of mentions it received. Frequently mentioned items have a bearing on the decision: they were either a positive inducement in that area or they present no constraint on the location decision. Infrequently mentioned items are factors that did not matter in the location decision and that received little consideration.

TABLE 4.1 Items that Influenced the Initial Location Decision

Rank	Item	Frequency	Percent
1	Proximity to Markets	141	45.5
2	Proximity to Family	117	37.7
3	Labor Availability	115	37.1
4	Commuting Distance	97	31.3
5	Cost of Property	92	29.7
6	Skill Level of Labor	66	21.3
7	Interaction with Other Firms	61	19.7
8	Availability of Business Services	51	16.5
9	Wage and Salary Levels	48	15.5
10	Cost of Living	43	13.9
11	Proximity to Research Universities	45	14.5
12	Good Schools for Children	41	13.2
13	Capital Availability	40	12.9
13	Availability of Land	40	12.9
13	Regional Surface Transportation	40	12.9
16	Proximity to Commercial Airports	32	10.3
17	Environmental Quality	31	10.0
18	Labor Productivity	27	8.7
19	Developed Local Infrastructure	25	8.1
19	Local Government Business Attitude	25	8.1
21	Taxes on Business Income and Property	23	7.4
22	Local Regulations	21	6.8
23	Crime Rate	20	6.5
24	Adequate Midpriced Housing	19	6.1
25	Availability of Recreational Activities	13	4.2
26	Availability of Cultural Activities	12	3.9
26	Weather	12	3.9
28	Cost and Availability of Energy	9	2.9
29	State Government Business Attitude	8	2.6
30	State Regulations	7	2.3
31	Taxes on Personal Income and Property	6	1.9

Note: Number of respondents = 310.

Source: Compiled by the authors from survey of advanced-technology firms.

The item most frequently mentioned in initial location is proximity to markets, 45.5 percent. This item was followed by proximity to family, labor availability, commuting distance, cost of property, and skill level of labor. The least mentioned item is personal taxes (1.9 percent), with the following items appearing progressively more frequently: state regulation, attitude of state government, cost of energy, and then a tie between weather and cultural activities.

Perhaps what is more instructive than the frequency of individual items is the aggregate nature, that is, the categories, of the items. Personal items such as proximity to family, commuting distance, cost of living, and good schools are important to these small, independent firms. Traditional cost items such as proximity to markets, cost of property, and availability of land are also generally important. Business items relevant to advanced technology and entrepreneurial-based businesses, such as interaction with other firms, availability of business services, proximity to research universities, and capital availability are important to initial location. Labor items, which rank high in almost all location studies, are also important for these firms (for example, labor availability, skill level of labor, and wage and salary levels). What is not found in the top half of the initial location list are amenity items such as climate, availability of cultural and recreational activities, adequate midpriced housing, crime rate, and environmental quality. The traditional manufacturing factor, cost and availability of energy, is also low on the list. Last, some of the tax and subjective business-climate items appear to have little influence on initial location decisions for these firms, including business and personal taxes on income and property, the state and local government's attitude toward business, and state and local regulations.

The influences on a possible expansion decision, however, are different from the influences on initial-location decisions (Table 4.2). Labor items and traditional business costs are important influences when considering expansion. Also, some of the tax and subjective business-climate items appear much more important in expansion decisions. For example, business and personal taxes, local regulations, and local government's attitude toward business generally are listed as much more important for expansion decisions. Three of the four entrepreneurial-based business items drop in importance for expansion decisions. Availability of capital becomes more important, but interaction with other firms, availability of business services, and proximity to a large research university are less important. Personal factors that were important for initial location drop appreciably in importance for expansion decisions.

TABLE 4.2   Items that Would Influence Future Expansion

Rank	Item	Frequency	Percent
1	Labor Availability	90	36.6
2	Proximity to Markets	82	33.3
3	Cost of Property	79	32.1
4	Capital Availability	74	30.1
5	Taxes on Business Income and Property	70	28.5
6	Availability of Land	55	22.4
7	Skill Level of Labor	51	20.7
7	Wage and Salary Levels	51	20.7
9	Interaction with Other Firms	41	16.7
10	Commuting Distance	40	16.3
11	Local Regulations	36	14.6
11	Local Government Business Attitude	36	14.6
13	Taxes on Personal Income and Property	34	13.8
14	Cost of Living	32	13.0
15	Proximity to Family	31	12.8
16	Availability of Business Services	28	11.4
17	Regional Surface Transportation	26	10.6
18	State Government Business Attitude	25	10.2
18	Crime Rate	25	10.2
18	Labor Productivity	25	10.2
21	Proximity to Commercial Airports	21	8.5
21	Developed Local Infrastructure	21	8.5
23	Cost of Energy	20	8.1
23	State Regulations	20	8.1
25	Good Schools for Children	16	6.5
26	Proximity to Research Universities	14	5.7
26	Environmental Quality	14	5.7
28	Weather	11	4.5
29	Availability of Cultural Activities	8	3.3
30	Adequate Midpriced Housing	7	2.8
31	Availability of Recreational Activities	5	2.0

Note: Number of respondents = 246.

Source: Compiled by the authors from survey of advanced-technology firms.

Items such as commuting distance, proximity to family, and cost of living lose importance in expansion decisions. Last, amenities such as environmental quality, climate, availability of cultural and recreational activities, and adequate midpriced housing are generally lowest in importance, much as in initial-location decisions.

Whether an item is important for an initial location or expansion decision depends on how that item appears to relate to two different periods in a firm's life cycle. The initial location decision occurs during the start-up period. Entrepreneurs living in a local community decide to start their firms close to their homes (Brennan 1983; Buck et al. 1984) as suggested by the importance of personal factors. Also important at this time is securing business services and locating vendors and clients necessary for establishing support services and assistance and for stable business relationships. The search for labor, services, and business clients is likely to be conducted initially at a local or substate regional level. Small and young firms have a greater dependence on markets within their state than do older, larger firms. Proximity to a local university may be important as a source of trained workers (Chapter 6) and a way to secure expert service and assistance that have not yet fully developed within the firm.

As a firm becomes successful and grows, new location influences emerge. Labor issues remain important; available, skilled, low-cost workers will certainly be needed for expanded business activity (Adcock 1984), but for any expansion to occur, available, low-cost land must be found and capital raised to pay for the expansion. By this time a stable local client and services base has been established, but markets must be expanded. Market proximity remains important, but it is now a wider area, probably a multistate region. As the firm develops an in-house capacity to conduct highly technical activities, the importance of proximity to a university diminishes.

Given fundamental differences between manufacturing and service industries, the type of industry is likely to have some influence on initial location and expansion decisions. Using the standard .05 level criterion of statistical significance, differences due to industry type were determined for the top ten items on the lists for either initial location or expansion. Four items for initial location and three for expansion exhibit a statistically significant difference based on industry type.[4] Labor availability, wage and salary levels, labor skill levels, property cost, and availability of land are favored by manufacturing firms (Table 4.3), and cost of living, business taxes, and proximity to a university by service firms.

TABLE 4.3 Differences* in Firm Characteristics for Initial Location and Expansion Decisions

A. Industry Type

	Initial Location			Item	Expansion		
	Manufacturing Percent/N	Services Percent/N	Rank		Rank	Manufacturing Percent/N	Services Percent/N
	59.8/55	40.2/37	5	Labor Availability	1	60.2/53	39.8/35
	54.7/35	45.3/29	6	Cost of Property			
	62.2/28	37.8/17	7	Skill Level of Labor	7	63.3/31	36.7/18
				Wage and Salary Levels	6	57.4/31	42.6/23
				Availability of Land			
	30.2/13	69.8/30	10	Cost of Living			
	34.9/15	65.1/28	10	Taxes on Business	5	41.4/29	58.6/41
				Proximity to University			
	43.8/134	56.2/172		Total Respondents		46.5/113	53.5/130

B. Size of Firm (employees)

	Initial Location			Item	Expansion		
	1-10	11 Plus	Rank		Rank	1-10	11 Plus
				Labor Availability	1	44.4/40	56.6/50
				Cost of Property	3	45.6/36	54.4/43
				Skill Level of Labor	7	43.1/22	56.9/29
	59.0/36	41.0/25	7	Interaction with Other Firms	9	65.9/27	34.1/14
				Taxes on Business	5	42.9/30	57.1/40
	53.2/165	46.8/145		Total Respondents		50.8/125	49.2/121

*All differences statistically significant at .05 level.

Source: Compiled by the authors from survey of advanced-technology firms.

The findings on industry type suggest that the location decisions of advanced-technology companies are not vastly different from location decisions in traditional manufacturing and service industries (Epping 1982; Lund 1984). Advanced-technology manufacturing firms focus heavily on labor and land items, two of their largest costs. Advanced-technology service firms focus on a different set of location characteristics, although the differences are not extensive in number or magnitude.

The size of the firm, however, is likely to significantly influence location decisions in two ways. First, larger firms are more likely to be labor intensive, so labor items should be more important to them. Second, larger firms are less likely to depend on other local firms for their economic vitality; consequently, business services and interaction with other local firms should be of less importance to them. The findings in Table 4.3 partially substantiate these two hypotheses. Still, size differences are relevant mainly to expansion decisions, an activity that larger firms are more likely to consider. Among the expansion items, larger firms favor labor availability, skill level of labor, cost of property, and business taxes. Smaller firms tend to emphasize interaction with other firms, for both initial location and expansion.

Much like the findings on industry type, these findings on firm size suggest that initial location and expansion decisions are not much different from those expected of less technology-intensive industries. Although these differences are statistically significant, they are not dramatic for all of the top ten items of the initial location and expansion lists. Neither are these differences widely divergent, that is, seldom is an item twice as important for one type of firm as for its complement.

CRITICAL MASS AND ADVANCED-TECHNOLOGY LOCATION

Advanced-technology firms tend to attract and breed other advanced-technology firms, and different areas' characteristics can be exploited to induce the attraction and startup of firms. Harding (1983) devised a five-part community typology that distinguishes advanced-technology-intensive areas by characteristics of development. The paragon community in the typology is the high-technology center. These communities (regions) have a high percentage of technical and professional workers, responsive research universities, large companies, and available risk capital. The two prominent high-technology centers are Santa Clara, California (Silicon Valley), and the Route 128 area around Boston (see Premus 1982, appendix).

Diluted high-technology areas are metropolitan areas where advanced technology is one element of a mature industrial base; Philadelphia and Chicago are examples of diluted centers. Spillover communities are areas adjacent to high-technology centers and diluted centers, like Lowell, Massachusetts, and the Route 202 region surrounding Philadelphia. According to Harding, diluted centers are locations close enough to advanced-technology concentrations to take advantage of the area's resources. Technology installation centers are communities associated with major federal-government, corporate, or research-university operations. Examples are Brevard County, Florida, and Los Alamos, New Mexico. Bootstrap communities lack extensive technology-oriented resource inducements but manage to successfully exploit local labor and amenity factors to attract existing companies. San Antonio, Texas, and Columbia, South Carolina, are bootstrap communities.

One element that all of these communities have in common is their ability to exploit features or resources that promote business location. Students of community-based, advanced-technology agglomeration processes have borrowed a technical phrase to name the process – critical mass. This concept refers to a threshold level of conditions, resources, activity, and so forth that must be reached to strongly promote the growth of technology-based companies.

A theoretical basis for the critical-mass concept is found in the classic works of Perroux (1956), Hoover and Vernon (1959), and Thompson (1954). A general consensus has evolved that cumulative causation and agglomeration economies have traditionally been associated with labor-intensive firms located in and around central areas of cities. Other trade-linked firms become interested in locating around this area and agglomeration effects are sustained, through a different process. For example, software and data processing firms in the business services industry are unable to achieve economies of scale because of labor intensiveness, but external economies can be generated for these firms. To the extent that they rely on high-velocity trade negotiations, external economies can be attained if a network that efficiently disseminates price and market information is established. With rapidly changing market conditions and where a multiplicity of buyers and sellers exist, such a spatially defined, person-to-person network is more likely to occur in densely populated areas.

Critical-mass explanations of growth suggest two interdependent development activities – attracting branches and new divisions of existing companies, and promoting the start of new firms. Of the two, critical mass is less a concern for advanced-technology branch plants or offices. Often these capital-intensive facilities, with their relatively low concentration of technical and professional workers, share many of the location characteristics of low-technology manufacturing industries. Location decisions for these facilities are likely to respond to the proximity of markets and to other company facilities, and labor and site cost issues (Ady 1981; Lund 1984; Epping 1982). Transportation, access to raw materials, and many other traditional manufacturing location characteristics are, however, less important for low-volume, low-weight, high-value-added advanced-technology goods (Speigelman 1964). Additionally, the higher the percentage of technical and professional staff in a company, the greater the emphasis placed on the quality of local living conditions (Battelle Memorial Institute 1982a; Stafford 1980; Schmenner 1982; Lund 1984). For example, the location of headquarters and R&D divisions are more likely to resemble the pleasant surroundings of a college campus or a research park. Also, many advanced-technology firms depend on cyclic defense contracts; if other companies do not exist in the area, technical and professional employees may be reluctant to move to the area knowing that similar work may be hard to find during the downside of a defense-spending cycle.

Start-up enterprises face a business environment that is more dependent on critical mass characteristics. Although young, small firms are concerned with labor and site costs, greater attention is placed on proximity to clients, service providers, and family. The environmental scanning strategies of start-up firms seem to be focused initially on the area most familiar to the entrepreneur – the community where he or she lives. The proximity to other advanced-technology firms allows the entrepreneur to keep in close contact with developing markets, products, innovations, pricing, and other specialized information and resources not readily available elsewhere (Browne 1982).

The critical-mass considerations of single plant, advanced-technology firms can be addressed with data collected from advanced-technology firms in Pennsylvania. Executives were asked to rate the attractiveness of their company's current location based on 31 items (the same set used in earlier tables).[5] Mean attractiveness scores were computed for each item and ordered from most attractive to least attractive (Table 4.4). The sample was then separated into two subsamples – firms in metropolitan counties, and firms in nonmetropolitan counties. Means were calculated for items in each sample, and statistically significant differences were determined.

Hypotheses are developed from knowledge about items of concern to small, advanced-technology firms. Metropolitan counties can be expected to receive more favorable ratings for the following entrepreneurial support items: availability of business services, proximity to research universities, interaction with other firms, and capital availability. The hypotheses are substantiated for the first three items but not sustained for capital availability (Table 4.4). Advanced-technology firms in metropolitan areas rate availability of business services and proximity to universities more favorably than firms in rural areas. Interaction with other firms is also rated more highly in metropolitan areas, but the urban/rural differences are not as great as with business services and university proximity. Apparently capital is fluid across local areas and is no more or less accessible in nonmetropolitan areas than in metropolitan areas.

In addition to these findings, the data can be used to examine other factors considered more favorable in metropolitan areas than in nonmetropolitan areas. Another study on small nonmetropolitan advanced-technology firms found that "nonmetropolitan based high-technology firms appear to attach greater importance on quality-of-life factors than on 'business factors'" (Buck et al. 1984, p. 54). As seen in Table 4.4, the quality-of-life factors – housing costs and environmental quality – are perceived to be superior in nonmetropolitan areas; still, recreational opportunities and schools for children are less attractive in nonmetropolitan areas. Metropolitan areas are also rated higher for cultural opportunities, skill level of labor, and proximity to a commercial airport. This indicates that, on balance, metropolitan areas may have the upper hand in attracting and keeping advanced-technology firms.

Although differences between rural and urban areas are apparent from the perspective of a chief executive officer, not all existing differences are important factors for initial location and expansion. Some important location factors differ, however, between metropolitan and nonmetropolitan areas. These factors – business services, interaction with other firms, and proximity to a university – are not directly manipulated by state and local governments, but they are indicators of development opportunities. These factors can and should be exploited in metropolitan economic-development strategies.

TABLE 4.4 Ratings of Attractiveness of Current Location for Metropolitan and Nonmetropolitan Areas

Overall Rank	Item	Overall Mean	Metro Mean/N	Expected Direction	Nonmetro Mean/N	Stat. Sig. α .05
1	Commuting Distance	6.7	6.7/324		6.7/37	
2	Proximity to Markets	6.6	6.7/299	>	5.4/32	*
2	Proximity to Family	6.6	6.6/299		6.5/38	
4	Availability of Recreation	6.5	6.5/306		5.7/38	*
5	Good School for Children	6.4	6.5/306		5.7/38	*
5	Labor Availability	6.4	6.5/305		5.5/36	*
7	Availability of Cultural Activities	6.2	6.4/311	>	4.3/34	*
8	Availability of Business Services	6.1	6.3/312	>	4.3/34	*
8	Proximity to Research Universities	6.1	6.3/269	>	4.6/30	*
10	Labor Production	6.0	6.0/299		5.6/36	
11	Skill Level of Labor	5.9	6.0/302	>	4.6/35	*
12	Wage and Salary Levels	5.7	5.8/301		5.7/36	
12	Cost of Living	5.7	5.6/324		6.1/38	
12	Proximity to Commercial Airports	5.7	5.9/289	>	3.7/28	*
12	Adequate Midpriced Housing	5.7	5.6/310	<	6.0/38	
12	Environmental Quality	5.7	5.6/313	<	6.4/37	*
17	Developed Local Infrastructure	5.6	5.7/292		5.2/34	
17	Interaction with Other Firms	5.6	5.7/292	>	4.5/33	*
17	Regional Surface Transportation	5.6	5.7/291		5.1/33	
20	Availability of Land	5.5	5.5/245		5.8/34	
21	Crime Rate	5.4	5.2/319	>	6.7/37	*

22	Weather	5.3	5.3/309	5.3/36
23	Cost of Property	5.2	5.2/279	5.4/34
24	Local Regulations	5.0	5.0/288	5.2/31
24	Local Government Business Attitude	5.0	5.0/298	4.9/36
26	Cost/Availability of Energy	4.9	4.9/291	4.5/34
26	Capital Availability	4.9	4.9/279	4.6/33
28	State Government Business Attitude	4.6	4.6/300	4.7/34
28	State Regulations	4.6	4.6/288	4.2/33
30	Taxes on Personal Income and Property	4.1	4.0/303	4.5/36
31	Taxes on Business Income and Property	3.8	3.7/307	3.9/37

Source: Compiled by the authors from survey of advanced-technology firms.

POLICY IMPLICATIONS FOR LOCAL
AND STATE GOVERNMENT

Government Influence on Location Behavior

The findings discussed in this chapter have two interdependent policy implications. The first concerns the amount of influence state and local governments have on factors important to location and expansion decisions (Vaughan 1983). From the list of 31 items presented to executives, ten items can be considered as directly or highly manipulatable by state and local government.[6] However, only one of these ten policy variables is ranked among the top ten items for initial location or expansion. An additional seven items can be considered indirectly or minimally manipulatable by state and local government, but only two of these indirect policy variables are ranked in the top ten initial location or expansion decisions.[7] In all, executives consider just 3 of 13 items (some appear on both lists) that may be influenced by state and local government important for the two types of advanced-technology location decisions.

Three different kinds of influences have a much greater effect on location decisions than do public-policy relevant items. First, national and international macroeconomic conditions influence such items as cost of living, and wage and salary rates. Certainly, interstate and intrastate variations exist among these items, but state and local governments are relatively incapable of offsetting macroeconomic influences. A second important influence on location decisions is related to local business markets, often called "business activity" in business-climate studies. Rapidly growing areas are likely to continue growing and therefore attract advanced-technology firms (Armington, Harris and Odle, 1984). Growing areas create a demand for new business interaction that is met by firms starting up near good sources of business trade relations. Similarly, a high level of economic activity is an indication of a healthy market for products and services that small firms provide to large firms. Even so, a significant increase in business activity takes time and until it happens, sustained multiplier effects do not occur.

A third influence on location decisions concerns geography and settlement patterns. States cannot change their weather nor their proximity to market centers. States also have little influence on settlement patterns that, over the last half century, have made property more available and less costly in suburban locations than in inner-city locations. Government also has virtually no influence on commuting distance and proximity to family; both are important personal factors influencing a firm's location.

The generalization made about government's influence over location factors does not apply in all instances. For example, government land-banking activities that started in the urban-renewal era of the 1950s may provide good development opportunities in the 1980s. As urban areas in general, and some center-city locations in particular, rebounded from recent fiscal distress, lack of private investment, and physical neglect, many renewal areas have become attractive sites for business develop-ment. The University City Science Center (UCSC) in Philadelphia is a good example of a deteriorated area transformed into a research park that fosters new business development. As of 1985, UCSC was the home of 80 organizations employing over 5,000 people. Research centers, laboratories, and companies are attracted to UCSC, primarily because of its business support services, the interaction with other firms, and the proximity to large universities.

Successful development ventures such as UCSC and other government-assisted business centers, like small business incubator facilities (Chapter 8), are testimony to the fact that a catalytic, supportive governmental role can effectively foster economic development. Many of the programs and policies discussed throughout this book stress limited governmental roles and public/private partnerships that take advantage of indigenous local technological development opportunities.

Analysis of Comparative Advantage

The second major policy implication derived from this analysis of location decisions involves determining a community's advanced-technology assets. Generally, those assets are items ranked in the top third of the location and expansion lists. Any community or state strategic economic-development planning should examine investment factors for new enterprises, expansion of existing businesses, and relocation of branches and large facilities (not part of this analysis). This examination may be in the form of economic-base analysis (primarily community export versus nonexport activities), target screening (matching commu-nity attributes with needs of an industry), shift-share analysis (changes relative to a larger economy), and/or business-inventory analysis.

Business-inventory analysis is most similar to the research on initial location and expansion reported in this chapter. Executives are interviewed to determine important attributes of the local, regional, or state business environment. Location strengths (major and limited assets) and location liabilities (correctable and not correctable) form the basis of an area's competitive advantage (Gregerman 1984).

One aspect of comparative advantage was addressed briefly in the preceding analysis and is a contemporary regional-growth theory. It was suggested that the differential importance of a particular location item was dependent upon the stage in the firm's life cycle. A simplistic, two-stage life-cycle model – start-up and early operations, and mature operations – suggests different location decision-making criteria for advanced-technology firms.[8] The ideas of Ady (1983), a site selection practitioner, coincide with the data and theoretical foundation presented in this chapter. Ady begins with theory-driven facilities represented by young firms at the cutting edge of technology. The firms locate plants where start-up costs are eased, that is, where technology can be transferred from a university, and where venture capital and business support networks are readily available. The second stage of the firm's development is characterized by a viable, unique product. At this time availability of skilled, productive workers, attractive living conditions, and a supportive business climate gain prominence. Ady contends that the importance of proximity to an R&D facility does not diminish during this second stage. The third stage starts when the firm becomes market driven due to the other firms' introduction of similar products at competitive prices. At this stage, the cost and availability of labor and utilities becomes much more important, and the firms may look for incentives, inducements, and exemptions for siting their facilities.

Comparative advantage analysis helps establish a common understanding of development opportunities and build support for organizational linkages and policy changes. The research process, if conducted as a cooperative public/private venture, forms the foundation for future intrasectoral collaborations. With an understanding of the business environment that most parties accept, agreement upon economic-development objectives and implementation strategies needed to achieve those objectives becomes much easier.

Strategic planning activities intended to guide economic-development decision making are becoming popular at all levels of government (Sorkin et al. 1984). Some are undertaken solely from an economic-development perspective (Governor's High Tech Cabinet Council 1984), while others are driven by a larger set of issues, such as housing, transportation, community revitalization, and so forth (Arthur Anderson Co. 1983;

Pennsylvania State Planning Board 1981). Governments that seek to nurture the advanced-technology industry must realize that a critical set of conditions must be in place or rapidly developing before advanced-technology growth can be expected. Attempting to attract industry with tax incentives is likely to yield minimal results. Conversely, creating a competitive advantage by building on existing technological support resources and activities is more likely to yield beneficial outcomes. The impact of the competitive advantage strategy will not be as immediate as a shotgun tax-incentive strategy, but it is more likely to promote sustained economic growth over the long run.

NOTES

1.   Conventional regional economic growth theories tend to ignore technology as a major component; technology is treated as a residual or indigenous variable for each region (Carlberg 1981, Richardson 1978). Attempts to include technology in wage and income differential models and price equalization theories (Moriarty 1978, Batra and Scully 1972) and in export-base theory (Thirwall 1980) exist, but they are not typical and have not found much scholarly support (Malecki 1983).

2.   The process of a firm's analysis and selection of a site may not follow the generalized methodology of an industrial location study because each firm has unique structural characteristics. For example, supply-side considerations may constrain a set of otherwise viable locations before any distance costs or area attributes can be considered. Manufacturing operations evolving toward the just-in-time inventory/supply method would be particularly constrained by supply characteristics. This manufacturing approach, however, presents other opportunities for locations looking to promote backward-linked industries.

3.   Another method of assessing the importance of items was used. As previously mentioned, respondents were asked to rank the items in descending order of importance. Given this condition, a weighting system was devised to determine the importance of items beyond their frequency of mention. Items mentioned first received weighting scores of five, items mentioned second received weighting scores of four, on down to the last item mentioned receiving a weighting score of one. The weighting did not appreciably change the ordering of items; therefore, the results of this analysis are not presented.

4.   A difference-of-proportions test, based on separate samples, was used to assess differences between the groups (Blalock 1972).

5.   Current attractiveness of the present location was rated on a scale ranging from zero to nine. A zero value indicated that the item was not applicable to the firm or its location. Lower values represented lower attractiveness; higher values represented higher attractiveness.

6.   The items considered highly or directly manipulable by state and local government are: taxes on business income and property, taxes on personal income and

property, local regulations, state regulations, local government's business attitude, state government's business attitude, developed local infrastructure, regional surface transportation, good schools for children, and environmental quality. With the exceptions of taxes and regulation, these items cannot be appreciably changed over a short period of time (less than five years).

7. The items considered as minimally or indirectly manipulable by state and local government are: skill level of labor, capital availability, proximity to universities, proximity to commercial airports, availability of recreational services, availability of cultural activities, and crime rate. Like many of the items more directly influenced by government, these indirectly influenced items cannot be appreciably changed over a short time.

8. Due to limitations in the data, a compressed two-stage life-cycle model is more appropriate for this analysis. This does not refute the presence of a three-stage model; rather, these data are not as sensitive to three stages as they are to two stages.

5 The Advanced-Technology Work Force

INTRODUCTION

The issue of the number of jobs technological change will create or eliminate has generated a lot of public attention. A related focus of interest has been the implications of this technological change for the composition of the work force. Three interrelated issues are of particular concern: the demand for labor, the adequacy of the existing labor supply, and the extent to which firms are involved in training new employees.

Advanced-technology firms may demand different types of workers than firms in the general economy. A "deskilling" of the work force as intelligent machines replace workers is one projected trend. Another is that technological change will increase firms' demand for sophisticated scientific and technical personnel. Conceivably both trends will occur simultaneously – increased demand for both very high-skill and very low-skill workers at the expense of those in the middle. The resultant bimodal skills distribution would imply a similar income distribution and a substantial decrease in the size of the middle class.

Concern is also expressed about the types of skills prospective workers supply and the adequacy of the existing labor pool to meet the needs of advanced-technology firms. Difficulties in recruiting skilled workers may be obstacles to growth at both local and national levels.

The extent to which advanced-technology firms train new entrants is the third issue of concern. Training is closely related to the role of colleges and universities, the topic of Chapter 6. Across all three areas (distribution of jobs, supply of workers, and training) patterns differ by type of firm and type of worker.

The analysis in this chapter examines single-period, cross-sectional data obtained from executives in advanced-technology firms in Pennsylvania. Job match is a dynamic process and "the advanced-technology work force" is an outcome rather than an entity. Workers move into and out of employment in advanced-technology firms in response to wage offers, benefits, conditions, and alternative opportunities in the rest of the economy. Firms make decisions about the mix of workers to employ depending upon both the marginal productivity and the relative prices of different classes of labor. Therefore, attempting to draw inferences about the future composition of the advanced-technology work force based upon contemporaneous data is risky.

Moreover, this book's definition of advanced technology is based, in part, upon the mix of workers employed in firms (see Chapter 2). Since the sampled firms were in industries with high average concentrations to technical and professional workers, it would be surprising if many such workers were not found in the sample. In addition, as shown later in the chapter, the labor requirements of advanced-technology firms are not monolithic – substantial diversity exists at any given time, and individual firms change profoundly as they move through the product-development cycle. Finally, the principal impact of the advanced technology sector on employment may not actually be within the sector itself, but rather through the impact of the sector's products and services on the rest of the economy.

Despite these limitations, a survey-based description of the distribution of jobs, difficulty in recruiting, and training policies within advanced-technology firms is important. Although it is generally agreed that technological change is responsible for basic change in the composition of the work force (and perhaps in the nature of work itself), little agreement exists concerning the magnitude or even the direction of these changes. This chapter examines the literature on the advanced-technology labor force, focusing on issues of occupational distribution, worker skills, and training, and relates these issues to data provided by executives in the sample of advanced-technology firms.

THE DEMAND FOR ADVANCED-TECHNOLOGY LABOR

Chapter 3 focused on the aggregate demand for workers within the advanced-technology sector. The focus in this chapter is on the demand for specific categories of workers. Specifically, this chapter focuses on the types of jobs these firms will create and the implications of these patterns for employment and income distribution. As technology changes the occupational distribution will change as well, but two radically different visions emerge of the skills required in an advanced-technology economy. Data presented in this chapter deal only with advanced-technology firms. It is important to note that technological innovation affects not only the demand for workers within these firms but, through its impact on production processes, the demand for labor generally.

Two Views of Skill Requirements

One view of the impact of technological change projects a substantial upgrading of the overall skills demanded by firms. The combined impact of robotics and low-cost competing foreign labor allegedly will result in a shift toward more high-skill occupations in the U.S. economy. "Most low-wage, standardized, non-defense production activities cannot be retained in the U.S.; it is inevitable that these jobs will be either robotized or moved abroad. . . . America's comparative advantage is in the high thought content . . . industries" (Choate 1982, p. 16).

Proponents of this view describe a "second industrial revolution" in which even production workers will need multiple skills (Tornatzky et al. 1982), and all workers will require skills in observation, communication, analysis, and problem solving (O'Toole, 1983). The introduction of computer-based tools into even such prosaic occupations as automobile mechanics, for example, has resulted in an increase in reading skills (Schuon 1983). Within advanced-technology firms themselves, proportionately more highly skilled professional and technical workers are required than in the economy in general (Doeringer 1982). These firms are characterized as demanding employees with an in-depth knowledge of the theories and principles of science, engineering, and mathematics (Riche et al. 1983).

An alternative view projects quite the opposite impact of technological change on the demand for workers in different skill categories. Levin and Rumberger (1983) note that new technology typically requires an initial increase in skill requirements followed by a decrease as new processes become mechanized. Advanced-technology products are frequently produced by low-skill production teams (Jackman 1983). For example, a substantial share of the most sophisticated electronic equipment currently marketed in the United States is produced by workers with little education or training (Rumberger 1984). Under this alternative view, "the proliferation of high technology industries and their products is far more likely to reduce the skill requirements of jobs in the U.S. economy than to upgrade them" (Levin and Rumberger, 1983, p. iii).

Organization of the Workplace

Another important dimension of this bifurcated view relates to the organization of work and whether advanced technology will result in increased worker participation or alienation. Those who subscribe to a vision of deskilling argue that "the new technologies provide opportunities to further simplify and routinize work tasks and to reduce the opportunities for worker individuality and judgement" (IFG Policy Notes 1983, p. 7). Others argue that advanced-technology processes require flatter organizational structures and a movement away from bureaucratic decision processes (Reich 1983; Gunn 1982). Technological changes may result in "major dislocations in organizational practice" (Tornatzky 1982, p. 14). Some evidence exists that this process is underway (Wall Street Journal 1983).

Advanced Technology and the
Distribution of Personal Income

The sustained economic slowdown of the early 1980s and the continued decline of smokestack industries have raised concerns about the impact of technological change on income distribution and reversal of the trend of the 1960s and early 1970s in reducing poverty. In 1974 the number of people in the United States living in poverty had dropped to about 23 million (Kuttner 1983); by the autumn of 1983, over 34 million in the United States were officially classified as poor, the highest poverty rate in 17 years (New York Times 1983). The problem is not simply employment; "half the heads of households living below the poverty level are employed . . . one-third work full time, year round" (Vaughn and Sekera 1983, p. 2). During the 15-year period 1965-80, the income share of the poorest 40 percent of the population dropped from 12 to 9 percent (Vaughn and Sekera 1983).

A major public policy issue is whether advanced-technology industries will demand primarily high- or low-skill workers at the expense of the middle class, or whether advanced-technology positions are equally distributed across occupational skill categories. Trends in the distribution of occupations in general suggest movement toward a bimodal income distribution with a shrinking middle class (Kuttner 1983). The size of the middle class declined from 28.2 to 23.7 percent of the population between 1967 and 1982 (Thurow 1984). In 1983 (a period of high interest rates), an average priced new house was beyond the purchasing power of 75 percent of all U.S. households (Kuttner 1983). Not all analysts agree that the long-term trend is in the direction of decline in the middle. Based on an analysis of U.S. Department of Commerce, Bureau of Labor Statistics' data, Rumberger (1984) argued that occupational distribution of jobs created between 1960 and 1980 was quite similar to that of older occupations.

Interest in the skills distribution within the advanced-technology sector is high, but findings on this topic are very sensitive to the way advanced technology is operationally defined. Advanced-technology industries allegedly demand a bifurcated labor force, with very high-skill and very low-skill workers, but fewer of the relatively well-paying jobs that have been characteristic of the post-World-War-II U.S. economy (Wiewel et al. 1984). Advanced-technology firms may lack the capacity to create middle income jobs for workers displaced in declining industries. Using the growing software industry as an example, Hall et al. (1983) argue that a scenario in which auto workers are retrained as paraprofessional programmers is unrealistic. Instead, they envision a future software sector with "a bifurcated labor market, with highly skilled Ph.D.s employed in small numbers . . . and a large group of computer specialists whose job responsibilities and pay levels might be akin to those in the clerical workforce today" (p. 60). Others disagree, arguing that the occupational distribution in advanced-technology firms is not bimodal. In an analysis of 1980 census data on manufacturing in Texas, Grubb (1984) finds no difference in occupational distribution between conventional and advanced-technology employers. Kuttner (1983) notes that the trend toward unequal income distribution is most pronounced in the service sector; advanced-technology manufacturing may not be characteristic of the entire advanced-technology sector.

Differences by Firm Characteristics

In terms of developing public policy and forecasting, the demand for workers (overall and at different skills levels) must be examined in light of the characteristics of advanced-technology firms. During initial stages of the product-development cycle, these firms use a large proportion of highly skilled workers (although total number of employees tends to be low). In a survey of 446 rural advanced-technology firms, Buck et al. (1984) found a strong inverse relationship between the ratio of scientific and engineering personnel and size of the firm. In the smallest firms (five or fewer employees), typically over 75 percent of the work force was composed of such high-skill workers. The availability of skilled technical and professional personnel is a key factor in location decisions of firms at this stage (Chapter 4).

At a second "product-driven" stage the firm moves toward a blend of research and manufacturing personnel; high worker productivity becomes more important to firms at this stage (Ady 1983). As advanced-technology firms move into a production phase, maintenance, clerical, and routine production activities become much more important, with the proportion of blue-collar and clerical workers exceeding those in technical and professional occupations (Doeringer 1982). One major difference between advanced-technology companies and traditional smokestack industries is that the former is much more geographically mobile. Electronics production facilities, unlike steel mills, can easily be moved to new locations attracted by low-wage labor (Malecki 1984).

PENNSYLVANIA'S ADVANCED-TECHNOLOGY WORK FORCE

One section of the questionnaire sent to executive managers of advanced-technology firms in Pennsylvania dealt with the composition of the firm's work force by skill level. Managers were asked to report the proportion of total employment in four skills categories: unskilled, semiskilled, technical, and professional. Unskilled workers included those with no specific skills or ability – workers occupying jobs that could be learned quickly with little orientation. Semiskilled employees were described as those with specific training acquired on the job or in a vocational-technical program.[1] Examples of semiskilled occupations are machinist or word-processor operator. Technical employees were those with postsecondary training and performing jobs requiring analytic skills and judgment (for example, electronic repair, drafting, laboratory technician). Professional employees were those with a four-year college degree (or equivalent) working in jobs requiring high-level analytic skills and judgment (for example, manager, engineer, scientist). In some of the analyses reported in this chapter, unskilled and skilled employees were combined to form a category labeled "low skills," and technical and professional employees were combined to form a "high skills" group.

All together, the 442 firms for which employment data were available reported 36,965 employees in the four skills categories (see Table 5.1). Employment was heavily concentrated in the technical and professional skills categories; almost one-quarter of the firms (23 percent) reported that over half of their work force was composed of professional employees. Over half the firms in the sample reported no unskilled workers; over one-quarter of the firms reported no semiskilled workers. Advanced-technology firms in this sample clearly provide a high proportion of high-skill jobs.

The single largest employee group consisted of semiskilled workers (over one-third), followed next by professionals (29 percent). The smallest cell was composed of unskilled workers (15 percent of the sample). When groups are collapsed to form two categories, the number of high-skill employees exceeds the low-skill group by a small margin. Wage data were not collected, but skill level serves as a rough proxy for earnings. The skills-distribution (and income-distribution) picture that emerges is broad based and balanced. The stereotype of large numbers of low-skill workers serving a small group of technical and professional workers is not at all consistent with these data. Using skills as an

TABLE 5.1 Distribution of Employees in Advanced-Technology Firms

(N = 442)

	Sample	Share
Unskilled	5,439	15.0%
Semiskilled	11,908	32.9%
Technical	8,546	23.7%
Professional	10,263	28.4%
Low Skill	17,347	48.0%
High Skill	18,809	52.0%
Total Number of Employees	36,156	100.0%

Source: Compiled by the authors from survey of advanced-technology firms.

earnings proxy, no evidence appears of a "disappearing middle class" within these firms.

It is worth reiterating that the skills mix within firms differs substantially among firms. As firms move through the cycle from basic research to application and production, the mix of skills needed in the labor force changes. Differences in the composition of the labor force, as they relate to firm characteristics, are examined next. Some major differences surface between manufacturing and service firms. Advanced-technology firms in the service sector are much more likely to have a high concentration of professional employees. Over a third of the service firms (35.2 percent) classified at least 50 percent of their work force as professional, compared to less than 8 percent of the manufacturing firms. Service firms are also more likely to employ technical personnel; almost a fifth (17.8 percent) of the service firms were composed primarily of technical employees compared to only 7.3 percent of the manufacturing firms. Conversely, advanced-technology firms in the service sector are much less likely to use unskilled and low-skill workers. Service-sector firms are almost twice as likely to have no unskilled employees as are manufacturing firms (65 and 33 percent, respectively).

The concentration of high-skill workers drops with firm size. Very small firms tend to employ predominantly technical and professional workers (92 percent of firms with fewer than five employees report a majority of high-skilled employees). The proportion drops to 58 percent for larger firms (over 50 employees). Differences are particularly pronounced in the professional category, with almost three-quarters of the small firms having a majority of professional workers compared to 45 percent of the largest firms.

Younger firms also employ relatively more high-skilled workers. For example, over 80 percent of the youngest firms (those in Pennsylvania for less than five years) report that the majority of their employees are professionals. This percentage compares to 53 percent of the oldest firms.

A more complex pattern exists between the use of high-skill labor and the "research intensity" of firms. Organizing firms into four categories according to the share of gross receipts devoted to research and development (less than 1 percent, 1-5 percent, 6-13 percent, and over 13 percent) results in a U-shaped pattern in the use of high-skill employees – firms with the highest research intensity are most likely to have predominantly (over 75 percent of total employment) high-skill workers. Firms reporting no research are also likely to have high concentrations of high skill employees. Firms doing moderate research are least likely to be staffed primarily by high-skill workers.

Slightly over half of the firms in the sample were located in counties with institutions of higher education that granted bachelor's degrees in advanced-technology-related fields. Firms in these counties were more likely to employ high-skill workers.

ADEQUACY OF THE LABOR FORCE

For advanced-technology firms, the most critical work-force issues relate to the adequacy (both in numbers and skills) of the available labor supply. This labor supply issue is, of course, a function of the advanced-technology occupational distribution already discussed. For example, a research or consulting firm requiring primarily high-skill technical and professional workers will have a very different definition of "adequate labor supply" than a firm using low-skill assembly workers in the mass production of electronic components.

Firms have four principal options available in obtaining workers. They can: 1) locate in an area with an adequate supply of workers with the skills they want, 2) compete with other firms in the area for employees, 3) recruit outside the local area, and 4) provide training for new entrants. From an economic-development-policy perspective, two questions are of particular interest. Are these four options substitutes or complements? What state and local activities are likely to assist firms in each option?

From a national perspective, shortages of workers with specific technical skills may constitute "bottlenecks" that prevent U.S. firms from being internationally competitive. A national report by the Business-Higher Education Forum (1983) argues that "the gap between the nation's needs and the capabilities of its work force is most evident in the growing shortage of skilled workers – particularly technical personnel, engineers and scientists" (p. 22). According to Choate (1982), the mismatch between the needs of employers and the availability of technically skilled workers is growing. This mismatch "is becoming a major structural barrier to meeting either national defense or domestic production requirements" (p. 37).

Moreover, concern is voiced regarding the adequacy of the work force in general. For example, one in five adults in the United States is functionally illiterate, and a growing proportion of the work force lacks basic skills in mathematics, verbal expression, and critical thinking (Business-Higher Education Forum 1983). Approximately 6 percent of the civilian work force is affected by alcoholism resulting in lost production estimated at almost $30 billion annually (Choate 1982). The work force is aging and specific skills may be lost as workers retire. In 1982, the average machinist was 58 years old; Choate (1982) projected a shortage of almost a quarter of a million machinists by 1985.

Other analysts present a more sanguine picture of the adequacy of the work force to support the development of advanced-technology firms. Job characteristics are viewed as less rigid with requirements changing to accommodate the availability of workers. A combination of on-the-job training, substitutability of one type of worker for another, and normal functioning of market mechanisms are seen as sufficient to avoid major shortages. In addition, advanced-technology innovations, in themselves, provide opportunities to substitute capital for labor in areas of skill shortage. Computer-assisted design (CAD) and manufacturing (CAM) allow a small number of high-skill workers to be extremely productive. The advanced-technology sector may have cleared a critical development point in terms of its dependence on large numbers of technical personnel. "We've peaked in terms of our need for the classical technician. The machinery is more and more self-diagnosing. There is less of a judgement factor. The computer spits out an instruction to change such-and-such a component, and you do it" (Kuttner 1983, p. 65).

The ability of small advanced-technology firms to recruit adequate numbers of high-skill workers is of particular interest. While most of the new jobs created in the economy are created by small firms, these firms are generally less attractive than large firms, paying lower wages, and offering less stability and fewer fringe benefits (Vaughan 1983). A study of small advanced-technology firms conducted by the National Science Foundation (1981) concluded that it is "difficult for small firms to compete with large firms for scientific and technical personnel" (p. 2). It is argued that small firms may end up serving a training function for larger firms (Doeringer 1982).

ADVANCED-TECHNOLOGY
RECRUITING DIFFICULTY

Four questions arise regarding the adequacy of the labor force to meet the needs of advanced-technology firms. How much difficulty do advanced-technology firms experience in recruiting employees? In what ways does recruiting difficulty differ by prospective employees' skills level? How do recruiting problems differ by firms' characteristics? How do employees' skills and firms' characteristics interact in affecting recruitment?

The survey sent to executive managers of advanced-technology firms in Pennsylvania included a set of questions about recruiting problems. Managers were asked to indicate the difficulty they encountered in recruiting potential employees in their local area. Data were collected separately for each of the four skill levels previously described (unskilled, semiskilled, technical, and professional) using a ten-point Likert scale. The scale was anchored on three general categories – no or minor difficulty, moderate difficulty, and considerable difficulty. When the data were collected, the national economy and the Pennsylvania economy were emerging from a recession. Unemployment was high and no doubt recruitment problems in general were atypically low. Therefore, the following picture may understate current recruiting difficulty.

The first row of Table 5.2 shows the percentage of firms in the sample experiencing moderate or considerable recruiting difficulty at each of the four skill levels (columns 2-5). While few (8.1 percent) firms reported difficulty recruiting unskilled workers, the proportion of firms encountering difficulty increases steadily with workers' skill level (semiskilled, 40.7 percent; technical, 53.8 percent; and professional, 57.4 percent). The data suggest substantial recruiting problems for high-skill workers; over half the firms in the sample reported difficulty in recruiting technical and professional workers.

The last three columns of the table use aggregate worker categories to show the proportion of firms encountering recruiting difficulty. Column 6 shows the percentage of firms experiencing difficulty in recruiting low-skill workers (that is, unskilled or semiskilled); column 7 shows corresponding figures for high-skill workers (technical or professional). The last column shows the percentage of firms encountering at least moderate difficulty in recruiting workers at any of the four skill levels. Over 40 percent of the firms encountered difficulty recruiting low-skill workers, and over two-thirds (68.4 percent) experienced difficulty in recruiting high-skill employees. Almost three-quarters of the firms reported some recruiting difficulty.

The data suggest that except for unskilled workers, recruiting is a substantial problem for advanced-technology firms and that the problem increases with skill level. About half (49 percent) of the firms reported

TABLE 5.2   Percentage of Firms Experiencing Moderate or Major Recruiting Difficulty

	Number of Firms	Unskilled	Semi-skilled	Technical	Professional	Low Skill (Un or Semi)	High Skill (Tech or Prof)	Any Level
ALL FIRMS	455	8.1	40.7	53.8	57.4	42.4	68.4	72.7
Size – Employees in PA								
up to 5	144	4.2	18.8	30.6	39.6	20.1	52.1	56.3
6-24	163	10.4	43.6	53.4	54.6	44.8	67.5	73.0
25-49	55	10.9	56.4	67.3	61.8	60.0	74.5	80.0
50+	93	8.6(ns)	60.2***	82.8***	87.1***	62.4***	91.4***	93.5***
Age – Years in PA								
1-4	103	4.9	25.2	36.9	48.5	26.2	56.3	62.1
5-9	108	6.5	35.2	48.1	57.4	37.0	67.6	73.1
10-14	114	5.3	45.6	63.2	64.9	45.6	75.4	77.2
15+	130	14.6*	53.1***	63.8***	57.7(ns)	56.9***	72.3*	76.9*
Sector								
Manufacturing	200	10.0	55.0	66.0	65.0	56.5	76.0	81.5
Service	250	6.4(ns)	29.6***	44.8***	51.6**	31.6***	62.8***	66.4***
Anticipates Growth								
Yes	272	6.3(ns)	44.1(ns)	58.8*	65.4***	45.2(ns)	75.0***	79.4***
No	183	10.9	35.5	46.4	45.4	38.3	58.5	62.8
LOCAL LABOR FACTORS IN PRESENT LOCATION								
Availability								
Low	74	5.4	18.9	39.2	47.3	20.3	59.5	62.2
Moderate	148	9.5	50.0	64.9	64.2	52.7	78.4	83.1
High	230	8.3(ns)	42.2***	52.2***	57.0(ns)	43.5***	65.7**	70.4***

Skill Labor								
Low	99	8.1	33.3	45.5	52.5	35.4	64.6	71.7
Moderate	170	8.8	50.0	66.5	67.1	52.4	78.8	84.1
High	183	7.7(ns)	36.6**	47.5***	51.9**	37.7**	61.7**	63.9***
Wages								
Low	88	9.1	23.9	38.6	51.1	27.3	56.8	65.9
Moderate	207	9.2	52.7	63.8	64.7	54.6	78.3	82.1
High	156	6.4(ns)	35.0***	50.3***	52.2*	35.7***	63.1***	65.6***
Labor Producton								
Low	82	6.1	26.8	35.4	51.2	26.8	57.3	65.9
Moderate	199	9.5	44.2	60.3	60.8	47.7	74.4	78.4
High	171	7.6(ns)	43.9*	56.1***	57.3(ns)	44.4***	67.8*	70.8***
UNIVERSITY PROXIMITY								
BA								
No	219	9.6	42.9	54.3	60.7	44.7	70.8	75.3
Yes	236	6.8(ns)	38.6(ns)	53.4(ns)	54.2(ns)	40.3(ns)	66.1(ns)	70.3(ns)
10 MAs in County								
No	266	7.9	42.1	53.8	59.0	43.6	69.2	74.1
Yes	189	8.5(ns)	38.6(ns)	54.0(ns)	55.0(ns)	40.7(ns)	67.2(ns)	70.9(ns)
Any Ph.D.s in County								
No	319	8.5	41.4	55.2	59.2	42.9	70.5	74.6
Yes	136	7.4(ns)	39.0(ns)	50.7(ns)	52.9(ns)	41.2(ns)	63.2(ns)	68.4(ns)
UNIVERSITY UNRESPONSIVE								
No	200	9.5	38.0	48.5	52.0	41.0	62.0	67.0
Yes	251	7.2(ns)	43.0(ns)	59.0*	62.5*	43.8(ns)	74.5**	78.1*

Note: Significance levels: *** = .001, ** = .01, * = .05.

Source: Compiled by the authors from survey of advanced-technology firms.

considerable difficulty in recruiting workers in at least one of the four skill categories. Given economic conditions in Pennsylvania at the time of the survey, these results suggest that skill shortages may be a major obstacle to economic growth.

Popular wisdom and available research suggest that small firms encounter more recruiting difficulty than their larger counterparts; in this sample, quite the opposite appears to be the case. When firms are divided into four groups based upon the number of employees in Pennsylvania, recruiting difficulty increases with size; this relationship holds across each of the four skill levels and for the three aggregate difficulty measures as well. For example, while only about half (56.3 percent) of the smallest firms reported recruiting difficulty, over 90 percent of the largest firms reported problems.

Established firms might be expected to have fewer recruiting problems than new firms for several reasons. Such firms might be better known in the area. The firms' executives are more likely connected in the network of civic, training, educational, and job-placement agencies, and these firms might be viewed as more stable. Survey responses indicate the opposite; older firms (as measured by years in Pennsylvania) encountered more recruiting difficulty overall and at each of the four skill levels. The relationship is less pronounced than that existing between recruiting problems and firm size. Firm age and number of employees are positively correlated ($r = .54$).

The consistency with which this pattern is repeated across skill levels and through the range of firm size and age indicates that it is not anomalous. Very small firms in the early stages of product development might not encounter recruiting difficulties because they are not yet recruiting. But this does not appear to be the explanation for the pattern observed across the range of firms in these data. Firms in the largest category (50 or more employees) consistently report more recruiting difficulty than the next largest category. It may be that smaller and younger firms encounter less recruiting difficulty because they are more likely "homegrown," that is, they have established local networks where key employees can be found relatively easily. In terms of economic-development policy, these data suggest that while small new firms may need assistance in a broad range of areas such as risk capital, management, and inexpensive space, they are not especially disadvantaged in recruiting new employees.

Except at the lowest skill level, manufacturing firms are more likely to encounter recruiting difficulties than their counterparts in the service sector. For example, fewer than half (44.8 percent) of the service firms in the sample reported difficulty in recruiting technical personnel, compared to two-thirds of the manufacturing firms.

Over half (56 percent) of the firms in the sample indicated plans for increasing employment. Except for the lowest skill level, those firms planning to increase employment reported greater difficulty recruiting new workers locally. Differences were most pronounced in recruiting professional employees. Fewer than half (45.4 percent) of the firms that did not anticipate growth reported difficulty recruiting professionals; almost two-thirds (65.4 percent) of the growth-oriented firms encountered difficulty.

The pattern has interesting implications for economic development. An effective strategy for assisting growing firms would be to emphasize the local area's attractiveness for professional workers. Issues relevant to critical-mass considerations discussed in Chapter 4 are pertinent here. Access to, and availability of, high-skill workers is another component of agglomeration effects.

Attractiveness of Labor Factors and Recruiting Difficulty

A section of the survey sent to executives asked them to rate the attractiveness of 31 local factors in their business operations. (See Chapter 4 for a discussion of these items.) Four of the 31 items pertained specifically to the local labor force (availability, skill level, wage levels, and productivity). Recruiting difficulty and the attractiveness of labor factors demonstrated a consistent curvilinear relationship. Those firms that assigned either a high or low attractiveness rating to labor factors were less likely to encounter recruiting difficulties than firms that assigned a rating of moderate attractiveness. For example, about two-thirds of the firms that assigned high or low attractiveness ratings to local wages reported recruiting difficulties at some skill levels. Over four-fifths (82.1 percent) of the firms that assigned a moderate attractiveness rating to local wages reported recruiting problems.

The pattern suggests an interaction between the attractiveness of local labor factors and recruiting problems and can be interpreted as follows. If recruiting new employees is not important to a firm, then both local labor factors and recruiting difficulty will be assigned low values. If recruiting is important, firms' ratings of the attractiveness of local labor factors is likely to be a function of the difficulty they encounter in finding skilled applicants. Firms that are successful will report less recruiting difficulty and assign a higher attractiveness rating than firms that encounter problems.

University Proximity and Recruiting Difficulty

A substantial literature exists on the relationship between universities and advanced-technology firms. Much of the interest focuses on collaborative research and interorganizational partnerships. Firms that are geographically proximate to colleges and universities should have an advantage in recruiting new employees. These firms are believed to have greater access to faculty and students, more opportunities to hire students for part-time and summer internships, and greater exposure through collaborative undertakings. In addition, proximity to a university allegedly increases the general attractiveness of an area, particularly to professional employees. Chapter 6 of this book is devoted to the topic of the university and advanced technology; the discussion here is restricted to the relationship between geographic proximity to colleges and universities and recruiting difficulty.

The National Center for Educational Statistics collects data annually on the number of degrees granted for postsecondary institutions by curricular area. Three indexes of advanced-technology-related training in 1982 were constructed for each of Pennsylvania's 67 counties. The indexes, which are described in detail in Chapter 6, were used to construct three dichotomous variables reflecting the existence of technology-related baccalaureate, master's, and doctoral programs in each county.

Over half (236) of the firms were located in counties with advanced-technology baccalaureate programs, about 40 percent (189) in counties with master's programs and about one-third (136) in counties with doctoral programs. No statistically significant differences were found between recruiting difficulty and these educational proximity variables. Several explanations for the absence of a relationship are possible. The county may be a poor measure of geographic proximity; county boundaries frequently fail to reflect patterns of commerce and communication. Pennsylvania has more rural residents than any other state in the nation; therefore, major universities may serve regions substantially larger than the counties in which they are located. Finally, contrary to popular opinion, universities may not be an important factor in labor recruitment.

As an indirect test of this latter possibility, firms were grouped into two categories depending upon whether they thought universities in the state were unresponsive in building working relationships with advanced-technology firms. Over half (251) of the responding firms indicated that they believed universities were unresponsive to their needs. Firms that saw the university as unresponsive were more likely to encounter difficulty in recruiting technical and professional employees.

These two relationships (geographic proximity and unresponsiveness) suggest that cultural rather than physical distance between firms and universities plays an important role in recruiting difficulty. From an economic-development policy perspective, programs designed to facilitate interactions and linkages between firms and universities may be more productive than those that simply attempt to transport university services to firms dispersed throughout the universities' service areas.

TRAINING FOR ADVANCED-TECHNOLOGY JOBS

If an imbalance exists between the needs of advanced-technology firms and the skills of the available labor force, employment-related training programs are an obvious way to reduce structural unemployment and support the advanced-technology sector. Substantial training occurs in the formal-educational sector, in proprietary schools, and through government-sponsored job-training programs. Although data on these activities are dispersed, a reasonably good picture of training activities can be constructed. Much less is known about company-sponsored training, particularly for advanced-technology firms.

Company-Sponsored Training

Estimates of the extent of industry investment in formal training generally vary from $30 to $60 billion annually (Doeringer 1982; Ehrbar 1983; Ripley and Franklin 1983; Office of Technology Assessment 1982; Randall et al. 1983). These investments in human capital (between $300 and $500 per employee per year) are dwarfed by investments in physical capital, which amounted to $3,300 per worker in 1981 (Choate 1982; Ehrbar 1983). One obvious reason why firms prefer to invest in physical capital is that, unlike human capital, physical capital remains the property of the firm when workers' employment is terminated.

Moreover, physical capital generally retains some resale value if an operation is dissolved. Human capital, which is embedded in the individual worker, provides no return to the firm when employment ends (Becker 1975; Mincer 1974).

In all likelihood, the $30 to $60 billion spent on formal training programs reflects a small part of the human capital investment occurring at work. Considerable learning in the form of informal on-the-job training occurs at work. Much of this training is undertaken by workers themselves, not financed by the firms that employ them.[2] Since on-the-job training is not formally organized, direct estimates of the dollar value of these investments are impossible to obtain. Yet Doeringer (1982) argues "that on-the-job training is the single most important source of skill development" (p. 29). Moreover, on-the-job training for advanced-technology processes such as flexible manufacturing may be especially important because skills evolve in response to situations in a collective process (Reich 1983).

Firm-based training may be particularly important for advanced-technology firms because processes and technology change very quickly making old knowledge obsolete. "In a rapidly advancing technological society, it is unlikely that the skills and information base needed for initial employment will be those needed for the same job a few years later" (Office of Technology Assessment 1982, p. 7).

Evidence exists suggesting that advanced-technology firms view training favorably. In a survey of 2,100 member firms in the American Electronics Association (1983), retraining and skills upgrading were rated most important for firms in meeting their manpower needs.

Publicly Sponsored Training Programs

While training programs are apparently important for firms, they may not be particularly useful as a policy tool in obtaining employment for displaced workers. Some analysts (Levin and Rumberger, 1983) argue that the growth of the advanced-technology sector will eventually reduce, rather than increase, the level of skill required in most jobs. Others (Kuttner 1983; McGowan 1984) observe that training programs have a generally poor record in assisting displaced workers and may waste resources and increase the frustration of program participants when they fail to obtain jobs. Ehrbar (1983) even suggests that support for job search may actually be more cost-effective than training.

Vocational training in secondary schools has also received substantial criticism. Such programs are frequently characterized as being excessively narrow, providing skills that are often out-of-date. The rate of return to such training (as compared to alternative secondary curricula) is frequently estimated at zero (Grubb 1984).

Given the disappointing record of vocational training and jobs programs, attention has shifted to business-education partnerships, customized job training, and advanced-technology education programs. The current trend is toward decentralization of decision making and participation of local businesspeople in the management of public education. The Job Training Partnership Act (JTPA), which replaced the Comprehensive Employment Training Act (CETA), reflects the Reagan administration's emphasis on decentralization and local partnerships.

At the state level, although training expenditures are relatively low, programs are growing rapidly and states are actively developing customized job training and advanced-technology programs. A study by the Congressional Budget Office (1984) reports that state expenditures for on-the-job training doubled during the two-year period 1983-84. In the most recent year for which data are available (1982), states spent over $120 million on training. Thirty-nine states fund customized training programs; of these, 31 are targeted at attracting new and expanding firms. Moreover, in 1983, 13 states were sponsoring advanced-technology education programs and 21 were offering labor training and technical assistance in advanced-technology areas. Most of these programs were initiated after 1980 (Gottlieb, 1983).

The customized programs usually concentrate on preparing workers for particular industries targeted by the state, or even for jobs in specific companies (Urban Institute 1983, p. 14). Training is typically targeted at firms considering locating or expanding operations within a state as opposed to those already in operation (Urban Institute 1983). In some ways, such preferential treatment is reminiscent of tax rebates associated with the "smokestack chasing" economic-development strategies. A study by the Congressional Budget Office (1984, p. 37) observed: "It can be argued that sufficient economic incentives exist both for workers to train themselves and for firms to train workers." Some contend that we may be publicly subsidizing businesses to do what they would have done anyway (Randall et al. 1983; Grubb 1984).

Small Firms and Training

Large firms provide more training programs (Choate 1982; Doeringer 1982; Randall et al. 1983). Yet small firms, which are the source of most new jobs, may have a greater need for training. It is argued that small firms are not large enough to support in-house training (Ressler 1983), are inaccessible to government-sponsored programs (Reinshuttle 1983), and often resist if contacted (Ripley and Franklin 1983).

Since most small firms are unable to maintain in-house training, firms must use outside facilities for entry-level training. Systematic information on the types of firms that provide training, the characteristics of employees most likely to receive training, and the interaction between firms' characteristics and employees' skill levels would be useful to policymakers.

FIRMS' TRAINING POLICY

Executive managers in the sample of 459 firms were asked to indicate the predominant mode of training new employees in each of four skill levels. Responses were grouped into three categories reflecting different training policies: no training, training exclusively in-house, and use of outside training facilities (Table 5.3). Firms reporting that they used outside training facilities (either predominantly or in combination with in-house facilities) were classified in the "outside" group.

TABLE 5.3 Percentage of Firms Providing Entry-Level Training by Skill Level of Employees (N = 442)

Skill Level	Type of Training		
	None	*In-House*	*Outside*
Any Level	4.1	15.8	80.1
High Skill	9.0	14.5	76.5
Low Skill	24.2	42.3	33.5
Professional	20.6	12.2	67.0
Technical	25.6	19.9	54.5
Semiskilled	28.7	40.0	31.2
Unskilled	60.2	32.1	7.7

Source: Compiled by the authors from survey of advanced-technology firms.

Over 95 percent of the firms in the sample report some type of entry-level training – over 80 percent use outside facilities. When training policies are examined in light of skill level, a clear pattern emerges. High-skill entry-level workers were likely to receive more training. Only 9 percent of the firms provide no training to high-skill workers (technical and professional), but almost one-quarter of the firms apply this policy to low-skill (unskilled and semiskilled) entrants. Over three-quarters of the firms use outside facilities for their high-skill employees, but only about one-third send low-skill workers outside for training.

A hierarchical pattern applies to the four skill levels in our sample. The probability of receiving no training decreases (from 60 to 20 percent) and the probability of receiving outside training increases (from 8 to 77 percent) as worker skills increase. In fact, for semiskilled, technical, and professional employees, the salient question appears to be where they will receive training. For unskilled workers, the relevant question is whether they will receive any training at all. In the analyses presented in the next section, firms that provide training for unskilled workers are contrasted with those that do not. For the other three skill categories, all contrasts are between firms that use outside facilities and those that don't; that is, they either provide no training or they train exclusively in-house.

Recruiting Difficulty and Training Policy

If company-sponsored training genuinely functions as a mechanism for producing human capital, firms that report difficulty recruiting employees should be more actively engaged in training. Table 5.4 contrasts recruiting difficulty (for a specific skill level) with the training policy for that skill level. For example, only 36 percent of the firms that reported no or minor difficulty in recruiting unskilled employees provided training for unskilled entrants. In contrast, 83.3 percent of the firms reporting difficulty in recruiting unskilled workers provided training.

At every skill level, a strong pattern is apparent. Firms that encountered difficulty recruiting new employees are much more likely to engage in training. For all columns except column 2 (unskilled workers), the figures in the body of the table show the percentage of firms providing training outside the firm. Firms that reported difficulty recruiting technical workers are twice as likely to provide outside training to these employees as firms that have only minor difficulty (70 percent and 35.5 percent, respectively).

TABLE 5.4 Percentage of Firms Providing Outside Training for Entering Employees

	Number of Firms	Unskilled	Semi-skilled	Technical	Professional	Low Skill (Un or Semi)	High Skill (Tech or Prof)	Any Level
ALL FIRMS	442	39.8	31.2	54.5	67.0	33.3	76.5	80.1
Difficulty Recruiting								
None or minor		36.0	23.7	35.5	46.4	26.4	64.7	77.2
Mod or major		83.3***	41.6***	70.1***	81.4***	42.9***	81.5***	81.0(ns)
Size – Employees in PA								
up to 5	134	15.7	14.9	33.6	53.7	17.9	65.7	70.1
6-24	161	41.0	35.4	58.4	65.2	36.6	77.6	82.0
25-49	54	53.7	44.4	66.7	77.8	50.0	83.3	85.2
50+	93	64.5***	39.8***	71.0***	82.8***	40.9***	86.0**	88.2**
Age – Years in PA								
1-4	102	25.5	25.5	49.0	67.6	28.4	77.5	80.4
5-9	104	36.5	30.8	49.0	62.5	33.7	74.0	79.8
10-14	108	38.9	29.6	60.2	64.8	31.5	76.9	79.6
15+	128	54.7***	37.5(ns)	58.6(ns)	71.9(ns)	39.1(ns)	77.3(ns)	80.5(ns)
Sector								
Manufacturing	197	56.9	35.5	61.9	71.1	37.6	79.2	82.2
Service	240	25.4***	27.5(ns)	48.3***	63.3(ns)	29.6(ns)	74.2(ns)	78.3(ns)
Anticipates Growth								
Yes	268	40.7(ns)	32.5(ns)	58.6*	70.5(ns)	35.1(ns)	80.6*	82.5(ns)
No	174	38.5	29.3	48.3	61.5	31.0	70.1	76.4
LOCAL LABOR FACTORS IN PRESENT LOCATION								
Availability								
Low	64	18.8	12.5	32.8	59.4	14.1	70.3	70.3

Moderate	147	42.2	33.3	59.9	70.1	36.1	81.6	84.4
High	229	44.5***	35.4***	57.2***	67.2(ns)	37.6**	75.1(ns)	80.3(ns)
Skilled Labor								
Low	89	29.2	20.2	40.4	59.6	22.5	67.4	67.4
Moderate	169	45.0	32.5	56.8	69.8	34.9	79.3	83.4
High	182	40.7*	35.7*	59.3*	68.1(ns)	37.9*	78.6(ns)	83.5**
Wages								
Low	78	29.5	21.8	44.9	65.4	24.4	74.4	75.6
Moderate	205	46.8	29.3	56.1	67.3	31.7	78.0	81.0
High	157	36.3*	38.9*	57.3(ns)	67.5(ns)	40.8*	75.8(ns)	81.5(ns)
Labor Production								
Low	74	28.4	20.3	43.2	64.9	24.3	73.0	73.0
Moderate	196	41.3	27.6	55.6	64.3	30.6	75.0	79.6
High	170	43.5(ns)	40.6**	58.2(ns)	71.2(ns)	41.2*	80.0(ns)	84.1
SHARE OF SALES IN PA								
0-5%	99	53.5	41.4	63.6	74.7	45.5	79.8	82.8
6-25%	85	52.9	27.1	54.1	70.6	27.1	78.8	80.0
26-85%	104	30.8	29.8	52.9	66.3	32.7	77.9	80.8
Over 85%	128	24.2***	25.0*	48.4(ns)	60.9(ns)	27.3*	72.7(ns)	77.3(ns)
RESEARCH INTENSIVE								
0% of sales	115	28.7	25.2	43.5	53.0	27.8	67.8	75.7
1-5% of sales	118	55.1	33.9	61.9	71.2	37.3	78.0	82.2
6-13% of sales	104	44.2	31.7	60.6	78.8	33.7	89.4	89.4
14+% of sales	96	29.2***	34.4(ns)	52.1*	65.6***	35.4(ns)	70.8***	72.9(ns)

continued

Table 5.4, Continued

	Number of Firms	Unskilled	Semi-skilled	Technical	Professional	Low Skill (Un or Semi)	High Skill (Tech or Prof)	Any Level
UNIVERSITY UNRESPONSIVE								
No	193	39.9	32.5	54.9	64.2	34.7	73.6	78.2
Yes	246	40.2(ns)	30.5(ns)	54.5(ns)	69.5(ns)	32.5(ns)	79.3(ns)	81.7(ns)
UNIVERSITY PROXIMITY								
BA								
No	214	42.5	36.4	58.9	72.4	38.8	81.8	85.0
Yes	228	37.3(ns)	26.3*	50.4(ns)	61.8(ns)	28.5*	71.5*	75.4**
10 MAs in County								
No	260	41.9	32.7	55.4	69.2	35.4	77.7	80.8
Yes	182	36.8(ns)	29.1(ns)	53.3(ns)	63.7(ns)	30.8(ns)	74.7(ns)	79.1(ns)
Any Ph.D.s in County								
No	312	41.3	33.7	55.4	68.9	36.5	78.2	82.1
Yes	130	36.2(ns)	25.4(ns)	52.3(ns)	62.3(ns)	26.2*	72.3(ns)	75.4(ns)

Note: Significance levels: *** = .001, ** = .01, * = .05.

Source: Compiled by the authors from survey of advanced-technology firms.

Columns 6, 7, and 8 of Table 5.4 show training policies in aggregate categories. For example, 26.4 percent of the firms that reported no difficulty in recruiting low-skill workers (either unskilled or semiskilled) provided training to at least one of these groups using outside facilities (column 6).

This pattern indicates that firms are willing to support training when skilled workers are unavailable. In terms of economic-development policy, the pattern suggests that programs such as customized job training may be effective, and that firms may be willing to pay a larger share of the direct costs of such activities. Over 80 percent of the firms in this sample use outside facilities at their own expense.

Firm Characteristics and Training Policy

Training policies vary systematically with the size of firms; a consistent pattern of large firms providing more training at each skill level emerges from these data. This pattern is consistent with the national data cited. For example, fewer than 16 percent of the smallest firms in this sample (one to five employees) provide training for unskilled workers; almost two-thirds of the largest firms (50 employees or more) provide such training. The behavior of the sample was consistent with national trends. Table 5.4 shows the probability of receiving outside training for each skill level by firm size. The first column (which describes policies for training unskilled workers) reflects the probability of a worker receiving any training at all.

Without exception, the probability of receiving outside training increases with firm size and, for any size firm, the higher the employee's skill level, the better the chances for receiving training outside. In part, this pattern may be related to the unexpected finding that smaller firms reported fewer recruiting problems. Nonetheless, the strength of the size-training relationship suggests that public job-training programs should commit resources to reaching smaller firms that provide substantially less training.

Older firms are slightly more likely to provide training to new employees. Differences are statistically significant only for unskilled workers where the oldest firms (over 15 years old) are twice as likely to provide such training as firms less than five years old. Manufacturing firms are more likely to provide training than their service-sector counterparts. Differences are significant, however, only for unskilled and technical personnel, the two groups most likely to be directly involved in production activities.

The probability of training for unskilled workers and of outside training for high-skill workers was systematically related to a firm's research intensity, but the relationship was nonlinear. The probability of receiving training was lowest for firms that either engaged in virtually no R&D or were research intensive. It may be that the former group of firms engages in very routine activities requiring few skills and little training. Skills for the latter group may be so specialized that outside training facilities are inadequate.

University Proximity and Responsiveness

If colleges and universities are an important source of training to advanced-technology firms, one would expect firms that viewed the university as more reponsive to their needs and firms located in close proximity to universities to engage in more training. In general, this was not the case.

Firms were organized into three categories depending upon the importance respondents attached to each of four traditional labor factors (availability, skills, wages, and labor productivity). The higher the importance rating assigned to these four factors, the higher the likelihood that firms would provide training to low-skill workers. The relationship was particularly strong for labor availability and productivity. This pattern suggests that training is viewed as a mechanism for producing human capital, and that advanced-technology firms concerned about the availability and productivity of low-skill workers are making such investments.

SUMMARY OF FINDINGS AND IMPLICATIONS

The distribution of occupations (which is treated as an income proxy) within the sample of 442 responding firms provides no evidence of a bimodal skills or income distribution within the advanced-technology sector. Employees tended to be highly trained; over half of all employees were categorized as either technical or professional. Contrary to the suggestion that advanced-technology firms require many unskilled workers, only 15 percent of employees fell into this category, and over half the responding firms employed no unskilled workers.

Substantial diversity in occupational distribution existed within the sample. A higher concentration of professional and technical workers was encountered in small and young firms, firms in the service sector, firms with moderate research intensity, and those firms located in counties with higher educational institutions.

The distribution of occupations in the sample suggests that advanced-technology firms are a source of high-skill jobs and that economic-development policies aimed at nurturing such enterprises do not imply increasing income inequality. The data also suggest that efforts directed at supporting service-sector firms near universities may be a productive strategy for generating high-income jobs. Patterns of occupational distribution and firm size, age, and research intensity are less policy-relevant since these characteristics of firms are likely to change as companies move through the product development cycle.

Evidence indicates that advanced-technology firms are encountering substantial difficulty recruiting skilled workers. At the end of 1982 (when the economy was emerging from a recession and unemployment was high), almost three-quarters of the sampled firms reported experiencing either moderate or considerable recruiting difficulty. Over 40 percent of the firms reported difficulty in recruiting semiskilled workers, and the incidence of difficulty increased with skill level. The data suggest that shortages of skilled workers may be a major obstacle to the growth of advanced-technology firms. About half the firms in the sample indicated that they had considerable difficulty recruiting qualified personnel at some level.

Contrary to popular wisdom, younger and smaller firms reported much less recruiting difficulty than older and larger firms. The largest firms tended to be twice as likely as the smallest firms to report difficulty recruiting technical and professional personnel, and three times as likely to have difficulty recruiting semiskilled workers. Economic-development and job-placement agencies are often criticized for being overly reliant on an "old boys' network" and for concentrating on the largest firms at the expense of smaller firms which are thought to be most in need of their services. These data suggest that, at least in terms of recruitment, older and larger firms are in more need of assistance. It is possible, however, that small firms are "homegrown," and that managers of these firms are local people, well connected with enterprise support networks (Chapter 10).

Service-sector firms encountered more difficulty than manufacturing firms, and firms anticipating growth reported difficulty recruiting technical and professional personnel. Geographic proximity to universities was unrelated to recruiting difficulty, but firms that viewed the university as being unresponsive had a significantly higher incidence of difficulty in recruiting high-skill workers. These patterns suggest that job placement services should be directed at service-sector firms and at firms that are expanding. Programs designed to facilitate communication between advanced-technology firms and the academic community may be more effective than extension programs in assisting firms in recruiting high-skill employees.

Advanced-technology firms are heavily involved in training entry-level employees. Over 95 percent of the firms sampled reported providing some form of formal training for new employees; over 80 percent reported using outside training facilities. The probability of a worker receiving training increases systematically with the amount of human capital that worker brings to the job. Most unskilled workers receive no training; the chances of such a worker receiving outside training are less than one in ten. Four out of five professionals, on the other hand, receive training; two out of three are trained outside the firms.

The evidence suggests strongly that firms provide training to compensate for recruiting difficulties. Firms experiencing difficulty finding workers are twice as likely to provide training (at every skill level) as those that have only minor problems. Manufacturing firms and firms concerned with labor issues such as labor availability and productivity also train more. The high incidence of training and its strong relationship to recruiting difficulty suggest that firms recognize training as an investment and are willing to pay for it. Critics of publicly subsidized customized job training may be correct in asserting that development agencies are subsidizing firms, especially larger ones, for doing what they would do anyway.

Overall, work-force patterns suggest a need for ongoing, lifelong training. The majority of advanced-technology jobs are in high-skill occupations. The high incidence of training provided by firms suggests that new workers lack critical skills. Moreover, those in the highest skill occupations (presumably with the most formal education) receive more training when hired. Clearly, an appropriate source of such training is the university, the subject of the next chapter.

NOTES

1. In the questionnaire itself, the category described in this book as "semiskilled" was labeled "skilled," and described in the following terms: "Skilled employees – some specific training and education required for job, either on the job or vocational-technical school. Job usually requires a substantial period of experience to master (examples: machinist, word processor operator)." To clarify exposition in the book, we refer to this group as "semiskilled."

2. The argument regarding worker finance of training builds upon the human capital model. To the extent that training is general, that is, increases a worker's productivity in any firm, employers have little incentive to finance training because they would have to increase wages upon the completion of training (see Becker 1964).

6 The Role of Colleges and Universities in Technological Development

INTRODUCTION

Despite the lack of consensus concerning the appropriate definition of advanced technology, near unanimity exists that colleges and universities play a central role in advanced-technology development (National Science Foundation 1983a; 1983b). A study of university-industry linkages commissioned by New York State summed up this pervasive belief as follows: "It has become a basic article of faith and conventional wisdom that institutions of higher learning play a pivotal role in both the development and the maintenance of high technology industry" (Battelle Memorial Institute 1982b, p. 5).

A number of national reports have strongly asserted that the education sector, through its contribution to technological change, will be a key factor in the United States' economic competitiveness (Education Commission of the States 1983; Business-Higher Education Forum 1983; AFL-CIO 1983). Enthusiasm for partnership between industry and education exists in a range of areas, but particular emphasis is placed on research-related advanced-technology linkages: "The highest degree of convergence between the university and industry is in high technology research where technology transfer is rapid and requires close proximity" (National Science Board 1982, p. 20). Enthusiasm for education's potential to contribute to economic development through its more traditional training function also exists; much of this enthusiasm, however, emanates from the education sector itself, which is facing substantial reductions in enrollment as the school-age population declines. "Allow educators to claim the rhetoric of economic development . . . and (it) gives the schools a centrality and 'relevance'. . . . Small wonder, then, that educators cannot resist jumping on the high-tech bandwagon" (Grubb 1984, p. 1).

This enthusiasm for linkages and partnership exists without any strong empirical evidence that higher education plays an important role in advanced-technology activities (National Science Foundation 1983). The limited literature that does exist has been categorized as "journalistic and anecdotal" (Office of Technology Assessment 1982, p. 4) and "more speculative and descriptive than empirical" (National Science Foundation 1983, p. 176). In fact, the dearth of information on university-industry research relationships was a central factor in the decision of the National Science Board to select this area as the topic of its 1982 Annual Report to the President and Congress (Peters and Fusfeld 1983).

The federal government is by far the biggest supporter of research in U.S. universities. Of the $7 billion annual academic basic research budget, $5 billion is contributed by the federal government. Less than 5 percent of basic research funding comes from private industry. It is no wonder that universities have concentrated on research rather than development. Industry resources represent a large undeveloped source of financial support for universities, but to tap into that resource base, universities must be responsive to industry's needs.

Substantial conceptual and theoretical work has focused on structural and organizational factors that might facilitate or hinder university-industry collaboration, but little empirical work has assessed: a) whether advanced-technology firms actually perceive universities to be important, b) the aspects of university services that are of interest to advanced-technology firms, and c) characteristics of advanced-technology firms themselves. One author (Ping 1983, p. 123) observed that "most business people still don't understand how or why they should collaborate with local universities." If this observation is correct, state and local initiatives designed merely to facilitate partnership arrangements may be futile. This chapter draws upon empirical data to explore the perceptions of advanced-technology firms concerning the importance of university services in their operations, and to address the three areas just noted.

In large part, current interest in university-industry collaboration is linked to a perception of national crisis and a sense that the higher-education sector represents a resource that can be mobilized to meet that crisis. The perceived crisis involves two interrelated components. First, the United States is seen as progressively less commercially competitive at the international level. At the same time, the university is perceived as a principal source of basic research that can be translated into commercial goods and services. The success of the transistor (a product of basic research at Bell labs) in transforming modern technology is frequently cited as an example of the potential return to basic research. Second, as suggested in Chapter 5, economic development may be delayed by shortages of workers with critical advanced-technology skills. The university is seen as a potential source of new workers for advanced-technology industries as well as a source of training and skills upgrading.

In short, universities are assumed to have two major dimensions of importance to advanced-technology firms: they are perceived as a source of research (basic theoretical inquiry and access to faculty and facilities) and as a source of skilled employees. At the state and local levels, programs focus on fostering university-advanced-technology linkages as a means of attracting and nurturing firms. In addition, demographic shifts (resulting in a decline in the college-age population) coupled with reduced growth in government support for university research, make industry linkages particularly attractive as a response to a higher-education funding crisis.

THE NATIONAL PERSPECTIVE

Patterns in Basic Research

The most common argument offered in support of increasing university-advanced-technology linkages concerns R&D expenditures. While impossible to observe directly, substantial indirect evidence suggests that R&D contributes significantly to economic growth and productivity (Wiewel 1984). In a widely cited study of the determinants of economic growth, Denison (1974) estimated that advances in knowledge accounted for more than 40 percent of the growth in the U.S. economy between 1950 and 1962. The share of GNP devoted to R&D is frequently used as an index of a nation's innovative capacity (Etzioni 1983). In the United States, the share of GNP devoted to R&D dropped from 3 percent in the late 1960s to 2 percent in the early 1980s (Reich 1983). During this same period, "the flow of innovation, as measured by such indicators as patents issued per year, began to shrink drastically"

(Business Week 1984d). New data suggest that this trend may be reversing (Fortune 1984).

Not only is the relative level of R&D expenditure considered an important determinant of innovation and productivity growth, but the mix of research activities between basic and applied research is thought to be critical as well (Peters and Fusfeld 1983). The long-term payoffs to basic research may be quite substantial, but the absence of immediate returns and competitive advantage cause firms to prefer applied research. In 1981, national R&D spending overall was estimated to total $69 billion; of this, only $9 billion (13 percent) was invested in basic research (National Science Board 1982). While academic institutions perform only 12.5 percent of all R&D (Office of Technology Assessment 1982), they perform over 50 percent of all basic research (Peters and Fusfeld 1983; Business-Higher Education Forum 1983) and perhaps as much as 70 percent (Ping 1983). University faculty clearly have a strong preference for basic research; two-thirds of the $6.6 billion spent on university R&D in 1981 were classified as basic research (National Science Board 1982). In contrast, only 4 percent of the industrial R&D budget is used for basic research (National Science Foundation 1983), down from 8 percent in 1960 (Business-Higher Education Forum 1983).

Given this concentration of basic R&D in universities, two issues emerge. First, changing demographic patterns and a decline in federal support of university-based research threaten the vitality of the university and its capacity to conduct research. Between 1975 and 1982 the proportion of university staff engaged in R&D activities grew by only 2 percent annually, compared with a 5 percent growth in industry. A second research-related concern is that important university-based discoveries may be delayed in reaching commercial application because of delays in knowledge diffusion. University-industry linkages are considered desirable because close interaction facilitates the flow of university-based research to commercial application.

Universities and Advanced-Technology Employees

The second major dimension of universities' contribution to advanced technology relates to their traditional role of providing high-level training. Recently, attention has focused upon potential shortages in computer science and engineering. Much of the rhetoric assumes the tone of international competition reminiscent of the post-Sputnik era. For example, Japan, with only half the population of the United States, is producing more engineering graduates annually. In the early 1980s, Soviet production of engineers exceeded that of the United States by a factor of five to one (Hayes 1983). Choate (1982, p. 37) has suggested that "the shortage of (technically skilled) workers is becoming a major structural barrier to meeting either national defense or domestic production requirements."

Part of the problem is that demand for technical personnel can actually diminish supply. Education is unusual in that an output of the process (graduates) also constitutes an input (instructors). "Nationwide, almost all engineering schools and computer science programs are having difficulty in recruiting engineering faculty" (Useem 1981, p. 20). At the start of the 1980-81 academic year, approximately 10 percent of university engineering positions were vacant (Office of Technology Assessment 1982); for junior faculty in fields such as computers and electronics, the vacancy rate neared 25 percent (Business-Higher Education Forum 1983). Increasingly, academic institutions have come to rely on part-time faculty to provide instruction; 23 percent of all academic scientists and engineers are now employed at their institutions on a part-time basis with part-time employment growing at three times the full-time rate (National Science Board 1982). Moreover, attractive salaries in industry serve to deter promising engineering students from graduate work and academic careers; currently, less than 60 percent of the Ph.D. engineering enrollment in U.S. universities consists of U.S. citizens (Pollack 1983).

This labor supply problem is exacerbated by the high rate of attrition of trained engineers. The accelerating rate at which new technical information is created makes engineering skills quickly obsolete. By one estimate, "the half-life of an engineer is about five years" (Pollack 1983, p. 14). A survey of 878 M.I.T. engineering alumni (classes of 1959-67) found that by 1978, 83 percent had left the profession (Pollack 1983). A report of the Business-Higher Education Forum (1983) projects a need for 100,000 new engineers annually for the forseeable future. Currently, U.S. colleges and universities are graduating only about 67,000 new engineers per year while estimates of the attrition rate run as high as 50,000 annually (Pollack 1983). Higher salaries and superior research opportunities outside the academic world are allegedly depleting the faculties of academic institutions (Tornatzky et al. 1982; Office of Technology Assessment 1982); however, a recent study of the American

Association of Engineering Societies found equal numbers of engineers entering the academic world from industry as leaving (Block 1983).

THE STATE AND LOCAL PERSPECTIVES

University-advanced-technology linkages are also of considerable interest at state and local levels; the emphasis, however, differs substantially. Concerns focus on building a strong indigenous educational system and fostering linkages to nurture, attract, and retain advanced-technology firms in the local area. State and local strategies emphasize the university's potential role regarding research and employees. An implicit assumption is that increased access to universities will make an area more attractive to existing firms considering relocation or expansion and will increase the likelihood that new home-grown advanced-technology firms will come into existence. These implicit assumptions regarding the importance of university-based activities to advanced-technology firms warrant careful consideration.

THE RESEARCH DIMENSION

Advanced-technology firms can benefit from university research activities in two principal ways: access to faculty and access to university facilities. Faculty members are experts in their technical fields, and their research activities at major universities often represent the cutting edge of knowledge, particularly in rapidly changing industries such as genetic engineering and microelectronics. The university provides firms with a "window" on science and technology. Industry's interest in faculty research tends to be general rather than specific; that is, advanced-technology firms do not typically look to university-based research for specific technological innovations that will directly result in new products or processes (National Science Board 1982; Peters and Fusfeld 1983). Rather, faculty research typically is seen as a source of general information on science and technology.

In addition to campus-based research conducted by universities, the faculty also serves as paid consultants to advanced-technology firms. National surveys of university faculty indicate that about 40 percent engage in paid consulting of some type (National Science Board 1982). In technology-related areas the participation rate is substantially higher;

62 percent of engineering faculty, for example, engage in consulting activities (Marver and Patton 1976). Consulting is more likely at universities than at colleges, at high prestige institutions, and among senior faculty members (National Science Board 1982; Marver and Patton 1976).

Consulting is important for several reasons. First, it provides a direct and flexible avenue for personal contact and interaction that bypasses obstacles associated with academic incentives and organizational rigidity. Second, consulting is seen as an important mechanism for direct knowledge transfer (Peters and Fusfeld 1983). Consulting can provide advanced-technology firms with direct access to faculty research. Third, consulting contracts are commonly used as a mechanism to fund basic research on university campuses (National Science Foundation 1983). Fourth, and perhaps most important, consulting has been found to be a critical precursor to more extensive interinstitutional research arrangements between universities and firms. In a study of cooperative research programs, 75 percent of all arrangements were based upon previous consulting agreements between the principal university researcher and the firms (Fusfeld 1983).

Another way that advanced-technology firms can access faculty expertise is through formalized joint research activities (Hise et al. 1980; Thornburg 1982). Underlying these arrangements is the presumption that both organizations will benefit (McCartney 1983). University administrators see such agreements as a source of financial support offsetting reductions in enrollment, declining federal support for R&D, and increasing operating and equipment costs. Firms' executives express interest in gaining access to technology, information, and manpower, and they also view such efforts as a means of providing support to research and excellence (National Science Board 1982). In addition, firms are motivated to affiliate with a major research university as a way to gain corporate esteem and to boost the morale of professional employees by providing opportunities for joint authorship in scientific publications (Peters and Fusfeld 1983).

Advanced-technology firms also establish links with universities to gain access to research-related facilities. An important research tool at any university is the library. Library holdings at major research universities represent a resource that all but the largest corporations are unable to duplicate. Moreover, a number of major university libraries also serve as repositories for government documents and technical reports, an important source of current technical data.

Increasingly, universities provide access to massive on-line data bases and maintain substantial machine-accessible data libraries. Also, university computer centers maintain state-of-the-art hardware and software. University libraries and information systems clearly provide important facilities for advanced-technology research.

Universities also provide a concentration of sophisticated laboratories and equipment. For many industries, access to university laboratories can represent a clear research advantage. Among advanced-technology firms, however, it is not clear that this is always the case. In fact, given the rate of innovation and change in the advanced-technology sector, equipment becomes obsolete quite rapidly. Some maintain that much university research equipment is outmoded and obsolete (Battelle 1982, p. 7). In some instances, university faculty seek collaborative arrangements with firms to gain access to state-of-the-art equipment that their own departments cannot afford.

THE EMPLOYEE DIMENSION

Traditionally, the higher-education sector has been a source of skilled employees. For advanced-technology firms, universities serve this function in two distinct ways: training employees and attracting employees. Universities not only produce skills; they also help attract skilled employees to an area.

Universities provide training services to firms in two ways. They provide a regular stream of graduates. In addition, many firms rely upon universities to provide additional training to current employees through on-site training or through regular degree programs. A number of studies indicate that industry's primary objective in establishing university relationships is to obtain competent and adequate personnel. The need for specific research "is far behind . . . as an objective" (Fusfeld 1983, p. 14). Moreover, even in cooperative research ventures, interest in acquiring skilled employees is of central importance (National Science Board 1982). In fact, access to high-quality manpower was described as "the single most important motivator" for support of university research by 75 percent of the firm representatives in one study (Peters and Fusfeld 1983, p. 34).

Proximity to universities is viewed as a particular advantage for recruiting graduates. Not only are recruitment and interview costs lower, but also firms frequently have the opportunity to use potential employees on a part-time basis during internships or joint research projects. This first-hand knowledge of prospective employees' characteristics may substantially reduce recruitment and interview costs and increase employee retention.

In addition to providing graduates, universities provide important training services by providing degree programs for current employees. Firms must "make a basic choice between retraining employees or simply replacing them" (Tornatzky et al. 1982, p. 19). Replacement, however, may not be a viable option in the advanced-technology sector. The High Technology Council expects that over the next five years the demand for technical people will significantly outstrip the supply (Kleinfeld 1984). A recent survey of member firms conducted by the American Electronics Association (1983, p. 44) reported that "retraining and upgrading current employees is the most highly rated course of action for companies."

In addition to the direct "production" of skills, local universities play an important role in attracting professional employees to an area by offering university-related opportunities and cultural amenities. As noted elsewhere, cooperative research arrangements and opportunities for joint publication are attractive to scientific personnel in advanced-technology firms. Professional employees with graduate training frequently hold adjunct appointments at local universities and teach part-time (Peters and Fusfeld 1983; U.S. General Accounting Office 1983b). The high level of part-time staffing in engineering and computer science programs (cited above) indicates that this practice may be pervasive. This pattern also appears common in community colleges where the part-time faculty is composed of employees of local advanced-technology firms (Useem 1981).

Another important aspect of proximity to universities is the cultural and recreational amenities that universities provide. For professionals seeking employment in regional or national job markets, "quality of life" issues are an important factor in job choice. Not only does the presence of a university increase the likelihood that such amenities will be available, but also the quality of public schools is generally high in university communities. Research indicates that on-campus cultural events are often seen as important to firms located in land-grant and public university communities (Buck et al. 1984).

A MODEL OF THE UNIVERSITY'S ROLE

Existing literature on the university's role in advanced technology, while limited and often anecdotal, does suggest a pattern of university-firm interaction. This pattern, drawn from the discussion above, is shown in Figure 6.1. University activities appear to fall in one of two major dimensions – facilitating research and providing employees. The research dimension can be further divided into activities involving access to faculty (on-campus research, consulting, and joint research) and those involving university facilities (information and laboratories). The employee dimension can be divided into training activities (graduates and programs for current employees) and activities that make the community attractive to professional personnel (adjunct appointments and cultural activities).

COLLABORATION: MEETING THE NEEDS OF BOTH PARTIES

Incentives for Collaboration

Extensive collaborative interaction between advanced-technology firms and universities is likely only if universities do, in fact, provide some or all of the advantages suggested in Figure 6.1. From the perspective of state and local economic development, collaboration should be

FIGURE 6.1 The Role of the University in the Activities of Advanced-Technology Firms

Needs of Firms	University Services and Capabilities	Interaction Activities
University		
Research	Faculty	Faculty Research
		Faculty Consultants
		Joint Research Efforts
	Facilities	Access to Libraries and Information Systems
		Access to Laboratories
Employees	Training	College Graduates
		Degree Programs for Employees
	Attracting	Part-time Teaching
		Cultural Activities

Source: Compiled by the authors from survey of advanced-technology firms.

encouraged for a number of reasons. If joint ventures are conducive to innovation and technology transfer, then policies aimed at facilitating communication will, in themselves, help firms in the region and enhance economic development.

Even if universities are actually not important to advanced-technology firms, they are believed to be important and substantial evidence suggests that this belief does affect location decisions (Premus 1982; Battelle Memorial Institute 1982b; Hall et al. 1983; Malecki 1984; Buck 1984). As state and local development agencies seek to attract advanced-technology firms, the adequacy of local universities is often a critical factor in this competition. For example, in 1983, 56 regional organizations in 27 states competed for the Microelectronic and Computer Technology Corp. (MCT), a new computer research consortium. The winning contender (Austin, Texas, in conjunction with the University of Texas) committed 30 new professorships and 75 graduate assistantships in its package of inducements. MCT executives acknowledged that the academic factors were the decisive element in the choice of location (Philadelphia Inquirer 1983).

In addition to helping existing firms, the university is seen as an environment for spin-off firms (Malecki 1984; Peters and Fusfeld 1983). The phenomenal success of such university-related firms in Silicon Valley and Route 128 provides impetus for encouraging collaboration. In a study of rural advanced-technology firms located near major universities, 35 percent of the responding firms indicated that the founder had been a faculty member, 44 percent were alumni, and 44 percent reported research interests paralleling a research concentration in the local university (Beck et al. 1984). Moreover, spin-off companies are believed to stimulate additional spin-off activity because these firms provide an example to other would-be entrepreneurs.

Attention has also focused on proximity-related policies such as university-based research parks and small business incubator facilities. Some well-publicized successes do exist, but the experience of research parks has frequently been disappointing (Smilor and Gill 1984). Advanced-technology incubators (Chapter 7) are fairly new and have not been the subject of extensive research.

Obstacles to Collaboration

Although many strong incentives for university-advanced-technology collaboration are apparent, a number of major obstacles exist, the most general having to do with the basic values and goals of each type of organization. Firms are profit oriented, ultimately answerable to shareholders; the university's mission is oriented toward creating, preserving, and transmitting knowledge. Ultimately, universities are dependent upon maintaining public credibility (Zollinger 1983).

These differences affect virtually every aspect of organizational and individual behavior. In terms of research, industry's approach typically has a commercial application and a quick payback orientation. Conversely, university research tends to be basic rather than applied. The reward structure for individual researchers also differs. Researchers in industry are rewarded for profitable applications; university researchers depend on peer approval and publications for promotion and salary increases.

Time is important in industry-university collaboration. Successful firms must be able to adapt quickly to changing markets. Universities are typically conservative and extremely cautious about implementing "faddish" changes. Firms often see universities as unresponsive and are frustrated by the "glacial pace of educational change" (Useem 1981, p. 5). Firms are anxious to complete projects quickly, particularly in highly competitive areas, while universities are "attuned to a less critical time frame" (Battelle Memorial Institute 1982b, p. 18) and graduate education is geared toward slow, long-term projects (Zollinger 1983). Faculty availability and requirements for graduate support tend to be tied to the academic calendar and university administrators are distressed when industrial support comes in short-term allotments (Peters and Fusfeld 1983).

Differences in goals are reflected in organizational arrangements. Industry is mission-oriented and the solution of complex problems often requires multidisciplinary teams. Graduate education is discipline oriented, and working units are organized into traditional academic departments. Firms use hierarchical authority arrangements. Universities tend to be more pluralistic and peer governed.

Another major difference between the two sectors concerns access to information, particularly as it pertains to publications and patents. There is a strong "university tradition that guarantees unfettered public access to university research" (U.S. General Accounting Office 1983b, p. 31). Freedom to communicate and publish are considered essential to graduate education and extension of knowledge; any limitation on communication is seen as a potential threat to academic freedom (Peters and Fusfeld 1983; Battelle 1982). Firms, on the other hand, view information as proprietary and are concerned with the possibility that open communication will help competitors (McCartney 1983). When firms are paying for research in a collaborative venture many of these concerns are well founded. Faculty members participating in externally supported research may confront a conflict of norms that is extremely difficult to reconcile (Hangfitt 1983).

Firms and universities frequently "hold distorted images of each other's concerns and capabilities" (National Science Board 1982, p. 28). University research is regarded as "self-indulgent, with too little application to real world problems; similarly, university researchers sometimes believe that industrial research is inferior" (U.S. General Accounting Office 1983b, p. 1). Universities are accused of expecting too much from industry, thinking that industry is obliged to offset reductions in government funding. Industry is accused of misunderstanding the value of basic research and the culture and tradition of the university (Block 1983).

The implementation of successful collaborative agreements can lead to tensions within the university. Some faculty resent the advantages associated with external support (faster promotion, additional space, summer support, consulting); others become burdened with deadlines and contract negotiations and frequently become engaged in work that they find less satisfying (Marver and Patton 1976). Faculty in traditional nonscience disciplines are also seen as obstructing the development of advanced-technology programs (Useem 1981). If university administrators attempt to counter these tensions by diverting income from externally supported programs, "countertensions" can result (Peters and Fusfeld 1983).

Despite the current enthusiasm for collaborative efforts on the part of economic-development organizations, relatively little systematic information exists on the extent or types of university-industry arrangements (U.S. General Accounting Office 1983b). State governments are moving forward quickly in developing programs to encourage collaboration. Given the complexity of such relationships, "the question is whether state involvement eases or exacerbates the problems" (Feller 1983, p. 13).

THE FIRM'S PERSPECTIVE

The rhetoric on local and regional incentives and institutional obstacles is moot if executives of advanced-technology firms do not believe that the university plays (or can play) an important role in their business activities. While some systematic empirical work has been conducted on the importance of universities in firms' location decisions, very little has been done to examine universities' importance to operating firms.

The existing literature (just reviewed) suggests nine specific university roles that may be important to advanced-technology firms. These are categorized into two major dimensions (research and employees), as shown in Figure 6.1. One section of the questionnaire was designed to examine this conceptual model. Executive managers were asked to rate the importance of each of the nine items to their business activities, using a ten-point Likert scale. The scale was anchored with zero representing "no applicability," values of 1-3 representing "minor importance," 4-6 "moderate importance," and 7-9 "major importance." Responses are summarized in Panel A of Table 6.1.

TABLE 6.1 Importance of the University in Nine Roles (N = 447)

PANEL A			
Individual Roles	*Avg. Rating*	*% Indi. Mjr. Imptn.*	*% Indi. Mod./Mjr.*
Research			
1. Faculty Research Activities	1.83	3.8	18.3
2. Faculty Consultants	2.18	5.8	22.8
3. Joint Research Efforts	1.67	4.7	15.9
4. Access to Libraries and M.I.S.	4.12	15.9	50.1
5. Access to Laboratories	1.88	4.0	18.6
Employee			
6. College Graduates	4.42	18.6	56.4
7. Degree Programs for Employees	2.87	8.5	34.7
8. Part-time Teaching Opportunities	1.79	2.9	16.3
9. Cultural Activities	3.12	6.3	36.9
PANEL B			
Aggregate Measures	*Avg. Rating*	*% Indi. Mjr. Imptn.*	*% Indi. Mod./Mjr.*
University (sum of 9 roles)	23.31	53.0	77.4
Research (sum of roles 1-5)	11.09	33.1	62.2
Employees (sum of roles 6-9)	11.61	46.8	73.6

Source: Compiled by the authors from survey of advanced-technology firms.

Averaged across the 447 firms that responded to this section of the questionnaire, university roles were not given high importance ratings (column 1, Table 6.1). Only two of the nine roles (Access to Libraries and College Graduates) were rated at least moderately important (higher than 4.0). Average ratings, however, can be misleading. For each of the nine individual roles, many firms indicated that a particular role was not important. However, these same roles were of importance to a substantial minority of the firms. Moreover, different types of firms identified different university roles as important.

Columns 2 and 3 of Table 6.1 show the percentage of respondents who indicated that a particular role was of major (column 2) or at least moderate (column 3) importance. Examined this way, a substantially different picture of overall importance emerges. The single most important role is apparently the university's traditional one of producing graduates. Over half (56.4 percent) of the responding firms indicated that this role was at least moderately important in their business activities. Almost one-fifth (18.6 percent) of the firms indicated it was of major importance.

Following closely in importance is the university's role of providing library and information services; over half (50.1 percent) of the firms rated this role of moderate or major importance. Over one-third of the firms rated degree programs for employees and university-related cultural activities at least moderately important. Faculty research activities and consulting were rated moderately important by fewer than one-quarter of the respondents. Part-time teaching opportunities were rarely cited as important (16.3 percent of responses). Interestingly, according to these 447 managers, the least important role was university-firm joint research activities. Yet, this is the single area that has received the most attention in regional economic-development efforts.

AGGREGATE MEASURES OF
UNIVERSITY IMPORTANCE

Building upon the approach shown in Figure 6.1, three aggregate measures of university importance were constructed from responses to these nine questionnaire items (Panel B, Table 6.1). The first, labeled "University," is the total score for each firm, summed across the nine items. Two subscores were also constructed: "Research" (the sum of scores for the first five roles listed in Panel A) and "Employee" (the sum of the last four). Columns 2 and 3 reflect this aggregation. For example, if a firm rated any of the nine university roles as of major importance (score of seven or higher), the university was considered of major importance. A principal components-factor analysis of the data strongly supports the concept of two factors.[1] (The information contained in Table 6.2 is discussed in Note 1 at the end of this chapter.)

It becomes quite apparent in looking at these aggregate measures that colleges and universities are viewed as quite important to these advanced-technology firms. Over half (53.0 percent) of the respondents indicated that at least one university activity was of major importance to them. Over three-quarters (77.4 percent) reported that some activity was at least moderately important. The aggregate measure of employee-related university activities (based on only four items) was more frequently reported to be important than was the aggregate research measure (based on five items). Almost half (46.8 percent) of the respondents reported that one (or more) of the four employee-related university roles was of major importance in their business.

DIFFERENCES BETWEEN FIRMS

Table 6.1 suggests that while at least one aspect of university activity is important to most of the firms in the sample, firms differ substantially in identifying the specific university roles that affect their business activities. The concept of advanced technology includes a broad range of quite disparate activities. Even firms that produce the same product or service might be expected to differ in their need for university services depending upon their size, stage in the product-development cycle, differences in staffing, or idiosyncratic differences in organization. Economic-development strategies require information about how the need for university linkages is likely to differ with a firm's characteristics.

Table 6.3 shows the average importance rating assigned by different types of firms to the three aggregate university measures developed above (Research, Employee, and University). The table also provides statistical tests for differences in mean ratings by type of firm. Of course, when looking at bivariate relationships, observed differences may be due to other factors.

Firm Characteristics

Substantial anecdotal evidence suggests that small firms are underserved by the higher-education establishment (Useem 1981;

TABLE 6.2   Factor Analysis of Nine University Role Variables Pattern Matrix – Oblique Rotation (N = 447)

		Factor 1 (Research)	Factor 2 (Employees)
1.	Faculty Research Activities	.73	.11
2.	Faculty Consultants	.75	.06
3.	Joint Research Efforts	.76	−.04
4.	Access Libraries and Info Systems	.36	.39
5.	Access to Laboratories	.84	−.09
6.	College Graduates	−.13	.82
7.	Degree Programs for Employees	.14	.57
8.	Part-time Teaching Opportunities	.34	.29
9.	Cultural Activities	.06	.62

Source: Compiled by the authors from survey of advanced-technology firms.

Doeringer 1982). Smaller firms are less likely to have elaborate laboratories and expensive equipment. Yet, they appear to be significantly more productive in R&D activities when measured by innovations per dollar (National Science Foundation 1983).

Such firms are also assumed to be disadvantaged in competing for skilled employees. Although they are responsible for between half and two-thirds of all new jobs in the economy, they have extremely high turnover rates among personnel. These firms are generally too small to support an internal training function (Ressler 1983) and are, therefore, particularly dependent upon attracting skilled workers. These firms tend to provide lower salaries and fewer benefits than large firms (Friedman 1983), however, and they are able to offer less, even when worker "quality" is taken into account (Business Week 1984c). These firms are also more likely to engage in short-term projects and to lay off workers during slack periods because of insufficient reserves. This reputation for unstable employment further exacerbates recruiting problems (Vaughan, Pollard and Dyer 1985). Despite this reputation, small firms in this sample experienced fewer recruiting problems (See Chapter 5).

The firms in this sample were divided into four groups based on the number of employees in Pennsylvania. A clear pattern emerges – university importance increases with firm size (Table 6.3). Firms do not differ in the value they assign to the research dimension of universities, but the data suggest that larger firms value the employee dimension of the

TABLE 6.3 Mean Importance Ratings of University Aggregate Variables

	N	Research	Employees	University
SIZE – Employees in PA				
up to 5	141	10.0	9.9	19.8
6-24	159	12.6	12.0	24.6
25-49	55	12.2	13.5	25.6
50+	92	12.5(ns)	15.3***	27.8***
AGE – Years in PA				
1-4	101	12.9	12.4	25.3
5-9	108	10.3	11.9	22.2
10-14	111	11.6	12.3	24.0
15+	127	11.9(ns)	12.2(ns)	24.1(ns)
SECTOR				
Manufacturing	194	12.1	11.9	24.0
Service	248	11.3(ns)	12.4(ns)	23.8(ns)
ANTICIPATES GROWTH				
Yes	268	12.1	13.6	26.5
No	179	11.3***	10.2***	20.0***
WORK FORCE COMPOSITION				
Percent Work Force Unskilled				
0	221	11.1	12.0	23.1
1-20	127	12.2	13.1	25.3
21-50	65	13.2	11.3	24.5
50+	22	11.5(ns)	11.6(ns)	23.1(ns)
Percent Work Force Skilled				
0	114	11.2	12.5	23.7
1-20	103	15.2	14.5	29.7
21-50	160	11.8	12.3	24.1
50+	58	6.7***	7.2(.005)	13.9***
Percent Work Force Technical				
0	101	9.1	10.8	19.9
1-20	124	12.2	12.4	24.6
21-50	152	13.4	13.3	26.7
50+	58	10.9*	11.4(ns)	22.3*
Percent Work Force Professional				
0	61	7.8	5.5	13.2
1-20	129	11.6	12.3	23.9
21-50	145	13.3	13.5	26.8
50+	100	12.2**	14.3(.005)	26.4***

continued

Table 6.3, Continued

	N	Research	Employees	University
LOCAL LABOR FACTORS				
Availability of Labor				
NA or Minor	73	8.1	8.5	16.6
Moderate	147	11.8	12.9	24.7
Major	224	12.8***	13.8***	25.9***
Skilled Labor				
NA or Minor	97	8.6	8.6	17.2
Moderate	168	11.7	12.4	24.0
Major	179	13.4***	14.0***	27.5***
Wages				
NA or Minor	86	8.5	9.7	18.1
Moderate	203	12.6	12.6	25.2
Major	155	12.4***	13.1**	25.5***
Labor Production				
NA or Minor	80	9.6	9.9	19.4
Moderate	197	11.3	12.0	23.3
Major	167	13.2*	13.7***	26.9***
LOCAL LABOR MARKETS				
Difficulty Recruiting Unskilled				
Considerable	20	9.9	9.5	19.4
Moderate	16	12.3	12.5	24.8
Little	410	11.8(ns)	12.3(ns)	24.1(ns)
Difficulty Recruiting Skilled				
Considerable	44	10.8	9.7	20.4
Moderate	137	12.5	12.7	25.2
Little	265	11.4(ns)	12.4(ns)	23.8(ns)
Difficulty Recruiting Technical				
Considerable	91	13.8	12.3	26.0
Moderate	132	12.1	14.0	26.1
Little	223	10.6*	11.2*	21.8*
Difficulty Recruiting Professional				
Considerable	95	12.8	12.3	25.1
Moderate	104	12.9	15.1	28.0
Little	247	10.7(ns)	11.0***	21.7***
TRAINING POLICY				
Train Low Skill Outside				
No	288	10.4	11.8	22.9
Yes	147	10.3*	13.7*	27.0*
Train High Skill Outside				
No	100	9.2	7.5	15.3
Yes	335	10.4***	13.9***	27.0***

continued

Table 6.3, Continued

	N	Research	Employees	University
RESEARCH INTENSITY				
0% of sales	120	9.2	8.8	18.0
1-5% of sales	116	10.9	12.1	23.0
6-13% of sales	103	13.1	13.9	27.0
14%+ of sales	99	13.8***	14.5***	28.3***
ATTRACTIVENESS				
Sum of 4 Attractiveness Variables				
Less than 20	124	7.8	7.3	16.3
20-25	160	11.2	8.8	24.1
Greater than 25	103	15.1***	8.2***	29.5***
University in Top 5 Location				
No	329	9.6	8.2	16.0
Yes	118	11.4***	8.8***	17.8***
UNIVERSITY UNRESPONSIVE				
Agree or Neutral	245	10.1	8.2	26.6
Disagree	198	13.1***	8.5***	21.0***
UNIVERSITY PROXIMITY				
300 BAs in County				
No	217	10.5	8.4	22.5
Yes	230	12.8*	8.7(ns)	25.2(ns)
10 MAs in County				
No	264	10.3	8.3	21.8
Yes	183	13.7***	8.7*	27.0***
Any Ph.D.s in County				
No	316	10.4	8.3	22.1
Yes	131	14.7***	8.8*	28.3***

Notes: T-tests were used to test for difference between firms in two categories. ANOVA was used in all other cases.

Significance levels: *** = .001, ** = .01, * = .05

Source: Compiled by the authors from survey of advanced-technology firms.

university most. Overall ratings of university importance increase with firm size as well.

This pattern suggests that larger firms may be better connected to the higher-education community. Small firms may not have adequate personnel to staff "boundary spanning" roles that facilitate such connections. Also, since most cooperative agreements are initiated by universities, small firms may be ignored because of their size. Finally, because larger firms in this sample reported more recruiting problems, they have more incentive to seek university linkages.

In terms of economic-development policy, these data suggest that special attention should be given to facilitating linkages between small firms and universities. While small businesses create most of the new jobs in the economy, about 45 percent of all new firms fail within five years (Rassmussen et al. 1982). This analysis supports the recommendations of a National Science Foundation Report that noted: "planning of university-industry linkages that does not take into account the specific role of the small firms is probably ill-informed" (1983, p. 174). Linkages, however, need not be primarily oriented toward assisting small firms in recruiting.

The firms were next divided into four groups based upon the number of years they have operated in Pennsylvania. Older firms might be expected to be more self-sufficient and to need less support from outside organizations. Conversely, such firms tend to be better connected with the higher-education establishment and, therefore, find it easier to make contact. The data in Table 6.3 suggest no relationship between firm age and the importance of the university overall or in either of its two major dimensions. It may simply be that even if the costs of establishing linkages are lower for older firms, the benefits are also lower.

Firms in this sample were about equally split (44 and 56 percent, respectively) between the manufacturing and service sectors. It is not clear which sector would be likely to value university linkages more. Manufacturing firms, with recent emphasis on automated and flexible process technologies, might be expected to require substantial support from engineering and science departments. Recall that many of the service firms in this group were involved in software design and computer-based business services. Such firms might require more interaction with university computer-science personnel. Analysis of the aggregate importance ratings indicated no significant differences between advanced technology in manufacturing and services. Service firms attached slightly less importance to research and more to employees than did manufacturing firms, but differences were not statistically significant.

Survey respondents were asked to indicate whether they anticipated increasing employment during the 1983 and 1984 calendar years. As noted, at the time of the survey (December 1982) the economy was still severely depressed. Despite this, 60 percent of the firms planned increases. Firms that anticipated expanding valued the university more overall and in both its research and employee dimensions. The data suggest that local economic-development agencies interested in increasing advanced-technology employment are well advised to support linkages between firms and universities.

A prevalent issue in the advanced-technology literature is the bimodality of work-force composition (see Chapter 5). Some argue that jobs in the advanced-technology sector are skills-intensive; others describe this work force as low or semiskilled, primarily involved in routine production-line and assembly operations. Clearly, the services of the university are highly valued by firms with high-skill workers.

The relationship between the distribution of technical workers and the ranked importance of the university is curvilinear (concave from below). Interestingly, the relationship is statistically significant for the university overall and for the research dimension but not for the employee dimension. This suggests that as the concentration of technical employees increases, firms may be interested in university linkages more as a means of obtaining technical assistance and information than as a source of technical employees. Beyond the 50 percent point, interest in the university declines, perhaps suggesting that firms with a high proportion of technical employees are more self-sufficient.

The importance of the university is also strongly related to the distribution of professional employees. In general, as the proportion of professional employees increases, so does importance assigned to the university. This holds overall and for both the research and employee dimensions.

From a policy perspective, these patterns suggest that very different interventions may be appropriate to firms that differ in labor force composition. Advanced-technology firms with a large proportion of unskilled workers may be responsive to initiatives directed at facilitating training-related university linkages. Firms with few skilled employees and those composed predominantly of skilled employees are less likely to be responsive. As the proportion of high-skill employees (technical and professional) increases, interest in the university is likely to increase. However, highly technical firms are more likely to be interested in the research dimension (at least up until the point where technical employees dominate the work force). Highly professional firms are more likely to be interested in both dimensions of the university, with interest in the university's employee-related roles increasing strongly as the firm's work force becomes more professional.

Local Labor Issues

If the higher-education sector is perceived as improving the quality of the advanced-technology work force, executives most interested in traditional labor issues, like wages and productivity, should value the university most. Four survey items dealt with the attractiveness of local labor factors (availability, skills, wages, and productivity) in the firm's current location (discussed in Chapter 4 under "firm location"). Firms were categorized into three groups depending upon whether each issue was of minor (or no) concern, moderate concern, or major concern (Table 6.3).

For all four items, the importance of the university overall, and in both research and employee dimensions, increased as firms reported that labor factors made their current location attractive. The consistency and strength of these relationships suggest that local economic-development agencies should explore the ways in which the higher-education sector and traditional labor factors are related in the immediate area.

A related measure of local labor markets concerns the difficulty firms encounter in recruiting local employees. For each of four skill levels, firms were categorized as having either considerable difficulty, moderate difficulty, or no difficulty recruiting locally (Table 6.3). (Firms reporting that the survey item was not applicable to their situation were included in the little difficulty category.)

Most firms (92 percent) reported no difficulty in recruiting unskilled employees. This measure was unrelated to university importance. About 40 percent of the firms reported at least moderate difficulty in recruiting skilled workers. No statistically significant relationships exist between recruiting difficulty and university importance for either type of employee.

For high-skilled workers (technical and professional), a complex and statistically significant pattern emerged. Firms reporting moderate difficulty in recruiting technical and professional employees assigned greater importance to the university (overall and to the employee dimension) than either firms having little difficulty or firms having considerable difficulty. On the research dimension, the highest university ratings were assigned by firms with difficulty recruiting technical personnel. For professional personnel, little difference existed in the research dimension between firms experiencing considerable difficulty and those with moderate difficulty. In all cases, firms reporting little or no difficulty in recruiting high-skill employees assigned the lowest importance ratings to the university.

The university is apparently not an important source of low-skill workers (unskilled and semiskilled). For high-skill workers, the univer-sity is most useful in helping to provide employees for firms experiencing moderate levels of recruiting difficulty. The implications for economic-development policy are that firms with high-skill employees and firms experiencing moderate, that is, less than major difficulty in recruiting, may value the university most. The university is viewed as helpful in addressing a labor shortage problem only until it becomes severe.

Training Policy

Training is a traditional role of higher education; firms that use outside training facilities should value the university more, at least in their employee-related roles. Firms were divided into two categories: those using outside training sources, and those either training exclusively in-house or not at all. Analyses were conducted separately for low-skill and high-skill workers.

Firms that trained outside valued the university more in both the research and the employee dimension for both types of workers. High-skill workers were much more likely than low-skill workers to receive outside training: over three-quarters of the firms provided outside training for high-skill workers compared to about one-third for low-skill workers. Differences in university importance were also more pronounced when firms were divided by high-skill training policy.

The analysis indicates that formal training activities conducted outside the firm are strongly related to the importance advanced-technology firms assign to the university. The strong relationship between research and outside training suggests that training activities may be an important source of technical information and a mechanism for building linkages with the local university community. Thus, economic-development programs would therefore be well advised to stress training-related activities in building linkages.

Research Intensity

A characteristic commonly associated with advanced-technology firms is that a large share of gross receipts is invested in research and development. Presumably more research-intensive firms would profit most from relations with major universities.

Firms in the sample were divided into four groups depending upon the share of gross sales devoted to R&D. A strong relationship between research intensity and university importance is apparent on all three aggregate measures (Table 6.3). As firms become more research intensive, the university increases in importance both in the research and in the employee dimensions. This finding confirms the implicit hypothesis that local development agencies should concentrate on building university linkages with research-intensive firms.

Some Geographic Considerations

Universities are important contributors to local ambience by providing recreational and cultural activities. Also, local public schools are typically better in university communities. Four survey items were related to the attractiveness of firms' current location (proximity to a major university, good schools, recreational activities, cultural activities). Responses to these four items were used to construct two measures of the attractiveness of education-related factors (Table 6.3). The first is simply the sum of respondents' scores of the four items. A second variable is based on whether executives indicated that each of the four items was among the top five (of a set of 31) in their initial location decision. This second variable is coded as one if a university factor is among the five most important location items, and otherwise as zero.

Measured in both ways, location factors were strongly related to university importance. As firms' executives assigned higher total ratings to these four university items, their perception of the university's importance increased. The pattern was more pronounced for the research than the employee dimension, for no obvious reason.

Using data from the Higher Education General Information System, collected annually by the National Center for Educational Statistics, a set of three dichotomous variables was constructed to measure each firm's proximity to universities. The number of degrees granted in 1982 in five advanced-technology-related academic disciplines (business administration, computer science, engineering, physics, and mathematics) was used as a rough measure of the size of the educational establishment in the county where each firm was located. Slightly over half the firms were located in counties that granted over 300 baccalaureates; 40 percent were in counties where over ten master's degrees were granted; fewer than one-third were in counties granting any doctorates in these five academic areas.

Without exception, proximity to a university was positively related to university importance. Firms that were located in areas with advanced-technology academic programs reported that the university was more important in both research- and employee-related activities.

University Responsiveness

A common complaint about university faculty is that they live in ivy-covered towers and are unresponsive to the needs of industry. Respondents were asked to indicate the extent to which they agreed with the following statement: "Colleges and universities in Pennsylvania could be much more responsive in developing working relationships with advanced technology firms." Over half (55 percent) of the firms in the sample agreed with the statement.

Those who disagreed with the statement assigned substantially higher importance ratings to the university overall and to both its research and employee dimensions. From an economic-development perspective, this pattern suggests that university rigidity is a serious obstacle to building linkages. At the time of this survey a major initiative directed at establishing linkages was being initiated in Pennsylvania (See Chapter 9). These strongly negative perceptions of university responsiveness may have decreased as a function of the program.

Multiple Regression Analysis

The bivariate patterns discussed above strongly indicate that the importance of university activities differs systematically with firm characteristics such as labor mix, training policy, and so forth. Of course, firm characteristics are not independent of one another. For example, younger firms tend to be smaller; firms with proportionally more low-skill workers must, by definition, have fewer high-skill workers. To discover the relationship between university importance and firm characteristics, stepwise multiple regression was performed on each of the three aggregate importance measures (Table 6.4).

Sixteen variables, measuring 11 dimensions of firm characteristics, were used as potential independent variables in each model. A number of categorical variables used in Table 6.3 entered the regression model as continuous variables. For example, firm size, which was shown as four categories in Table 6.3, was entered as number of employees in the regression model (Table 6.4). Dichotomous variables were not changed.

Stepwise regression is a technique that attempts to statistically select the set of independent variables best suited to explaining variance in an independent variable. As used here, the statistical program added variables to the model, one at a time, using an inclusion criterion of statistical significance at the .10 level. That is, if chances were greater than one in ten that the next variable to be selected would enter the model purely as a chance event, no more variables were added. In the technique used for Table 6.4, any variable entering the model was retained in subsequent steps.

In the three models (Table 6.4), eight of the possible 16 independent variables were selected for the research model – nine for the employee model and 11 for the model of overall university importance. Twenty percent of the variance in ratings of research importance and 30 percent of the variance in employee and university variance were explained.

Findings in the multivariate analysis were generally consistent with the observed bivariate relationships, with a few important exceptions. Firm size, which was significantly related to importance in Table 6.3, was not included in any of the three models. Firm age, on the other hand, was positively related to all three aggregate measures, controlling for other variables.

As with the bivariate analysis, a firm's sector was unrelated to university importance. Growth was still positively related to university importance overall and to the employee dimension, but not to the research dimension. A labor skill index was constructed as the percentage of employees in technical or professional jobs. Skill level was strongly related to the employee and overall importance variables. Controlling for other variables, measures of labor scarcity, training policy (for high-skill workers), research intensity, and measures of educational/cultural ambience were positively related to the three measures of university importance.

Two significant differences between the bivariate and multivariate analyses concern university proximity and responsiveness. Controlling for other factors, the only measure of university proximity statistically important was the presence of a doctoral program. This measure was unrelated to the employee dimension.

Interestingly, controlling for other factors, firms that rated the university unresponsive reported it of greater importance on all three scales. That is, when looking only at the two variables – perceived responsiveness and university importance – firms that perceived the university as responsive also thought it was important. Statistically controlling for the effect of other firm characteristics on importance,

TABLE 6.4 Firm Characteristics and University Importance – Stepwise Multiple Regression (N = 412)

	Descriptive Statistics		Stepwise Multiple Regression		
	Mean (1)	Standard Deviation (2)	Research Dimension (3)	Employee Dimension (4)	University Total (5)
Independent Variables					
1. Size – number of employees in PA	86.1	28.5	—	—	.12***
2. Age – years in PA	15.4	18.7	.05*	.06***	—
3. Sector – designated as primarily non manufacturing by Dun & Bradstreet (D)	.53	.52	—	—	—
4. Growth – projected growth in employment next 2 years	.61	.49	—	1.57**	2.60*
5. High Skill Labor Index – percent of total employees in technical or professional	61.3	30.0	—	0.5***	0.9***
6. Labor Scarcity					
– perceived importance of availability	6.0	2.5	.48**	—	.99***
– difficulty in attracting high skill workers	4.1	2.5	.34*	.58***	.85***
7. Training Policy					
– train low skill entrants outside firm (D)	.34	.47	—	—	3.02*
– train high skill entrants outside firm (D)	.77	.42	3.56***	3.99***	6.81***
8. Research Intensity – percent of gross sales allocated to R&D	10.0	15.4	.11***	.07***	.16***

9. Educational/Cultural Ambiance

– attractiveness of university related items	22.7	8.0	.17***	.14***	.28***
– education/cultural factor on top five location factors (D)	.27	.44	4.37***	1.90**	6.30***
10. Responsiveness – university rated unresponsive (D)	.56	.50	2.91***	2.04***	5.14***
11. Proximity to University					
– over 300 local B.A.(D)	.51	.50	—	—	—
– over 10 M.A. (D)	.40	.49	—	—	—
– any Ph.D. (D)	.29	.45	3.00***	—	3.92**
Adjusted R^2			.20	.30	.30

Note: Significance levels: *** = p ≤ .01, ** = p ≤ .05, * = p ≤ .10.

Criterion for inclusion in stepwise regression is significance at the .10 level.

Source: Compiled by the authors from survey of advanced-technology firms.

however, reverses the relationship. Firms that saw the university as unresponsive are the very firms that also saw its activities as most important.

POLICY IMPLICATIONS

Empirical evidence indicates that university activities are important to advanced-technology firms. The specific activity that firms perceive to be important differs significantly with firm characteristics, but over half the firms report that at least one university role is of major importance in their business activities. Over three-quarters indicate that one or more roles are at least moderately important. These findings suggest that economic-development programs are correct in focusing on university-advanced-technology linkages, although the linkages are multifaceted.

The data are consistent with a descriptive model in which university activities fall into two major dimensions – research and those that produce or attract employees. The analyses suggest that economic-development strategies should differentiate clearly between these roles in designing programs. The university represents very different things to different types of firms. Linkage activities should be targeted.

Conventional wisdom suggests that small, young firms may be in greater need of university interactions and that development initiatives have frequently ignored the needs of smaller firms. The data reported here suggest that small firms do not differ from larger firms concerning the value of university research activities, but small firms seem to value the university less as a source of employees.

These data provide little evidence to indicate that manufacturing firms differ from service-sector firms in their overall responsiveness to university linkages in either the research or employee dimensions. Of course, specific services will differ by sector. Firms with high-skill workers and those anticipating growth assign greater importance to the university, especially in the employee dimension. Clearly, economic-development initiatives should be targeted at linking these firms with local universities.

Firms that are concerned with traditional local labor issues such as availability, productivity, and wages, and those that report difficulty recruiting high-skill workers report that the university is more important and are likely more responsive to linkage initiatives. Firms that use outside training facilities, particularly for high-skill employees, also see the university as important.

Research intensity is strongly related to university importance in both the research and employee dimensions. These firms are obvious potential partners in collaborative agreements. Firms that rate cultural and recreational ambience highly are also most likely to value the university. Apparently, close geographic proximity to universities is not an essential factor in the importance assigned to university activities. This suggests that university-related economic-development initiatives operate in multicounty settings.

Firms are generally dissatisfied with the responsiveness of universities to their needs. Moreover, multiple regression analysis suggests that, controlling for other factors, the firms that value the university most, find it least responsive. This suggests that university rigidities may be major obstacles to implementing collaborative linkage arrangements. Those pursuing economic-development strategies would be well advised to obtain specific commitments from local universities prior to implementing linkage programs.

The overall pattern of findings suggests that the academic community is potentially very important to the growth of advanced-technology enterprises, but major obstacles exist to productive collaboration. These obstacles are imbedded primarily in the cultures of the two groups. Although physical proximity of universities and firms is not strongly related to importance, what the firm does, who does it, and other characteristics are related to university importance.

These findings are significant since virtually every university and college in the country is examining a more active role for itself in technological and entrepreneurial development. To overcome obstacles that have traditionally created a poor fit between universities and industry, support throughout the two groups must be strong and extensive. As discussed briefly in Chapter 1 and more extensively in Chapter 9, interorganizational networks are only as strong as the match between individual and organizational objectives, incentives, and activities that occur within the diverse interorganizational contexts of participants. As universities move to formalize their industry ties by pursuing technology-transfer mechanisms, cooperative research ventures, targeted educational programs, small business incubators, and other arrangements, they must focus on overcoming institutional rigidities that inhibit responsive collaboration (Doyle and Brisson 1985).

NOTES

1. As a test of whether the nine university items were actually related as suggested in Figure6.1, a factor analysis was conducted. Table 6.2 shows the pattern matrix of an oblique (nonorthogonal) factor analysis of the nine questionnaire items. Two principal factors emerge from the data (the zero-order correlation between factors was .59). The first, labeled "research," is strongly associated with the five university roles as hypothesized. A strong positive relationship exists between this factor and importance assigned to part-time teaching opportunities. This suggests that opportunities for an adjunct appointment may be viewed as leading to university-based research opportunities.

The second factor, labeled "employees," is strongly associated with the remaining five university roles as suggested in Figure 6.1. In addition, access to libraries and information systems is also positively related to this factor, suggesting that the availability of university research facilities makes an area more attractive to prospective employees.

The factor analysis provides strong confirmation for the patterns suggested by the literature. Advanced-technology firms do appear to be interested in two principal dimensions of university activity as suggested in Figure 6.1.

7   Financing Start-Up Ventures

INTRODUCTION

Small, advanced-technology firms can grow only if they receive capital infusions at regular intervals. Although it is important to remember that capital " . . . cannot make up for a lack of markets or management, labor or raw materials" (Litvak and Daniels 1979, p. 17), a recent report on small business identifies capital availability as the most important issue affecting small companies (Heller International Corporation 1984). The problem of start-ups' access to capital is not new; it simply has not abated.

This chapter examines the critical issue of capital formation for new, small, growing firms. Because venture financing is a complex topic, only a broad overview is presented in this chapter. The discussion focuses on some of the major problems, approaches, and innovations in development finance. Financial intermediaries, organizations that mediate between investors and the investment positions that investors seek to achieve, will be explored in depth.

The justification for public-policy intervention to promote small business was partially established earlier in the discussion of employment potential (Chapter 3). Additional justification for intervention is the failure of private markets to provide adequate access to capital. Many new ventures that have the potential for success and job creation never fully develop because of undercapitalization. The profitability of small business, though mainly a motivation for investors, is important for any community seeking to generate wealth. Evidence suggests that small, rapidly growing firms are more profitable for investors over the long run than larger, more established companies (Hansen 1981; Litvak and Daniels 1979). Small businesses also have been characterized as very active in the invention and innovation process (U.S. General Accounting Office 1981). Given the superiority of small firms in generating jobs, profits, and innovations, why are these firms often unable to obtain capital to begin operations and sustain growth?

The Burden of Financial Responsibility

One aspect of the capital problem is the degree to which financial responsibility is the burden of the firms' principals. Executives of advanced-technology firms were asked what percentage of their company is owned by current managers. Of the 441 valid respondents, 308 (69.9 percent) said 76 percent or more of the company is owned by current managers. These data indicate that current managers own a significant percentage of smaller, younger firms. Service-oriented firms, firms with a high proportion of professional employees, and firms with primarily state-based sales markets also have greater percentages of ownership by current managers.

These findings are similar to those of other studies, which point out the heavy investment burden assumed by entrepreneurs, their families, business associates, and other nonprofessional investors. Shapero (1983, p. 4) succinctly summarizes the financial situation of innovating companies: ". . . it is clear that the vast majority of capital for startups is personal and local. Between 85% and 98% of the funds for pre-venture capital come from personal savings and from loans and investments from local sources. By far the predominant share comes from personal savings of the entrepreneurs, between 50% and 75%. After personal savings the primary sources of pre-venture capital are bank loans, an estimated 10% to 20%, and investments by local investors, about 5% to 10%."

Undercapitalization of New Enterprises

Experts disagree about the availability of risk capital for enterprise formation (Osborne 1980; Vaughan 1980). Some claim that capital is generally available for good investment prospects, while others suggest that many such prospects are not properly capitalized, thus severely inhibiting growth. Few argue that the cost of capital for new enterprises is as serious a constraint as the problem of unavailable capital. Market failure, resulting in an inefficient allocation of capital, can be addressed through public-policy intervention. Recent policy changes at federal and state levels have undeniably increased risk capital availability, but many fundamental reasons for undercapitalization remain.

One of the foremost reasons for new enterprise underfinancing involves the lack of information about a firm's potential. Small, advanced-technology start-ups are typically targeted toward a narrow market niche, created either because large firms do not operate in that area or because a new market area is being pursued (Cooper, Willard, and Woo 1984). Information gathered by investors about new products, markets, and prospects for growth is initially costly, though it may be priced at virtually zero for additional investors. High initial costs will keep all except the most interested investors away, and will generally inhibit investment information. Consequently, a large number of investors may not be well informed about a new firm's growth potential.

The information problem also cuts in the opposite direction; for example, entrepreneurs looking for investors. Searching for potential investors is costly for entrepreneurs, many of whom are unfamiliar with financing arrangements. As different investors are contacted, different transaction arrangements are pursued. Entrepreneurs interested in exploring these various transactions have to work with a host of professionals, such as attorneys, accountants, and existing investors. Often the complexity of the situations and the regulations imposed by public bodies make transaction costs prohibitive, resulting in incomplete deals and unfunded enterprises.

A second reason for undercapitalization of new ventures, in this case equity capital, concerns the establishment of a large pool of investors to spread risk. Each investment in a portfolio has unique risk features associated with any firm, industry, or region. When these risks are distributed in a nonsystematic fashion and pooled so that the variability of the overall return is below the average variability of each investment, the risks tend to offset one another (Litvak and Daniels 1979, pp. 19-20). Many investors must have a financial position in the firm, or if a large share is taken by one investment group, that group must have a large number of investment members. Unless the nonrandom risks associated with each individual's portfolio cancel out, the portfolio will be characterized by systematic investment risk. For example, a portfolio heavily invested in the microcomputer industry is under considerable systematic risk as a shakeout occurs among small-scale producers in that industry. In a noncanceling situation, higher potential economic reward will be necessary to offset risk or the enterprise will not be fully capitalized.

A third reason for undercapitalization of small, growing firms relates to the basic nature of new enterprises: they have little retained earnings to reinvest in growth. This is particularly true of product-oriented firms as opposed to professional, service-oriented firms where an income stream may flow as soon as business operations commence. Advanced-technology firms are typically unable to begin providing services or selling products at the beginning of operations. Early-stage operation of advanced technology firms involves mainly product and market development, and sales. Hence, retained earnings may not begin for quite some time.

Macroeconomic conditions also have an affect on start-up capitalization (Hansen 1981). For example, during the mid-1980s, real interest rates (the difference between the discount rate and inflation) have been, and are expected to remain, high relative to rates experienced over the last 30 years. Investors are able to attain reasonably high economic reward for some relatively low-risk investments. Consequently, the initial public offering market has remained relatively dormant. The turbulent economic conditions of the past decade have made fixed rate, long-term debt difficult to secure. In such situations, long-term expansion strategies give way to short-term incremental growth strategies.

Institutional bias against lending to small firms is another constraint on start-up financing. This bias takes two forms. First, many major institutional investors do not consider companies below a "level of $200 million in sales . . . despite the fact that small firms are more profitable than large multinationals" (Osborne 1980, p. 137). Second, lending bias takes the form of discrimination against minorities, and against geographic areas considered bad investment risks. Problems concerning contacts with financial institutions and inadequate managerial skill have traditionally plagued black-owned enterprises (Bates and Bradford 1979). Lending institutions have had little experience dealing with minorities, and they often have prejudicial attitudes when screening for credit. Recent expansion of government regulatory authority over lending decisions, such as the Home Mortgage Disclosure Act and the Community Reinvestment Act, may significantly broaden the public responsibilities of pirvate lending institutions (Fisher 1983). By increasing information on individual credit worthiness rather than relying on generalizations of ethnic, class, or gender characteristics, fair lending procedures emerge and access to capital is enhanced.

Many regulations designed to protect investors and curb abuse have had a negative impact on risk capital availability (Hansen 1981; Marcus 1982; Stoll 1983; Zock 1983). These regulations cover reporting and provision of information, transaction costs, portfolio risk, and financial intermediary activities. Some of these restraints have been relaxed in the recent environment of regulatory reform. For example, financial intermediaries offer new services and have greater flexibility in arranging deals (U.S. General Accounting Office 1983). After considering these reasons for undercapitalization, it becomes apparent that financial regulatory arrangements have an important impact on access to capital and are highly susceptible to public policy intervention.

Because the tax structure traditionally has contributed to the unavailability of equity capital by discouraging risk taking (McCaleb 1983), tax policy changes have the potential to free capital for development financing. For example, changes in the capital gains tax made in 1978 and 1981 appreciably increased the availability of venture capital (U.S. General Accounting Office 1982). Similarly, relaxing pension trust fund investment rules in 1979 also expanded the venture capital industry (U.S. General Accounting Office 1982).

Poor capital availability seriously affects the ability of start-ups and existing small firms to grow and prosper. Firms have different financing needs at different periods in their growth. These different needs are best handled by different financing arrangements. The remainder of this chapter discusses the capital needs of firms at different stages of development and examines mechanisms that meet these needs.

GROWTH STAGES AND CAPITAL NEEDS

Investments in small, advanced-technology enterprises are risky. For example, the risk of loan default for a small firm is higher than for a large firm with a lower rate of return, even if both have the same debt-to-equity ratios (Rasmussen, Bendick, and Ledebur 1982, p. 25). Long development cycles (Richards 1983, p. 25) and increasingly shorter product life cycles (Choate 1982) only serve to increase the nature of risk for advanced-technology firms. These and other unique features of advanced-technology firms' growth suggest special problems for development finance.

Categorization schemes for company growth abound (U.S. Small Business Administration 1977; Cooper 1978; Churchill and Lewis 1983; Vozikis and Glueck 1980). Most of these growth schemes do not consider financial need as a critical variable that sets the boundaries between stages. The venture-capital industry, however, has devised a fairly standard approach to enterprise growth (National Association of Small Business Investment Corporations 1983). This approach does consider capital need and is therefore appropriate in this discussion.

The initial stage of an enterprise involves the conceptual formulation of the product. At this time a small amount of money, usually less than $50,000, is needed to allow a product inventor or creator to refine the idea into a tangible entity, such as a prototype. Financing at this stage, called "seed" or "adventure" financing, is highly speculative and is seldom undertaken by anyone other than a technically oriented individual with entrepreneurial aspirations.

Once a prototype is developed and the decision to proceed with production is made, the "start-up" financing stage begins. Although the product is not ready for commercial sale, the company is legally constituted and key management personnel are in place. These people develop a business plan and undertake market analyses. At this point professional investors from a seed-capital fund may provide operating funds. Typically though, capitalization at this stage is primarily the burden of the firm's principals, and their family and friends.

The third phase of a firm's growth marks a transition from product development to commercialization. This phase, called "first-stage financing," begins with commercial manufacturing and sales. To initiate commercial production, capital must be made available for personnel, inventory, plant, and equipment needs. Money earned from sales is reinvested, salaries are kept low, low-interest trade credit with suppliers is arranged, and leasing is undertaken to eliminate the purchase of fixed assets. Financing by the firm's management decreases during this time, while professional investors and financial intermediaries, such as local banks, assume a much larger role in providing capital.

The fourth phase of growth occurs when the firm undertakes its initial production expansion. For this "second-stage financing," working capital is needed for equipment and material purchases. Production processes may still be going through significant revision and restructuring, resulting in productivity-induced savings. Established accounts are generating income, but the firm is unlikely to be showing a net profit.

Major plant and market expansions signal the beginning of the fifth growth phase. An increasing sales volume and favorable future sales projections can be handled only with major expansions. Financing for this "third stage" begins to take on more of an institutional flavor. Commercial banks and insurance firms become interested as the firm turns the corner on profits and an annual break-even point is attained. Professional investment groups, such as venture capital funds, continue to support their earlier investments with financing at these later stages.

The venture capital growth scheme being described has one last phase: "mezzanine," "fourth-stage," or "bridge" financing. At this time, usually about six to eight years from inception, the firm is looking for the right "window" through which to proceed into public financial markets. Under pressure from its early equity partners who want to liquidate their previous investments, the firm must either go public, be acquired by another firm, or be recapitalized by the founder and early partners. Of course, if the firm is fortunate enough to make it to this growth stage, it no longer faces the financial constraints imposed on small businesses.

Some unique features of seed, start-up, and first-stage financing make equity financing more appropriate than debt financing. The nascent firm is not generating net income, but an inflow of funds is necessary for product development, marketing, and planning activities. To impose fast repayment of loans could be a crushing burden. In fact, debt financing is hard to obtain, given the lack of assets, credit history, and uncertainty of future profitability. Financial intermediaries do not have an incentive to provide debt financing unless their risk is substantially reduced through some guarantee mechanism. Equity financing is more suitable during these early stages. Cash flow is not jeopardized by exchanging capital for a share of future growth.

Enterprises face many problems during their early growth stages. The vast majority of enterprises vanish within five years of their inception (Richards 1983, pp. 15-17; Cooper 1982, p. 195). Many of those that do last five years do not obtain sustained growth and mature operations. Obviously one key to continued growth during these early years is a steady infusion of operating capital. The two types of capital, debt and equity, have unique features for development finance and merit further attention.

DEBT AND EQUITY FINANCING ARRANGEMENTS

Small firms have problems securing financing when most needed. The availability of capital from different sources is not only limited by investors' predispositions toward large established firms, but limitations specific to a particular firm also present financing problems. For example, a firm with a high debt-to-equity ratio has large portions of income going to loan payments, thus limiting equity capital expansion.

Debt Financing

Loan financing by intermediaries, such as local commercial banks, plays an important and unique role in enterprise formation. One element of this uniqueness is that commercial banks do not require and are commonly prohibited from obtaining equity shares in the business to loan money, although a very small percentage of bank credit is through equity participation agreements (Brophy 1984). Also, over 14,000 commercial banks exist; an entrepreneur does not have to go far to find one. Many different types of loans and financing are available from banks depending upon the needs and circumstances of the firm. Perhaps the greatest role banks play in development finance is in term loans. Term loans mature in more than one year and can be secured to meet company needs. The longer the term of the loan, the more advantageous it is for a firm with poor cash flow. Term loans to young ventures are often secured through personal guarantees required of and made by the firms' principals. As the firm grows, the secured debt against the principals can be retired and replaced with security of stocks, equipment, inventories, and other assets. Should the firm survive to this point, financial institutions, such as insurance companies, commercial finance companies, trust companies, pension funds, and others become active in debt capitalization. Liens against existing assets, however, are not easily established by new advanced-technology firms with long development periods and poor early-stage cash flow.

The poor financial relationship between advanced-technology firms and commercial lending institutions is evident in the survey of Pennsylvania's executive officers. Executives of advanced-technology firms were asked whether they believed that private financial institutions in Pennsylvania did not understand their company's "product, market, or risk position." Executives responded to a five-point Likert scale ranging from "strongly agree" to "strongly disagree." "Neutral" was a valid (middle) response. About half the respondents, 220 of 446 valid cases or 47.9 percent, agreed that financial institutions did not understand their company's product, market, or risk position. Only about one out of five (20.3 percent) of the executives disagreed with the statement. This negative perception concerning financial institutions was greater under the following conditions: smaller firm size, fewer years of operation, greater R&D commitment, greater capitalization by firm managers, and greater employment growth. Whether the firm has a manufacturing or service orientation has no bearing on executive perceptions of financial institutions. Although small, advanced-technology firms have difficulty getting financial institutions to understand their capital situation, government policies can ease the problems of obtaining debt capital.[1]

One important way that governments encourage lending to small business is through guaranteed loans. The U.S. Small Business Administration (SBA) or private financial intermediaries can make a loan, and the state or federal government can guarantee it against default risk. Guarantees typically apply to firms that do not have the credit to secure loans on their own merits, but that are reasonably good prospects. Although some problems exist with collateral for securing SBA loans (U.S. General Accounting Office 1983a), loan guarantees are becoming increasingly popular and may soon completely overshadow other forms of government small business loan programs. The SBA, under section 7(a) of the Small Business Act, guarantees loans will be repaid to the lender for the lesser amount up to 90 percent or $500,000.[2] SBA loan guarantees and immediate participation loans can help finance plant construction, conversion, and expansion; equipment and facilities; and working capital. Over 18,000 guaranteed loans were made in 1983, averaging $107,000 each (Farrell 1984, p. 56). Although questions of whether the guaranteed loans help firms secure otherwise unavailable capital or merely lower bank risks cannot be resolved easily (Bates 1983), the loans are generally perceived as highly beneficial to small firms. One additional aspect that promotes their usefulness is their longer maturity period, about six years, compared to less than three years for SBA nonguaranteed loans, and less than one year for non-SBA loans (U.S. General Accounting Office 1983a).

The SBA also administers the Small Business Investment Act Section 503 program that certifies state and local development companies, called certified development companies (CDCs) and local development companies (LDCs). Small businesses use the money to acquire and upgrade buildings and equipment. A second mortgage is taken out with a CDC approved debenture. The SBA guarantees the debenture, and it is then sold to the public through the Federal Financing Bank (Grossman 1984). CDC debentures typically cover 40 percent of the project, with 50 percent coming from a first mortgage with a private sector-lending institution and 10 percent covered by equity capital from the small business. Private lenders' interest in this program stems from their ability to take first position on 100 percent of the collateral while usually providing 50 percent of the project's financing.

In addition to the SBA, one other federal agency guarantees loans that are available to advanced-technology firms. The U.S. Department of Commerce, Economic Development Administration (EDA), through its Title II program, guarantees up to 80 percent of the principal and interest of loans made to provide borrowers with fixed asset and working capital loans to start up and existing companies in designated distress areas. It services larger financial needs with a $550,000 minimum loan. The EDA also supports the establishment of local revolving loan funds through Title IX providing economic-adjustment assistance to areas experiencing long-term economic deterioration. Grants are made by EDA to eligible counties that loan money to businesses from the revolving loan fund. Local lending discretion is high with the general purpose of creating and retaining jobs. The U.S. Department of Agriculture, Farm Home Administration has a business and industry guaranteed loan program limited to rural areas. These SBA, EDA, and FMHA loan programs represent $3.4 billion in development assistance for fiscal year 1984 with the largest program being the SBA 7(a) at $2.6 billion (SBA 1984).

Industrial Development Bonds (IDBs), indistinguishable from Industrial Revenue Bonds (IRBs), also play a key role in business debt finance. Local and/or state authorized organizations issue tax-exempt bonds to raise funds for companies (Price 1981). Bond purchasers, the largest group being commercial banks (American Bankers Association 1982), accept lower interest rates in exchange for tax exemptions. The reduced-interest savings permit a lower interest rate for the borrower. Small firms with poor or nonexistent credit ratings can obtain back-up letters of credit from banks. IRBs are not typically used for start-up ventures, however; they pertain primarily to larger firm relocation and expansion activities.

The economic efficiency of IRBs has gained recent attention (Congressional Budgeting Office 1981; Pascarella and Raymond 1982). In 1984 the Congress acted to offset the $50 billion tax revenue lost through IRBs by passing the 1984 Deficit Reduction Act. The subsidy to business was appreciable. One estimate is that the federal government loses $1 for every 75 cents a firm saves in financing through an IRB (Pierce 1984). The legislation limits states' issuing of IDBs to $150 per resident or $200 million, whichever is greater. Other restrictions and limitations were made but small-issue (manufacturing) IDB tax-exemption was extended to 1991. Although most states do not expect the restrictions to affect them immediately, many have looked at targeting bonds, interindustry and interjurisdictional allocation formulas, and alternative financing schemes.

Many of the programs sponsored by federal agencies present mix-and-match financing situations. For example, a firm may be capitalized by $200,000 SBA 7(a) and $50,000 from a local revolving loan fund. In general, small-firm debt financing is not easy, nor is it particularly desirable unless a long-term, low rate can be secured. Equity financing, however, does have some features that are attractive to small growing firms.

Equity Financing

Equity capital is permanent business capital that stockholders have invested in a firm. Unlike debt, equity is not repaid on a fixed schedule. Not having to make payments on loans is particularly important for a young company that is not in a net income producing stage. Equity capital finances primarily fixed assets such as building and equipment, but can also be used for working assets such as inventory and accounts receivable.

Ownership of a firm is determined by the amount of stock an individual or an organization possesses. Various types of stock represent alternative voting rights, asset dissolution, dividend guarantees, and rewards for initial participation. Stock offerings range from private placements to public sales underwritten by investment bankers. Most small firms are unable to afford the high costs of the Securities and Exchange Commission's registration, audit, and documentation requirements; consequently, they initially raise capital by relying on private placements to managers, key employees, and nonprofessional and professional investors. Nonprofessional investors are typically family, friends, and business associates. Professional investors, such as wealthy individuals and venture-capital groups, are often assisted by an investment banker working with the firm.

New Business Ventures and Venture Capital

The glamour of the high-risk/high-reward start-up financing environment is exemplified by the venture-capital industry. Venture-capital investors have become very active in advanced technology-enterprises and other potential high-growth industries. Investments are made in emerging companies that have difficulty raising money from conventional sources, such as commercial banks and the public market.

The fundamental financial transaction is exchanging company ownership privileges (stock) for funds (capital) necessary to develop and market products, and to expand operations. Some venture-capital investors provide seed capital to firms during the early stages of development when few other financial options are available. This financing may continue until the firm goes public or other investors are found. Venture-capital investors typically liquidate their accrued equity between the firm's sixth and eighth year. Per annum, pretax notes of return are currently down, after averaging about 30 percent in the late 1970s (Osborn 1980). The rapid growth of venture capital also appears to be slowing (Shaffer 1984).

Venture-capital investments are structured in a number of ways and often the financing arrangements are combined (National Association of Small Business Investment Corporations 1983). One way of structuring a deal is common stock. Common stock confers voting rights and, therefore, some control over management. Control over management is limited because venture-capital financiers seldom take a majority position, leaving sufficient economic risk and reward with founders and managers to assure high company performance.

Preferred stock is another equity instrument used by venture-capital investors. If the firm dissolves, this investment has priority over common stock in the distribution of assets and dividends. The liquidation and dividend preferences are exchanged for voting rights. Preferred stock is often converted to common stock over time.

Two types of debt financing are also used by venture-capital investors. In convertible debt financing, firms make a commitment to repay the loan and interest, and the investor is given the right to convert the debt note into common stock. In this manner the investor obtains principal and interest, and the potential to gain stock appreciation. The second common type of new-venture debt financing is long-term debentures. In this arrangement, senior creditors who have superior claim to the company's assets, in the event of default, are paid off before the venture capital lender. The most desired forms of venture-capital financing are preferred stock and convertible debt (Osborne 1980). These two instruments afford investors the greatest opportunity to cushion risk yet attain high reward should the firm do well.

The venture-capital industry is comprised of five different kinds of organizations that finance start-ups (Gill 1984). The first and most common organizational form is the private independent venture-capital partnership. Here, general partners, usually experienced managers and investors, manage the investment portfolio, while limited partners and individual investors, supply up to 80 percent of the capital. The second organizational structure is the business-development company. A business-development company is organized as a public corporation, but secures capital from private funds as well as from public-investment companies. By law (the Small Business Investment Act of 1980), a business-development company must retain at least 25 percent of a firm's equity in its portfolio and must become actively involved in that firm's management.

A third source of venture capital is large corporations, which become involved in risk financing by setting up nonpublic subsidiaries. Corporate bank and insurance subsidiaries generally make investments in many industries (to diversify portfolios). Subsidiaries formed from manufacturing corporations mainly seek investments that are related to the parent company and have the potential to increase its productivity and/or to expand its product offerings.

More than 500 Small Business Investment Companies (SBICs) and Minority Enterprise Small Business Investment Companies (MESBICs) constitute the fourth type of venture-capital investment organization. They exist as government-supported, for-profit companies that finance risky small ventures, at favorable rates, on a long-term basis. The government guarantees loans, allowing these companies to leverage their capital as high as four to one. SBICs typically make investments through the purchase of preferred stock. Many tax advantages are available to SBICs, but restrictions are also placed on investments. The tax advantages cushion losses, allowing SBICs to make risky investments and share in the high reward potential of risky firms. A growing movement is emerging to create a privately funded SBIC bank. Legislation has been offered to create a Corporation for Small Business Investment that would be capitalized by SBICs and subsequently would sell its guaranteed se-curities to private investors for later reinvestment (Kravitz 1984b, p. 64).

The fifth form of venture capital is relatively new and is almost exclusively oriented to advanced technology firms – the research and development limited partnership (Merrifield 1984; Meyer 1984). This arrangement allows a pooling of technology among companies. The pooling overcomes many cost constraints, yet equity is not lost or debt incurred. Typically one or a few separately held, sponsoring companies act directly, or through proxy, as the general partner. The general partner contracts with various research organizations in designated technology areas. If the product is successful, it may be manufactured by the general partner, licensed to others, or both. Upon product commercialization, limited partners receive royalties or they can be bought out. Investment tax incentives and depreciation allowances help offset the limited partner's risk. Some recent failures of these limited partnerships and subsequent litigation has dampened the interest of individual investors, but corporate investors' interest in these partnerships is likely to remain strong.

Venture-capital investment has some characteristics that make it worthy of public support. Innovative development concepts are supported by long-term "patient" money, not subject to the short-term whims of public money managers, which are thought deleterious to the economy (Business Week 1984b). Financing is not the only benefit to fledgling businesses, however; investors become involved in company management, often sitting on boards of directors and providing free, expert assistance. Gill (1980, p. 105) notes " . . . the venture capitalist's goal coincides with societal interests of economic development." That goal is to nurture a promising new company until it achieves a significantly mature stage to function as a successful entity in the public marketplace. Although some venture-capital and public interests coincide, very few of the business plans that venture-capitalist groups receive are seriously considered, and even fewer actually funded.

Nevertheless, the top 100 venture-capital firms invested $2.33 billion in 1983, nearly 54 percent more than the top 100 invested in 1982 (Kravitz 1984a, p. 60). For the top 100, the largest percentage of financing – 30 percent went for follow-on investments in existing portfolio companies. Seed and start-up investments comprised 29 percent of the deals, for a total of $571.38 million for 833 deals. The venture-capital industry is expansive and until very recently was growing rapidly, but many small firms still find it difficult to obtain early financial assistance, in part because of the cluster of venture-capital firms in New England and the West coast.

As part of the survey of advanced-technology firms, executives were asked whether the firm had ever tried to obtain venture-capital financing.

Because the question defined venture capital as "capital necessary to allow a business to start-up and/or grow through early stages of development," firms over seven years old were excluded. Of the 176 firms under eight years old that responded to this question, 82 (46.6 percent) said they had not undertaken a search for venture capital. And of the 94 firms that had searched for venture capital, 24 (25.5 percent) had no success while 70 (74.5 percent) secured at least one successful venture-capital deal. Overall, for the firms seven years old or under, 70 of 176 (39.8 percent) responded that they had at least one success in securing venture capital. The 40 percent success rate of these young firms seems favorable, but comparison data are not available.

The search for venture capital is not related to a firm's size, age, R&D commitment, industry type, percentage of capitalization by current managers, or employment growth. These same variables were also examined for their effects on the success of the search; only size has a statistically significant association. Larger firms had greater success securing venture-capital financing than did smaller firms.

Respondents were also asked to "rate the availability of venture capital for business startups. . . ." The rating scale went from zero to nine with anchors given as follows: "ø represents no knowledge of venture-capital financing; values 1 to 3 represent low accessibility; values 4 to 6 represent moderate accessibility, and values 7 to 9 represent high accessibility." Data from individuals who expressed no knowledge of venture-capital availability were deleted from the analysis. The average rating for the accessibility of venture capital was 3.8, in the low to moderate accessibility range. The variables mentioned earlier, representing company background characteristics, were cross tabulated with a three-level, ordinal configuration of venture-capital accessibility. Again, only the size of firm was associated (weakly) with the perception of availability. As firm size increases, the perception of venture-capital availability increases (Table 7.1).

In summary, no systematic self-selection of firms searching or not searching for venture capital financing appears to exist. Venture-capital groups are not systematically rejecting any particular kind of firm for financing except the smallest ones. In turn, these small firms perceive venture-capital financing as generally inaccessible.

These findings on venture capital, along with similar findings on financial intermediaries, suggest two conditions. First, communication and understanding between the financial community and small advanced-technology firms is lacking. Second, this lack of communication and

TABLE 7.1 Perceptions of Venture-Capital Availability by Size of Firm

Frequency Column %	1 to 4 Employees	5 to 10 Employees	11 to 50 Employees	51 or More Employees	Row Total
Low accessibility	26 61.9	19 51.4	19 45.2	3 50.0	67 52.8
Moderate accessibility	16 38.1	14 37.8	15 35.7	2 33.3	47 37.0
High accessibility	0 0.0	4 10.8	8 19.0	1 16.7	13 10.2
Column total	42 33.1	37 29.1	42 33.1	6 4.7	127 100.0

Tau C = .16.

Gamma = .26 statistically significant at .05 level.

Source: Compiled by the authors from survey of advanced-technology firms.

understanding has led to the undercapitalization of many small firms. Recently many state and local governments have established financing and information/referral programs to help overcome undercapitalization problems (Chapter 9).

DIRECT GRANTS AND LEASING ARRANGEMENTS

Two other common forms of financial assistance to small growing firms are direct grants and leasing arrangements. Grants, payments in the form of cash, services, or property, have an immediate positive impact on a firm's financial condition. The grant award increases equity and consequently the ability to raise debt capital. This direct benefit for the firm may also be viewed as having a secondary, indirect benefit for the public in the form of jobs. For the direct grant to have a social benefit, however, the firm must experience expansion and greater profitability. Because of the simultaneous private benefit of profitability, grant awards seldom take the form of direct cash payments anymore. Direct grants of business capitalization issued by federal agencies have been drastically cut or eliminated, with the exception of the Community Development

Block Grants, Urban Development Action Grants,[3] and Small Business Innovation Research Grants. Conversely, state direct-grant programs to support advanced-technology firms, often predicated on matching funds, are rapidly growing. Increasingly, grants are disguised as infrastructure improvements, tax abatements, tax-increment financing, land cost writedowns, and interest subsidies (Richards 1983).

Leasing arrangements are a popular way of financing new plant and equipment expenses. Andrews and Eiseman (1981) estimate that in the United States, about one-third of all new business equipment is leased. Leasing is particularly advantageous to a young, small firm unable to finance a loan or afford the outright purchase of equipment. Depreciation and investment tax credits may also be passed on to the firm to reduce its leasing costs.[4]

Though important because they assist small-business development, the financial arrangements reviewed in this chapter have two important limitations (Levy 1981). First, the economic efficiency of any scheme depends largely on who (individually, governments, etc.) pays and who benefits (Rasmussen, Bendick, and Ledebur 1982). Many financial programs simply result in subsidies between levels of government, in many ways equivalent to intergovernmental fiscal transfers. Second, many financial arrangements are seen merely as windfalls to business, having little effect on inducing activity that would have occurred anyway (Jacobs 1979). Nevertheless, even though the problems remain unresolved, state and local governments have forged ahead with new development finance approaches.

NEW DIRECTIONS FOR FINANCIAL ASSISTANCE

As state and local governments seek to promote advanced-technology development, they must deal sooner or later with the problem of access to capital by young, growing firms. New financial-assistance arrangements are unfolding at a rapid pace, as state and local officials push themselves up the development-finance learning curve (Ioannou 1985) and federal development assistance cuts loom large in the future.

One way to examine the government's role in development finance is through a three-part intervention typology (Litvak and Daniels 1979). Government may pursue any of the three approaches, or a combination of them. First, government may directly regulate or influence financial institutions. Second, government may assist firms through the influence of economic incentives directed at financial institutions. And third, a government unit may set up its own financial intermediary to deal directly with company financing needs. The general concept of the government/financial-industry partnership applies to each of these three approaches.

Legal authority for operating a financial institution derives from state or federal charters. Charters can be obtained and maintained only if the financial intermediary meets certain obligations concerning the use of funds. For example, states typically exercise control over asset holdings; that is, reserve amount requirements, and over liability; that is, the terms under which banks accept deposits (Litvak and Daniels 1979). The fluidity of capital and banks' desires to assure investors' liquidity, however, can counteract governmental attempts to promote risk-taking through asset and liability regulations.

In the current climate of the deregulation of financial intermediaries, the government's influence, or, more precisely, the withdrawal of its influence, can be clearly seen. For example, emphasis on increasing competition by opening new markets for financial intermediaries serves to increase financial access points for small business. The desire to promote capital efficiency and to finance small, growing firms is evident in recent state legislation concerning public pension funds (SBA 1984). The potential for economic-development investment of public pension funds is great. In 1981 public pension funds held $221 billion in assets (Employee Benefit Research Institute 1982, p. 69). Legislation recently passed in Michigan and Utah allows state pension funds to use up to 5 percent of their assets for investment in venture-capital partnerships. In the Michigan case, the majority of the money was invested in growing, advanced-technology firms. Pennsylvania recently enacted more conservative legislation intended to allocate 1 percent of the state and public school employees' retirement funds for venture-capital investments. Even at 1 percent, this amounts to about $100 million risk-capital pool. According to Posner (1984), 15 state venture-capital programs existed; one year later, Ioannou (1985) identified 20 new state venture-investment funds.

Venture-capital investing is new to retirement funds, and is not consistent with the conventional, low-risk investment strategies of their managers. Many obstacles must still be overcome (Litvak 1981), but traditional standards of investment prudence can be maintained while economic-development objectives are achieved.

A second public-policy approach to funding capital-starved growth companies is using incentives to influence financial intermediaries.

Incentive approaches yield less deterministic outcomes than regulatory approaches, but they are generally perceived as more viable politically and allow greater investor choice. Many financial incentives are available to financial intermediaries, but some are more effective than others. For example, interest-rate subsidies reduce capital costs for a firm while loan guarantees increase capital accessibility. Small, growing firms have less of a problem with capital costs than with access to capital; therefore, many state incentives are directed to loan guarantees, not to interest subsidies (Urban Institute 1983).

One area where incentives can be used to effectively increase the availability of capital is through tax changes that affect financial intermediaries. Tax credits have been applied to venture-capital investments in Louisiana, Indiana, Iowa, Montana, and North Dakota, and to research and development limited partnerships in Utah, to name a few. Disman (1983, p. 15) suggests a general approach in which a statewide development finance corporation could be capitalized by financial intermediaries in exchange for tax credits on profits earned by the investments.

Ohio has created incentives for small-business loans by using up to 10 percent of its $1 billion investment portfolio to make one- and two-year deposits with financial intermediaries willing to loan money to small businesses on equal terms. The purpose of the linked deposit program is to create new jobs and preserve existing jobs. The state trades a loss of up to $6 million on below-market interest for a potential gain of up to 5,000 jobs, and the tax revenue and social program savings that go with the increased employment.

State and local governments can also play an important direct role in overcoming the problems associated with the information and transaction costs of small business financing. The Venture Capital Network, a nonprofit corporation started by the Business and Industry Association of New Hampshire, brings informal risk-capital investors ($50,000 to $500,000 range) together with entrepreneurs. Wetzel's (1983) study of these informal investors called "business angels" suggests that these individuals represent a large pool of risk capital and that they are inclined to invest close to home. Many localities are creating networks to bring entrepreneurs and investors together. Some examples of these activities are monthly gatherings of venture capitalists where entrepreneurs and their products are introduced, venture-capital fairs where many entrepreneurs are introduced to prospective investors and computerized matching that encourages venture-capital companies to open a branch in other cities. When these network activities are combined with the third approach – direct government financial intermediation – investment risks can be pooled and more deals completed.

The third strategy, which amounts to a development-financier role for state and local governments, has expanded to the point that small, growing firms are gradually becoming able to secure equity capital. All states assist business through IDBs at little risk to themselves, and a few are now moving toward direct intermediation and consequentially to greater financial and political risk exposure.

The few state seed capital programs that exist serve the advanced-technology industry. One of the oldest, the Connecticut Product Development Corporation, a quasi-public agency, supplies up to 60 percent of the equity capital to small businesses to develop or expand products in exchange for a 5 percent royalty on the products sold (Grossman 1984, p. 11). Standard venture investment criteria, such as business-plan practicality, technical feasibility, and management expertise are examined in the assessment process. Assistance with business plans is provided to applicants, and referrals are made for those who do not qualify. One unique aspect of this program is that the payback to the state is made through product sales, not through a public offering or buyout, as is usually the case in venture-capital financing.

The publicly sponsored, nonprofit Massachusetts Technology Development Corporation supplies seed capital to start-ups in the form of subordinated debt. From its inception in 1979 to 1983, this fund has invested $3.4 million in 20 start-ups and leveraged over $22 million from private sources (National Governors Association 1983, p. 83).

Pennsylvania recently established seed-capital funds to work in concert with its four Ben Franklin Partnership Program Advanced Technology Centers (Chapter 9). The advanced-technology centers receive the money from the state (financed through general obligation bonds) to create a privately managed fund for investment in new ventures. Like the New York Corporation for Innovation Development, The Pennsylvania Seed Capital program seeks a 1:3 ratio of public funds to private money. By 1985, four regional seed-capital funds had been created by the Pennsylvania program.

The examples of regulation, incentive influences, and direct state role in financial intermediation cited in this chapter are characteristic of emerging government and financial industry partnerships in development finance. The key to success for these new approaches is in understanding the mutual interests of the partners. For example, private-sector financial intermediaries must be assured of adequate economic reward while public-sector financial organizations must achieve desired economic development outcomes. The challenges facing development finance partnerships, according to Richards (1982, p. 184) can only be met through significant mutual adjustments: "To ensure that local development finance programs are designed to operate as effectively and efficiently as possible, local economic development specialists and private sector lenders and investors must learn new skills and new ways of working together toward a common goal. Each must learn the other's expertise, capabilities, and limitations and also fully understand the problems facing business in their locale."

Neither sector can afford to act recklessly, nor can they afford to ignore the profitability and social benefits associated with small, growing advanced-technology firms.

NOTES

1. As of this writing President Reagan has proposed the elimination of most direct federal development-assistance programs. He proposed similar cuts during his first term but was unable to secure enough congressional support to significantly reduce these programs.

2. Changes in the 7(a) program will probably reduce the percentage of the guarantee.

3. UDAG is slated for elimination by President Reagan and CDBG received a 10 percent cut for fiscal year 1985-86. Since 1980 both programs have withstood elimination attempts.

4. Many changes in the tax codes that will affect depreciation schedules are proposed.

8 Entrepreneurial Development and Small-Business Incubators

INTRODUCTION

Entrepreneurship has received little attention in traditional economic-development literature (Kilby 1971; Kent 1982). Although definitions of entrepreneurship abound, the simplest and most useful definition for economic-development purposes is "the process of creating a new business." This chapter examines aspects of entrepreneurship including individual motivations and constraints involved in becoming entrepreneurs, and public-policy approaches to promote entrepreneurship. The small-business incubator facility is a new, rapidly growing approach used to nurture the development of new enterprise. Business incubator facilities support a wide range of enterprise activities, one of which is advanced-technology business development. Incubator facilities also exhibit a general characteristic consistent with emerging economic-development policy: many are devised as public/private partnerships. The role of incubators in economic development is examined using the results of a survey of 12 incubator facilities and their tenants.[1]

ENTREPRENEURSHIP, INNOVATION, AND ECONOMIC DEVELOPMENT

Entrepreneurship is distinguished from small business by temporal and stage-oriented features. Entrepreneurship refers to enterprise creation while small business refers to an established, ongoing company (Vesper

1983). A second, though somewhat less precise distinction between entrepreneurship and small business concerns innovation. Schumpeter (1934) identified innovation as the distinguishing element of entrepreneurship. Others have since refined his early work and introduced more conceptual rigor into the distinction that entrepreneurs are innovative, while small businesses may not be (Brockhaus 1980; Carland, Hoy, Boulton, and Carland 1984).

The topic of innovation is important as a justification, along with job creation and profitability (discussed in Chapters 3 and 7, respectively), for examining start-ups and small, growing firms in the context of technological development. Innovation is the process of transforming a product or technology from invention to commercial application (Drucker 1985; Mansfield 1977). According to Vesper (1983, p. 19) "all new ventures, almost by definition, contribute innovations to the economy." Start-ups exhibit characteristics conducive to product innovations, such as informal management processes, few ties to the past, and fewer concerns about how developments or modifications in a product will affect sales (Cooper 1979). Conversely, start-ups are less conducive to production process innovations and to managerial or behavioral innovations (Shapero 1982). Even in the product area, where start-ups excel, weak marketing capabilities inhibit innovation (Roberts 1969; Brunn 1980).

Despite some limitations, start-ups and small business play an important role in productivity and in innovation-induced growth. By building on creative initiative, direct competition, individual performance rewards, personal accountability, and long-term outcomes, productivity is enhanced (Vesper 1983). Start-ups and small firms contribute significantly to innovation, out of proportion to their R&D expenditures (Charpie et al. 1967). Undeniably productivity and innovation are important for economic vitality. For example, technological innovation is estimated to have been responsible for 45 percent of the nation's growth from 1929 to 1969 (Daniels and Barber 1981, p. 34), and productivity has been called the economy's only "free lunch."

ENTREPRENEURS AND START-UP DECISIONS

The decision to start a new firm depends upon a number of factors coming together at the right time. Some of the important influences are personal and background characteristics, previous employment experiences, and the entrepreneurial business climate (Cooper 1979). Personal and background characteristics of successful entrepreneurs include a need to achieve, the desire for financial gain, a belief in controlling one's destiny, a tendency to take risks, familial role models, and educational achievement (Brockhaus 1982; Liles 1974; Powell and Bummerele 1980; Quinn 1979). The linkages between individualistic and personal characteristics with successful enterprise are often tenuous (Gasse 1982).

Previous employment experiences have a bearing on personal "pushes," discontent with work situation for example, and on personal "pulls," knowledge about a particular market niche capable of being exploited (Vesper 1983). Prior employment experiences are particularly important for advanced-technology start-ups (Cooper 1971). Organizations where entrepreneurs have worked most recently are generically called "incubators" (Johnson and Cathcart 1979; Mescon and Adams 1980). When the organization specifically refers to a large firm (as opposed to say a university) the term "parent" or "mother" firm is frequently used. The incubator organization is important because it is where the entrepreneur gains business experience and knowledge about an industry. It also places the entrepreneur in the geographic area where he or she is likely to start the new firm (see Chapter 4). In this home community, the entrepreneur has developed a business reputation, accumulated savings or made personal investments, and established a network of colleagues and associates who may eventually become business partners or employees. A frequently cited example of this process is the Fairchild beget tree (OTA 1984, p. 38). From 1957 to 1970, the Fairchild Corporation was directly or indirectly responsible for starting 35 companies, including notable firms such as Intel and National Semiconductor.

A start-up company influenced by a larger or parent company is called a "spin-off." Two distinct forms of parent/spin-off relationships exist (Malecki 1981; Rees and Stafford 1983). First, a backward-linked spin-off results from sponsorship by the parent company. In these sponsored spin-offs, the parent company usually maintains trade relations with the start-up and frequently takes an equity position (Cooper and Riggs 1975). Larger companies often have difficulty internally initiating new endeavors (intrapreneurship), and backward-linked spin-offs help the parent company move into new markets.

A second major form of spin-off is independent of the parent company. In the independent spin-offs, employees leave the parent company and establish a product that is usually similar to the product they worked on while with the parent company. These start-ups may become direct competitors to the parent company by marketing virtually identical products, or the start-ups may market products that were never fully developed by the parent company. In the latter case, called forward-linked spin-offs, the product may not have been developed by the parent company because critical employees left at an early stage in the product's R&D. Such happenings have ired many parent-company executives and have resulted in considerable litigation.

Another major influence on start-ups, the entrepreneurial business climate, is rather broadly defined (Bruno and Tyebjee 1982). Entrepreneurial business climate generally refers to the constellation of regulatory, tax, and expenditure policies; the general economic atmosphere; access to business services and consulting assistance; and other factors that create an environment favorable for new business formation. Although entrepreneurs may have personal drive, specialized industry knowledge, and so forth, they typically lack a full array of business skills necessary to manage an enterprise, especially if they have no small-business background.

Entrepreneurs are competitive, strategic-thinking individuals with the commitment and enthusiasm for a successful business. But despite this, and even though they may be young with a proven track record, experience, and savings, a far greater number fail than succeed. This high failure rate highlights the need for, and the promise of, small-business incubator facilities.

SMALL-BUSINESS INCUBATOR FACILITIES

A new approach for nurturing small, growing businesses is the incubator facility.[2] Incubators are one of the fastest growing trends in economic development. National and state conferences are being held on the topic, state and local governments are devising or reorienting policy to promote incubators, large and small firms are getting into various facets of incubator development, and the national press has taken an interest in the topic. An incubator facility aids firms by providing rental space, services, and assistance. An incubator facility is different from an incubator organization or "mother firm," not because aid is provided – both do that – but because the facility is an independent organization that serves many firms (tenants) at one place (Cooper, Dunkelberg, and Furta

1985). An incubator firm, such as a large corporation, may possibly sponsor an incubator facility, but this is not a common arrangement.

A second trend occurring simultaneously with large firms' incubating and spinning-off small firms is based on multitenant buildings (Plosila and Allen 1985). The economic-development results of industrial parks in the 1960s and 1970s were not as successful as originally expected (GAO 1980). Park managers sought to fill vacant space by building multitenant buildings. The demand for space created by information- and service-based small firms was also met by multitenant professional office buildings, often located in rapidly growing suburban areas. At the same time, spurred by changes in tax laws, rural and urban areas gave increased attention to the rehabilitation of older buildings. A combination of these forces and the resultant multitenant management capacity gained through the years has helped ease the way for small-business incubator facilities.

No agreement has emerged, or is likely to emerge, concerning what constitutes an incubator facility. This lack of agreement and uniformity is due primarily to the differing needs and resources of communities and states where incubator facilities have evolved, and to the different purposes that incubators serve. For example, some of the earliest incubator facilities are located in industrial areas of the northern and central United States. Their major purpose was to diversify local economies, promote entrepreneurship, provide new jobs, and transform vacant buildings into usable space. Conversely, incubators in the South and West operate from recently constructed buildings and more often build upon a diversified entrepreneurial-oriented local economy.

It is difficult to generalize about incubator facilities because they are relatively new and few; about 65 were in operation nationwide at the end of 1984.[3] In less than one year, the number of incubators doubled. In Pennsylvania alone, more than 20 incubators were operating by the end of 1985.

Four different organizational support arrangements exist for incubators: public/nonprofit, educational institutions, private/corporate, and the hybrid public/private partnership.[4] Public/nonprofit facilities are typically sponsored by local governments, industrial or enterprise development corporations, and community-based development associations. The main objective of this type of incubator facility is job creation, with economic diversification, linkage with existing industry, and tax base expansion also important. Educational institutions (predominantly research universities, though some vocational-technical schools are involved) seek many of the same objectives, but also use incubators to promote their image, provide investment opportunity, and create a practical learning environment for students (Business Week 1984a). Private firms and corporations sponsoring incu-bators are interested in collecting fees for organizing facilities, developing real estate, transferring technology, new enterprise investment, as well as many of the previously mentioned interests (Demuth 1984). Public/private partnerships, by far the most frequent and varied arrangement, may seek any or all of the objectives mentioned.

Just as the interests of various sponsors vary, the types of tenants in incubator facilities vary. Generally, three kinds of tenant organizations exist. Product-development firms are attracted to incubators because of unique cost and location requirements. Firms in the early stages of product development, like the prototype, pilot, or feasibility stages, do not need expansive space, nor do they have a positive cash flow to pay high rental fees. These tenants often occupy university-sponsored incubator facilities. University faculty and students may be involved in these enterprises, and because of close proximity, access to university laboratories and other facilities is maximized.

A second kind of incubator tenant is the manufacturing firm. Facilities that house these firms have unique structural and site characteristics, such as high bays and railroad sidings. These buildings are often descendants of industrial parks or large manufacturing facilities. In many cases unoccupied "white elephant" buildings are renovated and subdivided to provide space for small manufacturers. Such incubators could be developed in all types of locations by any kind of sponsoring organization, limited only by costs of operations, availability of services, and a ready market of tenants (Plosila and Allen 1985).

A third kind of tenant is a service firm or organization. Service firms that cater to narrowly defined local markets typically employ few people. Firms of this nature, such as personal services (attorney, doctor, and so forth), and retail and wholesale operations, have short start-up periods and minimal business assistance needs; these firms could just as easily locate in conventional commercial space. Other service firms, especially ones with high growth potential such as data processing and computer software, are appropriate tenants and fit much better into a community's development strategy. Organizations and firms that provide services to incubator tenants, for example, word processing and photocopying, are appropriate permanent tenants for incubator facilities. An incubator that places no restrictions on tenants or has many kinds of tenants is called a mixed-use facility.

INCUBATOR-FACILITY PUBLIC POLICY

The earliest incubators were developed in the private sector.[5] Local and state governments are just beginning to understand incubators and realize their potential for promoting economic activity. Legislation for incubator programs has been enacted in eight states (Chapter 9). Of these states, Pennsylvania is clearly at the forefront in developing incubator policy (Table 8.1). In Pennsylvania, a number of state and federally sponsored programs operate at substate levels, often in conjunction with research universities. The leading program, the Ben Franklin Partnership (see Chapter 9), is integrated with the $17 million small-business incubator loan program and the $3 million seed-capital grant program passed by voters in 1984, part of a $190 million economic-development bond issue. The Pennsylvania Industrial Development Authority provides low-interest loans for facility acquisition, and the Pennsylvania Capital Loan Fund provides capital to small firms. Some federally sponsored programs, such as the Federal Job Training Partnership Act, Title IX Economic Adjustment Assistance and Urban Development Action grants (Small Business Administration 1985), and other state programs are also available for incubator facility acquisition, renovation, and operation.

Central to state and local incubator-development policy is local commitment, flexible funding approaches, and assurance of achievable public objectives. An incubator can be successful only if local government, business-services providers, private investors, financial institutions, and entrepreneurs support it. For example, if an incubator is to receive support from realtors, they must understand that tenants will eventually move out of the subsidized space and into local commercial space. Likewise, public officials must realize that large numbers of jobs will not be created until firms leave the facility and begin full scale manufacturing operations in the local community.

Incubator developers should seek a wide range of funding alternatives since community financial support bases, even within a state, are diverse. If segments of the local community are being asked to take risks in supporting the incubator, they must also be assured that public objectives can be achieved. Publicly supported incubators should only assist firms that truly need help, and they must be certain that the firms receiving help will contribute to the community by creating jobs. These demands for appropriateness and efficiency can be met by clearly specifying entry and exit rules for companies.

Entry and exit rules specify who may participate in an incubator and for how long. Tenants able to start operations without management or service assistance, such as doctors and lawyers, are not appropriate candidates for incubator tenants. Similarly tenants holding minimal promise for adding new jobs, such as retail and wholesale operations, do not promote efficient use of public resources. Tenants unable to leave the incubator after approximately three or four years are unlikely ever to do so, and their space should be made available to other more promising entrepreneurs.

As already noted, privately sponsored incubators do not have the same purposes that public incubators have. Less demand is made for tenant performance while greater demand is placed on them for full occupancy of the facility. But, private incubators that take an equity holding in tenants are likely to have some kind of entry and exit criteria, but probably related to return or investment, not job growth.

To summarize, all new businesses begin with entrepreneurship. The business incubator facility is one tool specifically designed to support entrepreneurial efforts. Incubators may be important for reaching so-called "latent entrepreneurs" – those who want to start their own business but are constrained by insufficient financial resources and management expertise. Every incubator is unique, but incubators as a group share many general characteristics.

AN OVERVIEW OF INCUBATOR FACILITIES

To understand various institutional arrangements, as well as the economic-development potential of incubators, 12 incubator facilities in Pennsylvania were studied (see Chapter 2). Seven of the 12 incubators contained advanced-technology firms, two housed manufacturing firms only, two were multiuse facilities, and one housed retail sales firms. Four of the 12 were privately sponsored and all but one of the remaining eight were public/private partnerships. Three were located on, or contiguous to, research universities, though only one was exclusively sponsored by a university. The following 12 incubators were studied:

TABLE 8.1 Pennsylvania's Incubator Support Programs

Incubator Development Components	Funding Source	Comments
1. Feasibility Studies	BFP, ARC, EDA	Focus on market for entrepreneurs, space, and service availability
2. Acquisition, Construction, and/or Renovation	PIDA, SBIL, ARC, CDBG, UDAG, SCBG	Emphasis on rehabilitation of older buildings and multiple funding sources
3. Equipment	SBIL	
4. Services	BFP, SBDC, ARC	
5. Operating Costs	No state programs	
6. Seed-Capital Financing	SCP, PCLF	With SCP, private fund matches of 3:1 are required to create new venture revolving loan funds
7. Employee Training	CJT, JTPA	

All components may be supported by local government, industry, and foundation sources.

ARC   Appalachian Regional Commission, Enterprise Development Program
BFP   Ben Franklin Partnership program
CJT   Customized Job Training (state administered program)
CDBG U.S. Department of Housing and Urban Development, Community Development Block Grant
EDA   U.S. Department of Commerce, Economic Development Administration
JTPA State plan for the Federal Job Training Partnership Act
PCLF Pennsylvania Capital Loan Fund
PIDA Pennsylvania Industrial Development Authority
SBIL Pennsylvania Small Business Incubator Loan program
SBDC Small Business Development Center (funded by Small Business Administration, state, local, and university sources)
SCBG State administration of U.S. Department of Housing and Development, Small Cities Block Grant
SCP   Pennsylvania Seed Capital Program
UDAG U.S. Department of Housing and Urban Development, Urban Development Action Grant

Source: Compiled by the authors with the assistance of the Pennsylvania Department of Commerce.

Private Incubators

- Control Data Business and Technology Center, Philadelphia
- Greater Easton Technology Enterprise Center, Easton, Northampton County
- Lansdale Business Center, Lansdale, Montgomery County
- Montgomeryville Technology Enterprise Center, Montgomeryville, Montgomery County

Public Incubators

- Liberty Street Market Place, Warren, Warren County
- Matternville Business and Technology Center, Matternville, Centre County
- Model Works Industrial Commons, Girard, Erie County
- North East Tier – Ben Franklin Advanced Technology Center, Bethlehem, Lehigh County (two incubator sites, one on the Lehigh University Campus, and one in Homer Research Laboratory, Bethlehem Steel Corporation)
- Ridgeway Industrial Complex, Ridgeway, Elk County
- Southwestern Pennsylvania Business Development Center, Wexford, Allegheny County
- The Pennsylvania State University, University Park, Centre County
- University City Science Center, Philadelphia

These 12 incubators housed 126 firms as of early 1984. Questionnaires were mailed to those firms' chief executive officers; 56 firms completed the survey (44 percent response rate). Information about the incubators was obtained through personal interviews with facility managers during site visits and follow-up telephone questions. Two types of data are presented here: characteristics of the 12 incubators, with the facility as the unit of analysis; and characteristics of the firm and its performance, with the firm as the unit of analysis.

Incubator Facilities

For this study, an incubator was defined as a facility that aids the growth of start-ups by providing low rent, common services, and business assistance. More than just common, shared physical/ maintenance services such as a lunch room or conference room had to be provided. Facilities that provided no management assistance were excluded from the study. These criteria served to exclude the following kinds of operations: human-service centers, "one stop shops" for permits and licenses, industrial parks or centers, professional office buildings, office or executive centers, and other multioccupancy facilities.

The size of the incubator facilities ranges from 2,000 to 25,000 square feet. Each incubator facility has space that varies in quality and usage. Although the larger incubators tend to have more tenants, the special needs of the firms vary widely and no correspondence exists between the size of the building and the average space allocated to each tenant. Flexible space in five of the 12 incubators had allowed firms to grow within the incubator, thus minimizing frequent moving.

Financing depends largely on whether or not the incubator is privately or publicly supported. Three incubators are entirely privately financed by sponsoring corporations, while a fourth received some money from city and state agencies for early development costs. This fourth facility also obtained $1.6 million through a state development authority for acquisition and rehabilitation of the building.

Each of the remaining eight incubators, sponsored by nonprofit organizations such as universities and regional economic-development authorities, had unique financing arrangements. Many of Pennsylvania's incubator assistance programs discussed earlier were not available when these facilities were initially developed. One incubator has two sites, one is on a university campus and the other in the research laboratory of a large steel company. Space for both sites had been donated to the sponsoring organization. Another does not own the building in which the incubator is located; rather, it leases a vacant building from the local school district at minimal cost. The school district contributes $40,000 rent-in-kind, and the local industrial development authority underwrites $14,000 for leasing costs. One incubator financed its purchase entirely with loans from local banks, then used federal and county monies to renovate and improve the building. A Ben Franklin Partnership Advanced Technology Center operated one incubator from a university building and has no rent or purchase costs.

Eleven of the 12 incubators have an executive board. The main duty of these boards is to establish facility policy. Other activities include reviewing admissions (five), advising the manager (four), overseeing finances (three), providing legal assistance (one), and fund raising (one).

Representatives from business are the most frequent board members. Other frequently represented groups are local development authorities and political jurisdictions.

Incubators have developed affiliations with organizations in their local communities. Both Industrial Development Authorities and Chambers of Commerce are involved in eight incubator networks. Small Business Development Center and Ben Franklin Partnership Center affiliations are also common.

Management responsibility rests with the owners of the incubator. In all but two of the incubators studied, sponsoring organization partnerships and corporations provide staff to manage the incubator. General managers working at the incubator, and secretarial/clerical support personnel are the most common staff. Only a few incubators have staff capability in the areas of legal, financial, and business consulting responsibilities. Also, very few of these types of business-assistance personnel have full-time duties at the incubator.

The critical duties of incubators include providing common, shared services and management assistance. Common, shared services, provided as needed, help keep a firm's personnel labor costs low. Management assistance is necessary because entrepreneurs do not always have the full array of skills and knowledge necessary for successful ventures. At the same time, on-site incubator staff are unlikely to provide a full range of management-assistance activities.

Each incubator manager was shown a list of 38 possible incubator services. These services can be classified into five groups: financial consulting assistance, management assistance, common business assistance, professional business assistance, and physical services.[6] The respondents indicated whether or not an individual service was provided and, if so, whether it was provided in-house, contracted out, or some combination of the two. The most frequent service provided is a copier; this was available in all but one incubator (Table 8.2). All but two incubators provide shipping and receiving, mail, and conference-room services. Business plan assistance and clerical support are provided in all but three incubators. The services that are available are most frequently provided by in-house staff. The exceptions are health and benefit packages, legal counseling and representation, and venture-capital assistance, all of which are more frequently provided through contractual arrangements or through the use of various organizations affiliated with each incubator, such as a small-business development center.

The least frequently provided services are off-hours answering services and inventory assistance; only two incubators help firms in these areas. Patent assistance and telex availability are provided in three incubators. Risk management, export assistance, audio-visual equipment, legal counsel and representation, and vehicle rental are provided in 4 of the 12 incubators.

Incubator Tenants

Overwhelmingly, the 56 firms in the sample are young – three years old on the average. Slightly over 10 percent are more than eight years old. Almost three-quarters moved into the incubator within the last two years, which is not surprising since almost all of the incubators are young. The firms are small, with a median of 4.5 employees. Gross sales also tend to be small, as is often the case with new, start-up firms. For the 36 firms reporting last-quarter sales, the median value given was $36,150.

The ages of entrepreneurs in the sample firms range from 23 to 63, with an average age of 39. Slightly over 70 percent of the entrepreneurs have a college degree. On average they completed 17 years of formal education.

Almost 70 percent of the entrepreneurs categorized their business start-ups as self-initiated but related to some other aspect of previous employment. Slightly over 16 percent characterized their start-ups as self-initiated but unrelated to previous employment. Four firms (7%) were characterized as sponsored spin-offs, and four others were subsidiaries.

Entrepreneurs rated the desire for self-employment as the greatest influence on their business formation. Previous employment experience was rated second. Whether that was considered a positive or negative experience cannot be determined. Rated third was the development of a new product. This reinforces research suggesting that entrepreneurs are major sources of innovation and that they are adept at finding unfulfilled market needs (Cooper 1979; Vesper 1983). Other lesser influences on the business formation were, in descending order: presence of a skilled work force, experience with other entrepreneurs, and access to higher-education institutions.

TABLE 8.2 Services and Assistance Provided by Incubator Facilities

	Not Provided	Provided In-House	Contract	Both
A. FINANCIAL CONSULTING ASSISTANCE				
1. Business Taxes	7	2	2	1
2. Risk Management & Insurance	8	2	1	1
3. Government Grants & Loans	5	5	1	1
4. Government Procurement Process	4	6	2	0
5. Government Contract Preparation	5	4	2	1
6. Equity & Debt Finance Arrangements	5	4	2	1
7. Export Development Assistance	8	3	1	0
B. MANAGEMENT ASSISTANCE				
8. Preparation of Business Plans	3	7	1	1
9. Employee Relations	7	5	0	0
10. Advertising & Marketing	6	4	2	0
11. Government Regulation	5	6	1	0
12. Health & Benefit Packages	7	2	3	0
13. Relocation Plans	5	6	1	0
14. Research & Development	7	2	2	1
C. COMMON BUSINESS SERVICES				
15. Audio-Visual Equipment	8	4	0	0
16. Shipping and Receiving	2	10	0	0
17. Mail Service	2	10	0	0
18. Copier	1	11	0	0
19. Clerical Service	3	9	0	0
20. Receptionist	4	8	0	0
21. Off-Hours Answering Service	10	2	0	0
22. Inventory	10	1	0	1
23. Word Processing	5	7	0	0
24. Telex	9	3	0	0
D. PROFESSIONAL BUSINESS SERVICES				
25. Legal Counseling	8	1	2	1
26. Legal Representation	8	1	2	1
27. Patent Assistance	9	1	3	0
28. Accounting	7	2	1	2
29. Computing & Information Services	6	4	0	2
30. Bookkeeping	7	3	0	2
31. Venture Capital Fund	7	2	3	0

continued

Table 8.2, Continued

	Not Provided	Provided In-House	Contract	Both
E. PHYSICAL SERVICES				
32. Conference Room	2	10	0	0
33. Cafeteria	7	5	0	0
34. Building Security	6	5	0	1
35. Vehicle Rental	8	3	1	0
36. Furniture & Equipment Rental	5	6	1	0
37. Library	7	4	1	0
38. Telephone Equipment	7	4	0	1

Source: Compiled by the authors from survey of incubator facilities.

Ratings of Usefulness of Services Provided

If one critical element of an incubator facility is business assistance, how useful are the various service arrangements? Incubator tenants were presented with a list of 38 services that many incubator facilities provide, and were asked to indicate whether or not each service was provided. If a service was provided, respondents were to rate its current usefulness in their business. If a service was not provided, they were to rate its potential usefulness. Most executives, though not all, completed the service ratings as instructed, but the data on potential usefulness are incomplete.

For the services provided, the ten most frequently rated as medium to high were (in descending order): risk management and insurance, building security, mail service, government grants and loans, receptionist, inventory, copier, advertising and marketing, health and benefit packages, and telephone equipment (Table 8.3). Of these services, four require considerable expertise to provide, that is, they are not general business or physical services. This list suggests that many of the services that can be readily provided by incubator management, like security, mail, clerical, receptionist, and copier services, are perceived as useful to entrepreneurs.

For services not currently provided, the 11 most frequently rated medium to high (three are tied at the ninth rank) were (in descending order): building security, clerical service, computing and information

TABLE 8.3 Tenant Ratings of Service Usefulness

Services	Service Provided			Service Not Provided		
	Low Use %	Med-High Use %	N	Low Use %	Med-High Use %	N
A. FINANCIAL CONSULTING ASSISTANCE						
1. Business Taxes	36.4	63.6	22	36.8	63.2	19
2. Risk Management & Insurance	0.0	100.0	8	53.3	46.7	30
3. Government Grants & Loans	10.5	89.5	19	36.4	63.6	22
4. Government Procurement Process	28.6	71.4	7	46.7	53.3	30
5. Government Contract Preparation	25.0	75.0	8	46.7	53.3	30
6. Equity & Debt Finance Arrangements	16.7	83.3	12	33.3	66.7	27
7. Export Development Assistance	66.7	33.3	3	67.6	32.4	34
B. MANAGEMENT ASSISTANCE						
8. Preparation of Business Plans	34.5	65.5	29	33.3	66.7	15
9. Employee Relations	37.5	62.5	16	63.0	37.0	27
10. Advertising & Marketing	12.5	87.5	16	39.1	60.9	23
11. Government Regulation	28.6	71.4	7	43.8	56.3	32
12. Health & Benefit Packages	13.3	86.7	15	56.5	43.5	23
13. Relocation Plans	42.9	57.1	7	64.3	35.7	28
14. Research & Development	40.0	60.0	15	63.0	37.0	27
C. COMMON BUSINESS SERVICES						
15. Audio-Visual Equipment	26.1	73.9	23	40.0	60.0	20
16. Shipping & Receiving	21.2	78.8	33	58.3	41.7	12
17. Mail Service	8.3	91.7	36	40.0	60.0	10

18. Copier	11.9	88.1	42	42.9	57.1	7
19. Clerical Service	18.9	81.1	37	22.2	77.8	9
20. Receptionist	11.1	88.9	36	50.0	50.0	12
21. Off-Hours Answering Service	25.0	75.0	8	46.4	53.6	28
22. Inventory	11.1	88.9	9	58.3	41.7	24
23. Word Processing	27.6	72.4	29	53.3	46.7	15
24. Telex	16.7	83.3	6	74.1	25.9	27
D. PROFESSIONAL BUSINESS SERVICES						
25. Legal Counseling	50.0	50.0	20	42.9	57.1	21
26. Legal Representation	50.0	50.0	8	40.7	59.3	27
27. Patent Assistance	41.7	58.3	12	69.2	30.8	26
28. Accounting	31.8	68.2	22	47.4	52.6	19
29. Computing & Information Services	21.7	78.3	23	31.6	68.4	19
30. Bookkeeping	27.8	72.2	18	55.0	45.0	20
31. Venture Capital Fund	61.6	38.4	13	57.5	42.5	40
E. PHYSICAL SERVICES						
32. Conference Room	16.3	83.7	43	50.0	50.0	6
33. Cafeteria	26.7	73.3	15	45.8	54.2	24
34. Building Security	2.8	97.2	36	20.0	80.0	10
35. Vehicle Rental	33.3	66.7	15	48.0	52.0	25
36. Furniture & Equipment Rental	35.0	65.0	20	47.4	52.6	19
37. Library	31.3	68.8	16	59.1	40.9	22
38. Telephone Equipment	14.3	85.7	35	40.0	60.0	10

Source: Compiled by the authors from survey of incubator tenants.

services, preparation of business plans, equity and debt finance arrangements, government grants and loans, business taxes, advertising and marketing, audio-visual equipment, mail service, and telephone equipment. Six of these 11 nonprovided services require considerable business expertise to provide. Apparently, many firms and incubator support staff lack this expertise.

One final observation: a service is generally rated less useful when not provided. Three execptions are legal counseling, legal representation, and business plans. One could interpret this to mean that, in general, incubators are providing services generally perceived as useful to start-ups.

Incubator Outcomes

Public-policy interest in business incubators stems primarily from the expectation that firms in incubators will be significant job generators. Of the firms in operation during 1983 (the year prior to the survey), the average job growth for that year was three employees (recall that the median size was 4.5 employees). About 30 percent of the firms did not grow during this period, slightly over 40 percent expanded employment by 3 to 21 jobs, the remaining 30 percent grew slightly. On average, four employees were expected to be added during 1984. Seventeen percent of the firms did not expect to add employees. Over the two-year period 1983-84, an average increase of seven jobs was expected; this amounts to an average employment percentage change of 200 percent. Although most of these firms apparently are growing rapidly, one must also remember that they are in early stages of development. Significant job growth, if it occurs at all, will not happen until the firm leaves the incubator and becomes self-sustaining.

The primary purpose of the incubator is to assure that the firm will become self-sustaining and move out of the incubator. As noted, private incubator sponsors are not as adamant about firms relocating; ten firms in the sample do not anticipate moving from the facility. Of those that do, the median incubation period (determined by adding how long firms have been in the incubator and how long they expect to remain) is 29 months or almost two and one-half years. The firms that expected to leave the incubator indicated overwhelmingly that they would relocate in the local area. Only one of the 44 firms that answered this question expected to relocate outside the local area.

INCUBATORS AND ECONOMIC DEVELOPMENT

As community leaders recognize the potential of small-business incubators, many are rushing to establish them. Incubator facilities exhibit many characteristics of the new economic-development approach of "homegrown" entrepreneurship examined throughout this book. They are excellent candidates for public/private partnerships. Most advanced-technology incubators are closely associated with a research university (Furst 1984). Incubators attract "latent entrepreneurs" from the local community rather than entrepreneurs from other geographic areas. The firms in incubators, though initially quite small, are likely to add to the local economic base after they move from the facility. But to relocate into the local area, they must be able to survive in a competitive business environment, one that takes a heavy toll of new ventures. This is where the incubator plays a key role. It provides assistance to fill management knowledge gaps, reduces early-stage development costs such as rent and service fees, and establishes the entrepreneur in a positive local business environment and support network.

Still, incubators are clearly not for every city and town. They are one tool to be used in a larger economic-development strategy in areas that have the resources to support them. Sponsors have to analyze how, if at all, an incubator fits into a development program. Also important is the vexing question of where is the threshold for unnecessary and inefficient subsidization of private enterprise. This caution reflects the criticism that most firms in industrial parks would have located in the general area regardless of the park's support facilities (U.S. General Accounting Office 1980). The responses to these challenges should be worked out at the local level where needs, commitment, and resources are best understood. States can play a supportive, catalytic role but the trials, errors, and subsequent learning must occur in local communities.

NOTES

1. Presentation of the data is based on a study of Pennsylvania's business incubators (Allen, Ginsberg, and Marx 1984).

2. The term incubator is used generically. Different sponsoring organizations call their incubators different names, such as enterprise development centers, innovation centers, business and technology centers, and entrepreneurial centers.

3. This figure is derived from a nationwide incubator study reported in Allen (1985).

4. For other typologies of incubators see Smilor and Gill (1984) and Temali and Campbell (1984).

5. Two corporations with extensive experience in business incubators are Control Data Corporation (CDC) and Technology Centers International (TCI). CDC had 16 business and technology centers operating by late 1984 and TCI had three. More are planned for both.

6. Some incubator managers (none included in this study) believe that services should not be provided unless requested by tenants. This approach may be economically efficient, but it may not be effective in meeting the unrecognized need of inexperienced business people.

9 States' Advanced-Technology Support Activities and Pennsylvania's Ben Franklin Partnership Program

INTRODUCTION

As technology becomes more sophisticated, the rate of technological change accelerates. Many states have a difficult time keeping up with rapid changes. Others are absorbed in an environment of change. No matter what situation a state finds itself in, it must constantly look forward. States cannot return to the days when they locked horns with one another, offering plum incentives in an effort to attract large-scale industrial facilities. Not only are the rules (policies) of the game changing, but the cast of players also is expanding and changing. Entrepreneurs, technologists, university faculty, and venture capitalists are sharing center stage with large corporations, while others, such as organized labor and less skilled workers, shuffle in the background.

This chapter describes the changing nature of state advanced-technology activities. The first section presents an overview of state economic-development activities. The select number of activities shows that state economic-development programs have evolved from just industrial attraction, although that is still a major focus. The second section of the chapter explains Pennyslvania's advanced-technology policies, centering on the Ben Franklin Partnership Program, and provides examples of development activities conducted as part of this program.

STATES' ADVANCED-TECHNOLOGY
SUPPORT PROGRAMS

All states are involved in economic development, though activities vary widely. The activities of state development agencies fall into eight general categories: planning, coordination of state activities, information dissemination, provision of business and technical assistance, financial assistance, coordination of foreign outreach, promotion, and research (Reinshuttle 1983, p. 1). In 1983, state budgets for economic development ranged from $278.6 million in Ohio to $900,000 in South Dakota, the average economic-development budget being about $28 million. Because many state technological and entrepreneurial development activities took place within the context of the eight major activities, it is often difficult to separate advanced-technology support activities from the larger set (Mazziotti and Savich 1984). Indeed, the coordination of technology support is one useful state-policy approach.

In response to the fairly recent ascent of advanced technology, most states have at least begun to examine development opportunities in this area; a few others have mounted extensive and diverse technological development programs. Almost 90 percent (44 of 50) of the states have responded to advanced-technology opportunities by creating an advisory council, advisory board, or task force (Table 9.1). Often these arrangements precede development programs. Most of these bodies are permanent with primary responsibilities to oversee operations of development programs.

State advanced-technology programs have grown rapidly since 1979 when four states had such programs.[1] By 1985, 35 states had developed some kind of advanced-technology program (Table 9.1). As states have attempted to emulate Silicon Valley with their own versions (Bonic Valley, Silicon Bayou, Polymer Valley, and so forth), policymakers have realized that traditional economic-development support will no longer suffice. New programs focusing on education and training, R&D, and entrepreneurship have sprung up across the country. In the majority of cases, these programs involve financial contributions or matching funds from the private sector. These public/private partnerships are gradually replacing traditional distributive development policies by focusing on the employment potential of the partnerships, not equal distributions across jurisdictional boundaries. Some states have targeted certain high-potential regions (mainly urban centers), industries (the emerging or "sunrise" industries), and strategies (industry attraction versus homegrown

TABLE 9.1   Advanced-Technology Strategies

State	A	B	State	A	B
Alabama	o		Montana	o	
Alaska	o		Nebraska	o	
Arizona	o		Nevada	o	
Arkansas	o	o	New Hampshire	o	o
California	o	o	New Jersey	o	o
Colorado	o	o	New Mexico	o	o
Connecticut	o	o	New York	o	o
Delaware	o	o	North Carolina	o	o
Florida	o	o	North Dakota	o	
Georgia		o	Ohio		o
Hawaii	o	o	Oklahoma	o	
Idaho	o		Oregon	o	
Illinois	o	o	Pennsylvania	o	o
Indiana	o	o	Rhode Island	o	o
Iowa	o	o	South Carolina	o	o
Kansas	o	o	South Dakota	o	
Kentucky			Tennessee	o	o
Louisiana	o	o	Texas	o	o
Maine	o	o	Utah	o	o
Maryland	o	o	Vermont		
Massachusetts	o	o	Virginia	o	o
Michigan	o	o	Washington	o	o
Minnesota	o	o	West Virginia	o	
Mississippi	o	o	Wisconsin	o	o
Missouri	o	o	Wyoming		
			Total	44	35

Source: For column A – State Science and/or Technology Advisory Council (Conway Data Inc., 1984, p. 10). For column B – State Advanced Technology Development Program (Office of Technology Assessment, 1984a, p. 13; Brody 1985, pp. 20-22; U.S. Small Business Administration 1982).

business). Other states have taken a broad approach by not limiting programs to any particular place, industry, or approach. Mirroring the economic diversity of states, advanced-technology development programs are highly diversified.

States' Training Programs

States engage heavily in training, but little information is available about advanced-technology training. States correctly perceive qualified labor as an important ingredient in attracting and retaining firms. All states support training of industrial employees (Table 9.2). Training approaches take the form of state financial support for employee training and retraining. Many states have also developed programs to support training directed at the structural or "hard-core" unemployed.

According to the findings reported in Chapter 5 and conventional wisdom about advanced technology, most of the workers eligible for the state training programs are not in critical demand by advanced-technology firms. Advanced-technology companies are not characterized by the mass production of high-bulk, low-value goods. Instead, they require precision, innovation, and specialized services. Consequently, training programs must emphasize productivity, specialization, flexibility, and continued learning. This kind of training occurs primarily in the educational sector.

Education and Research Programs

State advanced-technology education programs are quite diverse. At the university level, administrators and governing boards have sought to offset the growing demand in science, engineering, and business disciplines by increasing resources in those areas. Some emphasis has been placed on increased technological instruction; in particular, computer literacy has received considerable attention in higher education.

A few states have devised special advanced-technology, high-school-level educational programs. Two areas receiving attention are teacher training, and math and science curriculums. Summer schools and financial incentives, such as scholarships and pay bonuses, are used to promote student and teacher interest in advanced technology.

Some of the more innovative, new approaches in the education sector involve research. All states permit university research facilities to be used

TABLE 9.2 Training Research and Education Programs

State	Training Programs					Research and Education Programs				
	A	B	C	D	E	A	B	C	D	E
Alabama	o	o	o	o		o	o			o
Alaska	o	o	o	o	o	o				o
Arizona	o	o	o	o	o	o	o	o	o	o
Arkansas	o	o	o			o	o			o
California	o	o	o	o	o	o	o	o	o	o
Colorado	o	o	o	o	o	o	o			o
Connecticut	o	o	o	o	o	o		o		o
Delaware	o	o	o	o	o	o	o	o		o
Florida	o	o	o	o	o	o	o		o	o
Georgia	o	o	o			o	o		o	o
Hawaii	o	o	o	o	o	o	o			o
Idaho	o	o	o	o	o	o	o			o
Illinois	o	o	o	o	o	o	o			o
Indiana	o	o	o	o	o	o	o	o	o	o
Iowa	o	o	o	o	o	o	o	o		o
Kansas	o		o			o	o	o		o
Kentucky	o	o	o	o			o			o
Louisiana	o	o	o	o	o	o	o	o		o
Maine	o	o	o	o		o	o	o		o
Maryland	o	o	o	o	o	o	o			o
Massachusetts	o	o	o	o	o	o	o	o	o	o
Michigan	o	o	o	o		o	o	o		o
Minnesota	o	o	o	o	o	o	o		o	o
Mississippi	o	o	o	o	o	o	o			o
Missouri	o	o	o	o	o	o	o	o	o	o
Montana	o	o	o				o			o
Nebraska	o	o	o	o	o	o				o
Nevada	o	o	o	o	o	o				o
New Hampshire	o	o	o	o	o	o	o			o
New Jersey	o	o	o	o	o	o	o	o		o
New Mexico	o	o	o	o	o	o	o	o	o	o
New York	o	o	o	o		o	o	o	o	o
North Carolina	o	o	o	o	o	o	o	o	o	o
North Dakota	o	o	o	o	o	o	o			o
Ohio	o	o	o	o	o	o	o	o		o
Oklahoma	o	o	o	o		o	o			o
Oregon	o	o	o	o	o	o	o	o		o
Pennsylvania	o	o	o	o	o	o	o	o	o	o
Rhode Island	o	o	o			o	o			o

continued

Table 9.2, Continued

State	Training Programs					Research and Education Programs				
	A	B	C	D	E	A	B	C	D	E
South Carolina	o	o	o	o		o	o			o
South Dakota	o	o	o	o	o					o
Tennessee	o	o	o	o	o	o	o	o	o	o
Texas	o	o	o	o	o	o	o	o		o
Utah	o	o	o		o	o	o	o		o
Vermont	o	o	o							o
Virginia	o	o	o			o	o			o
Washington	o	o	o	o	o		o	o	o	o
West Virginia	o	o	o	o	o	o	o			o
Wisconsin	o	o	o	o		o	o	o		o
Wyoming	o	o	o	o			o			o
Total	50	49	50	42	34	44	44	24	14	50

Sources: Training Programs – column A: State Supported Training of Industrial Employees (Conway Data Inc. 1984, p. 10); column B: State Retraining of Industrial Employees (Conway Data Inc. 1984, p. 10); column C: State Recruiting, Screening of Industrial Employees (Conway Data Inc. 1984, p. 10); column D: State Supported Training of "Hard Core" Unemployed (Conway Data Inc. 1984, p. 10); column E: State Incentive to Industry to Train "Hard Core" Unemployed (Conway Data Inc. 1984, p. 10). Research and Education Programs – column A: State Program to Promote R&D (Conway Data Inc. 1984, p. 10); column B: Three or More University Base Centers (Brody 1985, pp. 20, 22); column C: Research Grants (Brody 1985, pp. 20, 22); column D: Educational Programs (Office of Technology Assessment 1984a, p. 13); column E: University R&D Facilities Available to Industry (Conway Data Inc. 1984, p. 10).

by industry, and all have some program to promote R&D. Almost half the states have research grants that create R&D partnerships between universities and industry (Table 9.2). In many of these partnerships, state monies are matched at a minimum one-to-one level with private and nonstate money. Often these research grant programs are tied to university-based technology centers.

University-based centers are new organizational arrangements created to span the boundaries between academia and industry. Interested firms, major and lesser universities, local, regional, and state development organizations, financial institutions, and other relevant groups are organized on a consortium basis. Often representatives from all sectors serve on centers' executive boards. The most typical university-based center arrangement is the single technology focus or "center of excellence" approach (robotics, biotechnology, flexible manufacturing technologies). A number of centers have multiple technology thrust areas that allow collaborative projects from different disciplines to emerge. Some centers operate in conjunction with a small business incubator (Allen 1985). Forty-four states have three or more university-based R&D centers (Table 9.2).

Tax and Financial Incentives

Tax and financial incentives portray how changing economic conditions affect business incentives. Traditional, large facility attraction strategies, oriented primarily to manufacturing firms with large fixed capital needs, were reinforced by tax and financial inducements. In response to these needs, states over the last three decades developed industrial finance authorities and local industrial revenue bond financing arrangements; 39 states have industrial finance authorities, and all have a state or local IRB authority (Table 9.3). Financing the expansion of existing plants and accelerated depreciation allowances (34 and 35 states, respectively) are also important elements in traditional industrial-development strategies.

As small-business and advanced-technology development opportunities became evident, state business inducement approaches started to change and expand. Many of the approaches just mentioned have been aimed at advanced-technology development opportunities, and new strategies have emerged. States have increasingly assumed the role of financial intermediary and investment partner, offering loans for buildings, equipment and machinery, loan guarantees, development finance corporations, and seed and venture-capital programs (Table 9.3).[2] New, flexible incentive programs to promote R&D operate in 13 states, and job creation incentives are available in 24 states (Table 9.3).

Business Assistance Programs

Business assistance programs also illustrate the changing nature of economic-development activities. Economic-development agencies have traditionally helped firms locate and expand within their boundaries. All 50 states conduct feasibility studies to attract new industry and help firms

TABLE 9.3 Tax and Financial Incentives

State	A	B	C	D	E	F	G	H	I	J	K	L
Alabama			o	o				o	o			o
Alaska	o	o	o	o	o		o	o	o	o		o
Arizona				o					o	o		o
Arkansas			o	o			o	o	o		o	o
California	o	o		o	o		o	o	o	o	o	o
Colorado				o			o	o				
Connecticut	o	o	o	o	o	o	o			o	o	o
Delaware			o	o					o	o	o	o
Florida	o	o		o		o		o	o	o	o	
Georgia				o				o				
Hawaii	o	o	o	o						o		o
Idaho				o				o		o	o	
Illinois	o	o	o	o	o			o	o	o		o
Indiana	o	o	o	o	o	o	o	o	o	o	o	o
Iowa				o	o	o		o	o	o	o	
Kansas				o	o	o		o	o	o	o	
Kentucky	o	o	o	o	o			o	o	o	o	o
Louisiana				o	o	o	o	o	o	o	o	
Maine	o		o	o	o	o	o		o	o	o	o
Maryland		o	o	o	o		o	o	o	o	o	o
Massachusetts				o	o	o	o	o	o	o		o
Michigan	o	o	o	o	o		o	o	o	o		o
Minnesota	o	o	o	o	o			o	o	o	o	o
Mississippi	o	o	o	o	o		o	o	o	o		o
Missouri	o	o		o			o	o	o	o	o	o
Montana				o	o		o	o	o		o	
Nebraska			o	o				o	o	o		o
Nevada				o				o	o			
New Hampshire			o	o			o	o	o			o
New Jersey	o	o	o	o	o		o		o	o	o	o
New Mexico	o	o	o	o	o		o	o		o		o
New York	o	o	o	o	o	o	o	o	o		o	o
North Carolina				o	o		o			o		
North Dakota	o	o		o				o	o	o		o
Ohio	o		o	o	o		o	o	o		o	o
Oklahoma	o	o	o	o						o	o	o
Oregon	o	o	o	o	o			o	o	o		o
Pennsylvania	o	o	o	o	o	o	o	o	o	o	o	o
Rhode Island			o	o		o	o	o	o			o
South Carolina	o	o	o	o			o	o		o		
South Dakota			o	o						o		

continued

Table 9.3, Continued

State	A	B	C	D	E	F	G	H	I	J	K	L
Tennessee				o						o		o
Texas	o	o	o	o					o			o
Utah			o	o	o	o		o	o	o	o	
Vermont	o	o	o	o			o	o				o
Virginia			o	o	o		o			o	o	
Washington			o	o	o			o	o			
West Virginia	o	o	o	o				o		o	o	o
Wisconsin			o	o	o	o		o	o	o		
Wyoming				o				o	o			
Total	27	24	39	50	27	13	25	39	35	35	24	34

Sources: Column A: State Loans for Building Construction (Conway Data Inc. 1984, p. 8); column B: State Loans for Equipment, Machinery (Conway Data Inc. 1984, p. 8); column C: State Supported Industrial Development Authority (Conway Data Inc. 1984, p. 8; Reinshuttle 1983, p. 18); column D: City and/or County Revenue Bond Financing (Conway Data Inc. 1984, p. 8); column E: State Venture and/or Seed Capital Program or Assistance (U.S. Small Business Administration 1982; Posner 1984, p. 110; Brody 1985, pp. 21, 23); column F: Research and Development Tax Credits (Brody 1985, pp. 21, 23; Conway Data Inc. 1984, p. 8); column G: Loan Guarantees (Conway Data Inc. 1984, p. 8; Posner 1984, p. 110; Reinshuttle 1983, p. 19); column H: Privately Sponsored Development Credit Corporation (Conway Data Inc. 1984, p. 8); column I: State 503 Certified Development Corporation (U.S. Small Business Administration 1982); column J: Accelerated Depreciation on Equipment (Conway Data Inc. 1984, p. 8); column K: Tax Incentive for Creation of Jobs (Conway Data Inc. 1984, p. 8); column L: State Financing Aid for Plant Expansion (Conway Data Inc. 1984, p. 8).

select industrial sites (Table 9.4). Although export assistance has recently gained the attention of small advanced-technology companies, states have long provided export assistance to large firms. Today, all states provide export assistance (Table 9.4), mainly information dissemination and overseas trade offices.

Enterprise zones are a relatively new state development; to date 26 states have enterprise zone programs (Table 9.4). States have filled the void in the much discussed, yet undeveloped federal enterprise zone program. Enterprise-zone programs are really an amalgam of various business incentives: tax credits are to encourage job creation, regulatory and permit relief, tax exemptions, and targeting other state programs. Although these programs lack administrative capacity, program marketing, and seed capital (CUED October 15, 1984), they are generally deemed successful urban-development strategies.

TABLE 9.4 Business Assistance Programs

State	A	B	C	D	E	F	G	H	I
Alabama	o	o	o			o	o	o	
Alaska		o	o	o	o	o	o	o	
Arizona			o			o	o	o	
Arkansas	o	o	o			o	o	o	
California	o		o		o	o	o	o	
Colorado			o			o	o	o	
Connecticut	o	o	o	o	o	o	o	o	
Delaware		o	o	o	o	o	o	o	
Florida		o	o	o	o	o	o	o	
Georgia	o	o	o		o	o	o	o	
Hawaii				o		o	o	o	
Idaho		o		o		o	o	o	
Illinois	o	o		o	o	o	o	o	
Indiana	o		o	o	o	o	o	o	o
Iowa		o				o	o	o	o
Kansas	o	o	o		o	o	o	o	
Kentucky		o	o	o	o	o	o	o	
Louisiana	o	o	o	o	o	o	o	o	
Maine	o	o			o	o	o	o	
Maryland	o		o	o	o	o	o	o	
Massachusetts	o	o	o	o	o	o	o	o	
Michigan	o	o	o	o	o	o	o	o	o
Minnesota	o	o	o	o		o	o	o	
Mississippi	o	o	o	o	o	o	o	o	o
Missouri	o	o	o	o	o	o	o	o	o
Montana	o		o	o		o	o	o	
Nebraska		o	o	o		o	o	o	
Nevada					o	o	o	o	
New Hampshire		o				o	o	o	
New Jersey	o	o	o	o	o	o	o	o	
New Mexico	o		o	o		o	o	o	
New York	o	o	o	o		o	o	o	
North Carolina		o	o	o		o	o	o	o
North Dakota	o		o	o		o	o	o	
Ohio	o	o	o	o	o	o	o	o	
Oklahoma		o			o	o	o	o	
Oregon		o	o		o	o	o	o	
Pennsylvania	o	o	o	o	o	o	o	o	o
Rhode Island	o	o	o	o	o	o	o	o	
South Carolina	o	o	o			o	o	o	
South Dakota			o	o		o	o	o	

continued

Table 9.4, Continued

State	A	B	C	D	E	F	G	H	I
Tennessee	o	o	o	o	o	o	o	o	
Texas	o	o	o	o	o	o	o	o	
Utah		o				o	o	o	
Vermont		o				o	o	o	
Virginia			o	o	o	o	o	o	o
Washington	o	o	o	o		o	o	o	
West Virginia	o	o	o	o		o	o	o	
Wisconsin	o	o	o	o		o	o	o	
Wyoming						o	o	o	
Total	30	37	39	34	26	50	50	50	8

Sources: Column A: Small Business Set-Asides (U.S. Small Business Administration 1982); column B: Small Business Development Centers (U.S. Small Business Administration 1982); column C: Minority Business Program (U.S. Small Business Administration 1982); column D: Procurement Assistance (U.S. Small Business Administration 1982; Conway Data Inc. 1984, p. 10); column E: Enterprise Zone Act (U.S. Small Business Administration 1982; Reinshuttle 1983, p. 18); column F: State Program to Increase Exports (Conway Data Inc. 1984, p. 10); column G: Feasibility Studies to Attract New Industry (Conway Data Inc. 1984, p. 10; Reinshuttle 1983, p. 10); column H: Industrial Site Selection Assistance (Conway Data Inc. 1984, p. 10); column I: State Incubator Program (Allen 1985).

Small-business assistance programs focus mainly on helping firms develop markets and internal management capacity. Given states' extensive purchases of goods and services (especially data services), state government itself is a potential market for small business. To promote entry into government markets, over half (30) of the states have devised small business set-aside expenditure policies (Table 9.4). Set-asides occur when a portion of the contracts from state government must be provided to small business. To promote federal government procurement contracts, 34 states provide procurement assistance to small business.

States also provide general types of assistance to specific groups, such as minorities and small-business enterprises. Technical and managerial assistance to small business is promoted through a network of Small Business Development Centers (SBDCs) now operating in 37 states (Table 9.4).[3] The SBDCs, located at universities, provide a full range of services to small business. Their funding comes from diverse sources: the SBA, states, universities, and local business and development organizations. Minority business programs, also extensively targeted at a small-business clientele, provide an array of services, ranging from low-interest loans and guaranteed loans, to technical and managerial assistance. Many small-business incubator programs, now operating in eight states, supply a wide range of technical and managerial assistance (Chapter 8).

The roster of incentives and assistance provided to advanced-technology firms is growing steadily. As states examine their development needs and resources, new and revised programs geared to helping businesses start and prosper have emerged. The gradual withdrawal of the federal government from this arena leaves the playing field wide open for state and local governments.

States and local governments have a different kind of challenge facing them today. They are no longer at the receiving end of categorical and entitlement grants provided by the federal government. Rather, they are beginning to work with the private sector to mold their own economic destiny. The states have learned many lessons during the past 20 years and their capacity to pursue economic development has improved. At the same time, the economy has changed rapidly and fundamentally, and governmental and educational institutions typically lag behind entrepreneurial companies, which are at the forefront of innovation. Many governmental policymakers understand the economic-development potential of advanced technology and realize the effectiveness of using state resources as leverage, consequently inducing the private sector's role in economic development.

The remainder of this chapter examines the conceptual basis and operational activities of one highly regarded state advanced-technology economic-development program – Pennsylvania's Ben Franklin Partnership (BFP). The BFP program was legislatively created in 1982 and has received considerable national media attention; many consider it a model state program.

OVERVIEW OF THE BEN FRANKLIN PARTNERSHIP PROGRAM

Historical Background

Faced with high unemployment and a decline of major industrial sectors (Chapter 3), Pennsylvania's business, labor, and governmental leaders began to examine strategies for reversing the state's economic decline. The Pennsylvania State Planning Board, a group of legislators, citizens, and cabinet officials that provides advice to the governor on planning issues, undertook a comprehensive effort to develop a state strategy and plan of action for economic development, community development, and resource management and conservation. This strategic planning report entitled, "Choices for Pennsylvanians" (Pennsylvania State Planning Board 1981) was instrumental in developing a broad consensus about the outlook of the state's economy and opportunities for economic development.

These leaders recognized, first, that Pennsylvania alone could not reverse the fundamental economic forces affecting the state. Pennsylvania's industries have gradually been losing their competitive edge. The state's manufacturing industries cannot be counted on as a source of new employment opportunities whether they continue to lose market share and decline, or whether they are able to modernize and regain a competitive world-market position. New replacement jobs created by enterprises have not flourished in many of the state's depressed regional economies.

A second conclusion reached was that traditional approaches to economic development, that is, recruiting large industrial facilities to locate within the state, have limited success. Concurrent with the increasing doubt about the efficacy of "smokestack" and "chip chasing" was the realization of small businesses' important role in job creation. Third, Pennsylvania was perceived to have a history of commercializing technological innovation and a large base of research and development. Several of the state's 140 colleges and universities have national reputations in emerging technologies.[4]

Despite Pennsylvania's resources in technology, little seemed to be happening there in comparison to New England, California, and Texas. A study by the Wharton Applied Research Center (1979) concluded that the state's inability to compete with other technology centers was the result of poor university/industry relationships and inadequate in-state financing for small high-risk entrepreneurial firms. The issue facing state policymakers was whether to create a set of policies and programs to overcome these problems by using the state's rich technological base as a seedbed for nurturing firms and industries of the future.

Program Structure

One of the major policy responses to the challenge of a changing economy was to create the Ben Franklin Partnership Program. The BFP is a state-funded program that provides challenge grants to four university-based advanced-technology centers (ATCs).[5] At least 50 percent of the funding for the program must be provided by sources other than state government with a strong preference given to private-sector financial participation. The ATCs are university-led consortia of other educational institutions, businesses, organized labor, local government, financial institutions, economic-development organizations, and other groups interested in stimulating economic growth. The program has three major goals: to maintain and create jobs in advanced-technology enterprises; to improve productivity, particularly among existing industries; and to diversify the state's economy, with special emphasis on increasing Pennsylvania's share of advanced-technology firms and employment. To accomplish these goals, innovation, risk taking, and cooperation must be infused into an economy not known for these characteristics.

The legislation creating the BFP received strong bipartisan support in the Pennsylvania General Assembly, passing both houses unanimously in late 1982. Ten million dollars was appropriated for the first full year of operation, matched by $28 million from the private sector and other sources. The state appropriation for the second full year was $18.6 million with a better than 3:1 nonstate match. The state contribution for third-year funding is $21.3 million with a nearly 4:1 nonstate match, which amounts to slightly over $100 million for 1985-86.

Each of the four ATCs is required to develop a regional advanced-technology strategy. This strategy serves as the basis for regional integration and coordination of advanced-technology efforts. Because the four regions are substantially different, no center is like another. In fact, the four ATCs vary considerably in structure, R&D focus, and linkage activity. Advanced-technology activities of the centers include: joint research and development, scientific education and technology training, and entrepreneurial development.

Conceptual Orientation

Technological development programs such as this one can be conceived of as two interdependent processes: technical innovation and organizational change (Chapter 1). Technical innovation encompasses the design, development, and marketing of new products and processes. The conveyance of innovation from inventor or initiator to product developer and eventually end user occurs within organizational contexts. Organizational processes of innovation and adaption occur at two levels of resolution. Macrolevel concerns are interorganizational issues and microlevel concerns are intraorganizational issues. One of the key elements in these organizational processes is the linkage of individuals and organizations. Linkages are exchanges of information and resources that support an environment for entrepreneurship and technological development.

The interorganizational linkage network for the BFP program is comprised of advanced-technology firms, ATCs, and technological support organizations such as universities, other educational service providers, financial institutions, and local development groups.[6] Firm-oriented linkages with ATCs are relevant for the three primary thrusts of the BFP program. First, firms and universities pursue R&D and facility-sharing arrangements. The second program thrust, education and training, can also occur through university/industry agreements. An increasing role is being played, however, by nonresearch collegiate institutions, proprietary schools, community colleges, and vocational/technical schools. For the third thrust area, entrepreneurial development, financial institutions (local banks, venture and seed capital funds, and government financial programs), community and industrial development organizations, and other governmental agencies play a key role in promoting and financing new enterprises. Other than linkages where firms are directly involved, technological support organizations are working together to further develop service and assistance networks that support the start-up and growth of advanced-technology firms and users.

Linkages between organizations require a process of change and adaption within organizations. The purpose of interorganizational change and adaption is to create incentives that support external linkages. In this context, the intraorganizational processes are bundles of rules, intentions, arrangements, and rewards that bring the organization's objectives in line with the interests of the organization's employees. For example, if universities are to be active in technological development, the proper incentives and facilitating structure must exist to support faculty collaboration with industry. Universities that give faculty little leeway or support are likely to see little emphasis placed on collaborative activity by faculty.

Linkages are clearly a focal activity of the Ben Franklin Partnership program. By definition, linkages do not occur unilaterally; they result from many activities of agents in the technological support infrastructure. The BFP program systematically plans and organizes those agents (consortia members), although many firms and agents with similar intentions exist outside the BFP program structure. Once linkages begin to occur, they may grow exponentially by building upon prior agreements. As successful linkages develop, a snowballing effect occurs in an organization, exhibited by changing beliefs, structures, and incentives, that is, positive adaptions to the interorganizational linkage process. In essence, organizational learning and adaption can occur only if a critical number of linkages develop over time. The eventual outcomes of new economic development approaches are not linkages. An enhanced or developed regional economy is the eventual objective. Linkages must first occur, however, if new jobs, economic diversity, and higher levels of productivity – all due to applications of advanced tech-nology – are expected to occur as a long-term consequence of the BFP.

Whether or not the model implicit in the BFP program operates as specified cannot yet be determined. Changes in technological support organizations have occurred, many new firms have started up, and older firms have introduced process and product changes. But, questions remain as to the magnitude of the program's long-run impact on Pennsylvania's economy. If appreciable change and impact are to occur, it will not be for many (perhaps 20) years.

BFP PROGRAM ACTIVITIES
AND EARLY-STAGE RESULTS

In order to provide an operational context for the interorganizational and intraorganizational constructs, some BFP program activities are illustrated. The activities mentioned in this section are not exhaustive of BFP activities; they merely highlight recent activity in the three focal areas (BFP Fund Board 1984).

Research and Development

- A project between a corporation and the University of Pennsylvania developed perfluorocarbon emulsions for use in treating cancer and stroke victims. Patent applications have been fixed in 11 countries and a wholly-owned subsidary has been formed to market the products.

- A project that links users between wire-frame models and solid modeling systems has delivered software to a large computer company. The small BFP-sponsored company is negotiating with Lehigh University to market this computer-aided-design software.

- A device has been developed that will improve the current systems for measuring blood glucose. A Penn State professor working with a medical laboratory company has developed an integrated test container that uses thin film polarographic sensors to follow the enzymatic reaction. Projections show sales could reach $100 million by 1990, creating approximately 100 jobs.

- Research is being conducted by a Carnegie-Mellon University engineering professor and a medium-sized robotics company on the effects of machining interactions on robot design and control. Researchers intend to build a prototype robot system that relies on force or position control in machining interactions and not upon template positioning methods.

Education and Training

- A program of labor-management working groups is identifying ways to improve productivity and worker satisfaction by adjusting training processes to meet technical innovations. Models of successful cases from the Northeast will be developed and disseminated to companies throughout the state.

- A network of advanced-technology companies created in the five-county Philadelphia metropolitan area is conducting courses on new technology applications. Companies design courses and provide the instructors, facilities, and access to equipment. Initial funding is oriented to upgrading the skills and knowledge of company employees.

- The western Pennsylvania ATC is supporting the development of a labor-force data base and employment trend forecast for use by educational institutions in planning curricula to meet the labor needs of area businesses.

- Representatives from four universities and colleges, five vocational-technical schools, one intermediate unit, and three private institutions have been recruited by the ATC of central northern Pennsylvania to participate in a training clearinghouse.

Entrepreneurial Development

- The four ATCs operate or support the operation of 14 of the 20 incubators operating across the state (Chapter 8). About 15 more are proposed for 1986. The BFP program provides matching funds for incubator feasibility studies and supports the provision of management services.
- The Utilization Center of the Council for Labor and Industry is being supported to provide business consulting, technology transfer, and financial assistance to new business ventures in the Philadelphia metropolitan region. The center, in cooperation with segments of industrial and academic communities, works primarily with firms to increase competitiveness by using advanced forms of process-related technologies.
- A regional development authority will provide business development and financial support services to projects emerging from the ATC of central and northern Pennsylvania. Primary attention is focused upon business plans, financial packages, and the expansion of investment capital intermediaries.
- The Pittsburgh High Technology Council, an association of advanced-technology companies in western Pennsylvania, provides direct entrepreneurial assistance and educational programs to firms of various sizes and industrial makeup. Some other similar BFP-supported organizations working in the western Pennsylvania region are the Southern Alleghenies Entrepreneurial Assistance Program of the Center for Technology Training and Development, The Enterprise Corporation of Pittsburgh, the Clarion University Entrepreneurial Technology Center, and the Foundation for Applied Science and Technology.
- In conjunction with venture-capital partners, four regional seed-capital funds have been organized, one involving each ATC.

Six other advanced-technology and enterprise-development support programs are linked to the BFP program. In April 1984, Pennsylvania voters approved a bond issue that funds the Economic Revitalization Act. This $190 million bond issue mainly supports new economic development programs. For three of the bond programs, the BFP Board acts as the policy body that approves guidelines, allocates program funds, and coordinates the ATC delivery systems. The previously existing program has been reoriented to promote enterprise development and advanced technology.

- Thirteen university-based Small Business Development Centers and 30 outreach facilities exist in the state. These centers support business assistance to new and existing small companies. The BFP program augments other state and SBA financial support for these centers.
- The state's Small Business Research Seed Grant Program provides $35,000 grants for R&D to small firms. This money is also used to complement the federal SBIR program, mainly as bridge financing. R&D activities not funded by this program are eligible for BFP funding, conditional on a firm's forming a linkage with a university. The seed-grant program does not require such a linkage.
- Engineering programs in universities across the state have the opportunity to purchase equipment for instruction through a $3 million grant program. State funds from the bond issue for the equipment purchases, distributed on the basis of number of enrolled students, must be matched 3:1 with new private funds.
- The Small Business Incubator Loan Program (Chapter 8) provides loan assistance to public and private incubator sponsors for acquisition, rehabilitation, furnishings, and equipment. The BFP program complements the incubator loan program by providing funds for feasibility studies, and for services in the facilities not available elsewhere.
- The Seed Capital Program, also established through the bond issue, helps capitalize four new-venture seed funds in the ATC regions. The ATCs act as limited partners with general management provided by an established partner. The $3 million designated for the four centers must be matched by $9 million in private funds.
- The Appalachian Regional Commission activities in Pennsylvania have been reoriented to promote enterprise development.[7] Local Development Districts (LDDs) administer business assistance, export development, incubator facilities, SBA 503 corporations, and Pennsylvania Capital Loan Fund programs. Close cooperation and resource sharing has been established between LDDs and ATCs.

Early Program Results

The BFP began operations at the four ATCs in March 1983. An internal review of program activities 30 months later highlighted substantial progress (Ben Franklin Partnership Board 1985). Some examples of positive results are 208 new start-up firms assisted and over 2,000 jobs created directly due to the program. Fourteen patents have been issued, and over $29 million in venture capital was committed to program-assisted firms. About $29 million in BFP funds have generated $86 million in nonstate matches. Of the $86 million, less than $10 million came from the federal government and less than $1 million from local governments. The majority of matching funds – over $50 million excluding foundations' funds – came from the private sector.

For the 1985-86 fiscal year, $21.3 million was allocated by the BFP funding board to the four ATCs. Financial resources were allocated by the board on a criteria of equalness ($6 million), quality of matching support ($9.3 million), and performance ($6 million). Equal allocations are intended to assure ATC administrative consistency and the funding of ATCs' high-priority items. Quality of matching support assures that private-sector funds, both cash and in-kind support, will be largely responsible for project funding. A distribution formula that uses weights for private sector, nonprofit and foundation, and other sources of matching funds is used for each year's allocations. Additionally, three direct performance criteria and five indirect performance criteria are used for fund distribution. Direct criteria are jobs at new and expanded firms affiliated with the ATC for two periods, and the number of new start-ups. Indirect criteria are the amount of venture capital attracted to the ATC; the number of higher-education institutions participating; the relative percentage of small firms participating in R&D; the number of projects benefiting women, minority, and displaced workers; and the ATC's success in meeting private-sector expenditures during the first six-month operating period. These guidelines assure that ATC and program participants become entrepreneurial; grantsmanship and distributional allocations seldom promote efficient use of public-development funds.

CONCLUSION

In a time of changing intergovernmental arrangements for economic development (Ledebur and Rasmussen 1984), states have begun to initiate their own advanced-technology-development programs. Many programs encompass new activities for states; others build upon existing activities to augment a growing technological support infrastructure. Whether the program is totally new or an adaption of prior activities, a main focus is linkages between the public and private sectors. In the public sector, new organizational arrangements and incentive structures are emerging to foster linkages. On the private side, entrepreneurs and firms are coming to rely on the resource base of technological support organizations that provide business and technological assistance.

Pennsylvania's Ben Franklin Partnership program is an excellent example of this new breed of state development initiatives. Other states have examined the program and emulated much of its structure and program (Plosila, Tellefsen, and Cook 1984). The BFP program was designed by policymakers as a flexible, market-driven program able to build upon existing resources of the state's advanced-technology industries and technological support organizations. The state's catalytic role seeks to orient existing and new resources toward meeting the changing needs of entrepreneurs and existing businesses.

These new state programs are large-scale experiments conducted in almost 50 laboratories across the country. Many years must pass for these programs to have a large-scale impact. But before a large number of firms and many new jobs are created, organizations must reorient incentives and activities to establish networks of support linkages. Participating organizations must communicate common purposes and work toward meeting mutual interests. State and local governments do have a role to play; they must integrate public resources and private interests to support mutually beneficial outcomes. As the pace of change increases, the need for coordinated efforts becomes increasingly evident.

NOTES

1.   Sources for information on state programs are diverse (see tables). The data represent whether or not the state has a program, not how many, how large, or how effective the program. Substate programs are not included unless they have considerable intrastate uniformity or are primarily a state initiative executed at substate levels.

2.   The seed- and venture-capital programs are financed and managed primarily as partnerships with existing venture-capital funds. Some states have legislatively authorized or mandated state retirement funds to invest in venture capital.

3.   The SBDC program is targeted for elimination by the Reagan administration. Other SBA programs, such as small business advocacy and minority enterprise, would be moved to the Department of Commerce.

4.   Some examples of Pennsylvania's universities and their areas of research excellence are: Carnegie-Mellon University – robotics and computers; Lehigh University – robotics, computer-aided design, and manufacturing technologies; The Pennsylvania State University – biotechnology, and materials engineering and processing; and the University of Pittsburgh – biological/biomedical technology.

5.   The four ATCs are: The Advanced Technology Center of Southeastern Pennsylvania, a consortium of 35 colleges and universities in the greater Philadelphia area including the University of Pennsylvania, Drexel University, Temple University, and area medical schools; The Western Pennsylvania Advanced Technology Center, a consortium of 39 public and private academic institutions, over 250 private firms, 7 organized labor groups, several venture-capital firms and regional development organizations organized by Carnegie-Mellon University and the University of Pittsburgh; The North East Tier Advanced Technology Center, organized by Lehigh University in Bethlehem, including 69 private and public colleges, 86 labor and industrial organizations, four small business development centers, and 21 local development organizations; and The Advanced Technology Center of Central and Northern Pennsylvania, housed at the Pennsylvania State University with satellite centers in Harrisburg and Erie, involving 34 other colleges and universities, 238 private sector firms, and numerous other groups.

6.   The concept of technological support organizations is taken from Wenk and Kuehn's (1977) notions about technological delivery systems.

7.   The Appalachian Regional Commission is also slated for elimination by the Reagan administration. The administration has sought to eliminate the program since 1980, but as yet has not found Congress willing.

10 Economic-Development Policy at a Crossroads

INTRODUCTION

Technological and entrepreneurial development is taking place all across the United States. Mature advanced-technology centers, such as Silicon Valley and the Route 128 area around Boston, are touted as examples of what technological-based new enterprise can do for an area's economy. Neither of these centers developed as a result of extensive state or local government technological development programs. Rather, during a 20-year span responsive quality universities, plentiful venture capital, and other market and amenity forces came together to develop a critical mass of entrepreneurial support activity that still promotes growth in these areas. In many developing and emerging advanced-technology centers (Conway 1985), such as Phoenix-Tempe, Denver-Boulder, Central Florida-Orlando, Minneapolis-St. Paul, Philadelphia-Route 202, Pittsburgh, Austin-San Antonio, Salt Lake City, and Seattle-Tacoma, just to name a few, public/private cooperation is much more deliberate. In this final chapter, problems and opportunities associated with publicly supported entrepreneurial and technological development are examined. Findings and perspectives from previous chapters are integrated to assess new economic-development approaches.

THE CHANGING DEVELOPMENT LANDSCAPE

We live in interesting, complex times. On the one hand, the world of advanced technology is heralded as creating an easier, more pleasant life

214

by increasing the standard of living and reducing much of the drudgery and danger associated with many labor-intensive tasks. On the other hand, it brings forth a new set of issues and challenges for developed and developing societies.

One fundamental trend that will continue to increase with technological development is the complexity of changing relationships. As the national economy changes from an extractive and transformative base to a producer and consumer-services base, interdependencies increase. The new "thoughtware economy," as Birch calls it (1984), relies upon innovation – the process of using resources in new ways to generate new goods and services. Innovation may come from new technical processes or new organizational arrangements used to support the further generation and integration of knowledge and information resources.

As this process continues through time, much of labor's and industry's old ways will be left behind. Worker skills and products created will become obsolete faster, given shorter skill and product life cycles. The pace of employment change is staggering. Birch (1985) estimates that 8 percent to 10 percent of the jobs in the United States are lost every year and have to be replaced with new jobs. This means that over a five-year period, the economy must replenish about one-half of the nation's jobs just to keep employment even. The very nature of an innovation-based economy is that it must continually change or face competitive pressures from lagging producers as they improve and standardize new technology. For example, in 1984, for the first time, the United States' electronics sector was in a net import-export deficit (Business Week 1985). Although consumer sales are high in the United States, U.S. firms are increasingly purchasing electronic components from abroad. Forces fueling this sea of red ink include high capital costs, insufficient research and development expenditures, minimal investments in improved manufacturing, domestic antitrust policies, foreign government trade restrictions, and deficient human-resource adaptions. Some of these problems are beyond the influence of state and local governments; some are not. What state and local governments can do is provide catalytic support for technological innovation, which, in the world's largest entrepreneurial economy, will help offset many of these forces. This is not to suggest that the federal government can sit idly by – it too must seek to alleviate problems within its domain by such means as antitrust policies, reducing trade barriers, and promoting the commercialization of defense technology.

The new homegrown approach to economic development, characterized by technological innovation and entrepreneurship, offers new challenges and problems for state and local policymakers and development officials. The attraction approach to economic development – distinguished by the process of creating policy instruments (for example, financial incentives) or preparing a site (for example, infrastructure improvements), and then marketing the inducement – is predicated on a firm or its consultant doing the site selection work. In essence, the locality prepares policies and inducements, disseminates that information, and waits for firms to respond. This attraction approach is becoming increasingly less applicable for entrepreneurial and technological development.[1] Areas that pursue attraction strategies often set their sights on branch plants. Such self-contained operations have minimal links to local suppliers, have centralized management functions, and generally do little to stimulate entrepreneurship in the local economy (Miller and Cote 1985). The new proactive agenda calls for development officials to work actively with private entities to arrange new enterprise opportunities and to help establish new firms and promote the growth of existing ones (Booth and Fortis 1984). One way to organize activities to promote new business is through strategic economic-development planning.

A STRATEGIC PERSPECTIVE ON ECONOMIC DEVELOPMENT

Strategic economic-development planning (Gregerman 1984) seeks to overcome typical implementation problems (Pressman and Wildavsky 1973) by incorporating planning and implementation into one sequential process. Although strategic planning and management techniques have been used in the business sector for nearly two decades, the approach is relatively new to nonprofit and government entities. Fundamental differences concerning goals, internal capability, and external environments make strategic planning different in the two contexts.

Strategic planning is a focused process that addresses an organization's internal strength, weaknesses, resources, and external influences on the organization (Sorkin, Ferris, and Hudak 1984). The overall intention is to better position the organization to perform in a dynamic, competitive environment. Strategic decisions are typically interdependent with long-term consequences that require considerable resources and broad-based support to achieve, but given the future orientation and complexity of external environments, knowledge about consequences is uncertain. Although strategic planning has a strong action orientation, achieving practical results occurs as part of strategic management. In the management of change, the organization attempts to divest itself of unproductive and declining activity, enhance productive and growth activity, and increase the efficiency of support services.

External Constraints

The constraints in governmental strategic planning and management come at various levels and through different influences (Advisory Commission on Intergovernmental Relations 1985). Citizen preferences can seldom be neatly bundled or ranked, but most decisions require the support of at least a majority of the electorate. This need to achieve a broad-based consensus frequently forces a distributional approach to development activities rather than a performance and/or focused approach. Narrow parochial interests, which are played out in "log rolling" and "pork-barrel" economic-development appropriations, usually form the basis of consensus. Equity issues, such as citizen demands for equal access to resources, may have a tendency to relegate economic efficiency secondary to distributional fairness. Similarly, the need for citizen involvement is fundamental to democratic government, even if it slows the progress of deliberations, delays projects, and increases costs.

Internal Constraints

The turbulence of external environments exists in apparent contrast to the high degree of certainty assumed to exist in large monolithic urban and state bureaucracies. In such hierarchical institutions, a high degree of predictability of output is assumed to result given rule-guided behavior, a uniform task environment, and information that flows along prescribed lines of authority and responsibility. Output, however, is not predictable in this environment. Prescriptions for work are difficult to enforce given extensive civil-service arrangements, task environments that change with administrations and economic conditions, and information that is fragmented over multiple agencies, each handling different segments of complex development problems. Reduced growth in government revenues, which results in minimal across-the-board salary increases (much less merit raises) and lower salaries than private-sector equivalents, mean considerable difficulty in hiring employees with skills and knowledge useful to plan and execute new development initiatives. The observation that strategic planning initiated by governors is often viewed with suspicion by legislators, who believe such activity is undertaken to advance governors' career objectives (Advisory Commission on Intergovernmental Relations 1985), points out the rather bleak internal environment for governmental strategic planning.

In general, public-sector economic-development strategic planning entails a high degree of intrapreneurship. New ideas and policy options have to find champions who will struggle as "true believers" to support what may go against accepted wisdom or practice. Those individuals who promote technological innovation and entrepreneurship as part of governmental strategic planning for economic development have to assume entrepreneurial traits themselves (Kysiak 1983).

Temporal Constraints

Public-sector temporal constraints to strategic planning and management are also formidable. To placate citizen demands for action, legislators enact short-term solutions that treat the symptoms of problems, not long-term solutions that deal with root causes. Political support has a tendency to line up behind short-term solutions (tradeoffs that serve as holding actions) because electoral cycles are also short. Additionally, when the rapid turnover of politicians and executive administrators occurs, new decision makers are eager to make their claim for change. The frequent result is policy inconsistency, regulatory uncertainty, and a bad reputation from business people who desire stability in governmental relations. Some of these problems can be presented as opportunities or checks against excess. For example, frequent political turnover results in incremental public policy, but major swings toward untested strategies are unlikely in such situations.

Although the constraints seem to outweigh the opportunities, economic-development strategic planning and management in the public sector is possible. The key to successful strategic planning is cooperation engendered from an understanding of mutual self-interests and a belief that such interests can be optimally achieved when all parties work toward common goals.

External and Internal Assessment

Public organizations that want to develop a competitive strategy for an area first need to understand the local entrepreneurial environment (Bruno 1982). Whether it be a state or local jurisdiction, an assessment of the external entrepreneurial environment should go beyond important resource or input factors common to business climate studies (Chapter 4). The comprehensive assessment should include the level of support for small technological businesses provided by existing industrial concerns, educational institutions, community-based organizations, other small businesses, and government jurisdictions.

The external assessment should also examine the appropriate market for entrepreneurs. A development organization working in an area with a strong external infrastructure and positive entrepreneurial culture may not want to cream the best enterprise prospects; rather, the group may want to work with disadvantaged or minority clientele. Conversely, development organizations located in areas not possessing a supportive external infrastructure and entrepreneurial culture may want their business support activities to act as a catalyst to improve these conditions, in essence, a showpiece that demonstrates something positive is being done for local economic development. Different objectives and external environments should lead to different expectations and outcomes. Part of the utility of a catalytic approach is that it can serve different purposes for different communities and sponsoring organizations by adapting to different needs and resources.

Organizations examining technological and entrepreneurial development concepts also need to assess their internal capacity to provide effective financial, technical, and management support. Many public and nonprofit groups have minimal experience providing these kinds of support. For example, business consulting capacity needs to be developed both internally and within external support groups. To develop this capacity internally, local economic-development officials must assume entrepreneurial traits, a gradual process that entails considerable cost and commitment. For this capacity to develop externally, new linkages must be forged with groups that economic-development officials have not previously worked with extensively (marketing analysts, accountants, technology specialists, and so forth). Support organizations will also have to reorient incentives and institutional arrangements. For example, if university faculty are to provide assistance to small firms, they must be rewarded for this by their institutions; these incentives are not common in U.S. colleges and universities.

Value and Wealth Multiplier Goals
Versus Redistribution Goals

Organizations involved in the strategic planning process should determine their common goals and the specific objectives they will use to monitor progress toward those goals by assessing external and internal resources and capacity capable of assisting new enterprises. Although various organizations have different goals (Chapter 1), a global goal that brings organizations together in the technological development process is the generation of new value (Vaughan, Pollard, and Dyer 1985). Added value may take a pecuniary form, such as increased tax revenue or stock value; a societal form, such as increased community cohesiveness due to higher employment; or a psychic form, such as increased reputation conferred on the public champion of local entrepreneurship.

Technological development programs are a response to many factors, one of which is a shift in public attitudes and public policy orientations. Public attitudes of the late 1960s and early 1970s generally supported public policies that sought to create equal outcomes from unequal resources. The federal government, using extensive fiscal-transfer mechanisms, tried to equalize opportunity and wealth outcomes across income groups and geographic areas. Many new public-policy purposes emphasize the generation of new wealth (value), not the redistribution of wealth. This trend is not absolute; human services provided to the most disadvantaged, that is, the "safety net," is a canon of social policy. But, the new policy perspective is applied to the disadvantaged as well as to low- and middle-income levels – a growing economy benefits all segments of society. By investing resources in an enterprise-development infrastructure the potential for self-sustaining growth increases (Hula 1985). Although this assumption has been challenged, it is the foundation of the current administration's domestic development policy.

Policies, Arrangements, and Outcomes: An Example

Following the external and internal assessments and the formulation and clarification of goals and objectives, the process of organizing a framework for technological and entrepreneurial development should start to take shape. The framework is created by alternative development approaches or choices that work within realized constraints and seek to optimize objectives. Advanced-technology economic-development programs recognize the uniqueness and similarity of different organizations' objectives. To meet different objectives, different structural arrangements and management approaches are created, resulting in different development outcomes. The emerging business-incubator industry is a good example of how objectives are translated in varied organizational arrangements.

Various organizations in private, nonprofit, and higher-education sectors sponsor business-incubator facilities. Sponsor's interests in incubators are similar to the development objectives described in Chapter 1. One additional objective specifically relevant to incubators is added value through property development (Allen 1985). This objective is often a primary interest of private groups; public organizations and universities are not in the real-estate-speculation business and look at property development as an ancillary result of incubators, not as an end in itself.

Given various objectives, sponsoring groups organize and manage their incubators differently. One important distinction in incubator management is entry and exit rules. Privately sponsored incubator organizations that invest in tenant firms are obviously selective; they seek ventures with the best investment potential. Conversely, sponsors of privately run incubators that are not interested in tenant-firm investments are likely to be interested in property development. Property development facilities have few entry restrictions; emphasis is on full occupancy rather than high valuation tenants. Publicly supported incubators are more apt to accept firms that promote job creation and economic diversification objectives. Consequently, retail, warehousing, professional personal services, and nonprofit organizations are often ineligible tenants (Plosila and Allen 1985). University-sponsored incubators are more apt to be concerned with product development, and therefore more apt to accept start-up tenants that have a university affiliation, thus building upon the university's research mission.

Objectives of incubator sponsors also influence whether or not an exit policy exists (Allen 1985). An exit policy relates to tenants' residency in the facility. If tenants are permitted to reside continuously in the facility, over time, the facility assumes characteristics of a multitenant commercial operation. Private facilities are more likely to allow tenants to remain in the facility indefinitely, thereby assuring greater certainty of occupancy and avoiding the financial risk associated with tenant turnover. Public and university incubators are more likely to terminate tenant leases when service assistance and rental subsidies are no longer needed. Some public facilities limit residency to (typically) three years. In all kinds of facilities, successful tenants move out into local commercial space if they outgrow the limited space available in the incubator. Slowly growing firms located in public and university facilities are usually asked to leave, which frees up space for more promising growth ventures.

This brief examination of one aspect of incubators demonstrates how sponsors' different objectives translate into different organizational arrangements and different development outcomes. Job growth is likely to be greater in public and university-sponsored incubators than in private-property development facilities. Conversely, investment-oriented incubators, primarily because of their rigid entry requirements, are likely to have higher firm survival rates, and also high firm growth rates.

Although differences in objectives and management of incubators are evident, incubators share a global purpose: to create a supportive environment that increases the chances of a fledgling firm's surviving its formative years. The realization that private profit motives create a desire for successful firms and that this objective is compatible with community wealth and job creation has led public agencies to promote privately sponsored incubators. This realization is not limited to the incubator industry; it is a widely accepted tenet of new economic-development programs (Vaughan, Pollard, and Dyer 1985).

A Targeting Strategy for New Enterprise

Public and private goals of new value and wealth generation are not met equally by all firms. Furthermore, different development policies and organizational arrangements result in different development outcomes, as argued in the preceding section. Given limited resources and constrained options, one result of a strategic development plan should be a finely tuned focus on the most appropriate development opportunities. Although each jurisdiction has different development needs, those jurisdictions that desire to promote homegrown technologically based enterprise should gain a sense of the variety of these new enterprises.

New firms can be categorized in various ways. One schema popular in the venture-capital industry proffers three categories (Wetzel 1983). Lifestyle firms are those that are started by individuals who want to maintain a satisfactory quality of life. Most new ventures are of this type, but they do not have the growth potential for job creation and diversified levels of income. In many areas, such as recreational regions, these types of firms are extremely important to the economy, and management assistance is of utmost importance to increase their chances of survival.

The second type of enterprise is the middle-market firm. These firms can be generally characterized as reaching a level of 50 to 200 employees and $5 to $20 million in sales five to ten years after start-up. Firms portraying these growth rates are the mainstay of new employment and new tax-generating capability. Because these firms are new wealth producers, development organizations should focus financial, technical, and managerial assistance on such enterprises.

The third category in the venture-capital schema is much less frequently represented than the other two. Firms that have high growth potential, that is, can exceed $20 million in annual sales and over 200 employees in a five-to-ten-year period, are unlikely to need the assistance provided by development agencies (with the possible exception of financial assistance). Managers of these firms have high business acumen, financial and managerial involvement with venture capitalists, and well-established technical capability.

Another typology of business start-ups also provides useful insight into maximizing wealth multiplier goals (Morrison 1985). A traded firm is one that sells products or services outside the local economy, thus increasing the wealth of the local area by exploiting the local area's competitive advantage. A sheltered firm is one that conducts business primarily within the confines of the local economy. Although wealth retention is enhanced by traded firms that substitute for externally created products (import substitution), these firms rely mainly on the traded firms to create the demand for goods and services provided by sheltered firms.

Advanced-technology product-oriented firms are typically traded firms. Demand for the specialized, high value-added products created by small advanced-technology firms is national or international in scope. Advanced-technology service firms are more likely to be sheltered firms, but even these firms are more likely to have external markets than are more traditional firms. Enterprise-development programs that target traded firms are more likely to generate higher value and increased wealth, the essence of economic development.

Although the economic-development strategic planning and management process can be described simply in a few pages, it is a complex endeavor that consumes considerable time and resources. The planning and management of economic-development strategy today incorporates a much broader scope of concern than it did two decades ago. The new approach assumes a close working relationship between the public and private sectors (Holland 1982; Wolman and Ledebur 1984). These public/private partnerships are a response to a long history of inappropriate and ineffective traditional community and economic-development programs (Brevard 1980). Without the cooperation of private industry and citizen and public interest groups, government development agencies have had limited success in resolving community economic problems. Given the complexity of technological development, the diversified interests of business and government, and local needs and resources, successful public/private partnerships encompass more than single-objective narrowly defined activities (Chapter 9). They have a wide variety of purposes and structural arrangements. Generally, they have both policy and operational components. The policy component centers on consensus about the purpose and institutional roles assumed by relevant actors in the community. The operational component centers on the work conducted to achieve the intended development outcomes. Effective partnerships link these two components to advance community interests while promoting individual and organizational objectives (Committee on Economic Development 1982).

In the advanced-technology environment of rapid change, plans quickly become obsolete; rigid plans do not fit well with the concepts of technical innovation and entrepreneurship. The role of centralized, top-down planning in economic development is gradually diminishing, while assisting local groups through information brokering and resource coordination gain importance. The operative concepts of linkage, network, and leverage, to cite a few, are dynamic activities that officials can pursue in response to comparative advantages in state and local economic environments.

OBSTACLES, CHALLENGES, AND RESPONSES

New obstacles and challenges are presented to state and local officials seeking to promote advanced-technology economic development. Some problems seem like old wine in new bottles, while other problems are truly endemic to this age of technological and entrepreneurial development. Isolating the problems is not an easy task; like the economic context that surrounds them, interdependencies abound. Hard and fast policy recommendations would be inappropriate, since each state and locality has to respond to different circumstances with unique approaches and resources. Perhaps it is better not to think in terms of solutions, but of guideposts that can lead policymakers and development officials to make the trade-offs that satisfy the needs of relevant communities of interest.

Public-Sector Entrepreneurship

The new mode of economic development has left many public-sector officials somewhat estranged from leading economic forces. Their professional training and experience has centered on industrial location and site preparation, activities not particularly relevant to entrepreneurs and managers of technological enterprises. Two good examples that characterize the distinctions and challenges faced by development officials are marketing and development planning.

In the conventional development approach, marketing consists primarily of selling the locality as an attractive place for a firm's relocation or expansion. Assembling information to be used in brochures and trade journal advertisements, and occasional international junkets and local receptions for outside dignitaries constitute an area's marketing strategy. The marketing called for in the new economic-development approach has little pomp. This marketing consists primarily of providing assistance to local firms and entrepreneurs by helping them develop new markets and expand existing ones. Topics such as market segmentation, sociobehavioral profiles of consumer groups, and backward linkages into the existing industrial base are not part of the mainstream of industrial-attraction marketing. Although marketing was used to juxtapose the two development approaches, other business-consulting assistance, such as financial management, risk management, business planning, debt and equity financing, and legal assistance, is also important to entrepreneurs and small-business managers who typically do not, at least initially, have a full range of business skills and knowledge (Rivchun 1985).

The second example that distinguishes the conventional approach from the new approach is economic-development planning. While no consensus exists as to what constitutes an economic-development plan, development plans commonly assess the needs of existing and expected industry by examining proximity to population centers; cost and availability of labor, energy, and commercial property; tax structures; and physical infrastructure. The conventional use of economic-development plans and/or studies has been to compare the study area to geographic competitors, and if the findings are favorable, to buttress industrial marketing activities. Plans have also been used to suggest recommendations for governmental action, but a high percentage of such plans are never executed.

The new agenda for development officials incorporates the strategic planning approach of assessing competitive advantage, but goes one step further. Recently a few communities have taken the next step to establish support networks that tie together entrepreneurs, enterprise opportunities, venture investors, business expertise, and potential product users. Two types of support networks operate in communities: formal and informal (Birley 1985). Formal networks include realtors, bankers, business accountants, investment brokers, lawyers, local government officials, and business assistance agencies. Informal networks include family, friends, and business associates. Birley (1985) found that informal actors in enterprise development networks were frequently consulted about business opportunities and local issues such as location and employee selection. Formal sources were used less frequently and at a later stage when the basic structure of the firm was set. In essence, a loose core of local support helps entrepreneurs develop the enterprise idea, while formal sources contribute financial support not obtained through an entrepreneur's personal resources, family, friends, or business associates. The length of time from start-up to small business depends largely on the entrepreneur's ingenuity, personal time, financial commitment, and ties to formal and informal local support networks. Many good venture opportunities never see the light of day because entrepreneurs cannot tie into a local support network, if any exists.

The challenge for economic-development officials is to understand the objectives and resources of disparate actors, and to organize support networks that promote the interests of all members with the primary objective of new enterprise development. Public development officials who pursue this challenge must assume the characteristics of entrepreneurs by taking risks, deferring gratification, learning new skills, and flexibly adapting to changing circumstances. One can easily see that these are not characteristics of a "bureau" personality. The transition process will be long and wrenching for communities and individuals unused to change. What is evolving on a growing scale is a new definition of local government's roles: "This new definition puts city government at the very heart of what happens to the community in all areas – from economic development to education, from cultural affairs to health issues – without the assumed responsibility for actually providing these services" (Moore 1983, p. 7).

Designing Economically Efficient Development Programs

One of the continuing vexing issues of economic development is whether or not an incentive or assistance program actually promotes economic development (General Accounting Office 1984). Subsidies perform two functions (Brooks 1983): they make a seemingly unprofitable venture profitable, as measured, for example, by long-term return on investment; and they provide a contribution that assures some social benefit that cannot be obtained from the market alone. When the first function outweighs the second and when the social benefits are largely uncertain, the subsidy is not warranted. The central question becomes: Is a subsidy needed to obtain social benefits and, if so, how much of a subsidy? Litvak and Daniels (1979, pp. 70-71) believe that given the difficulties in properly evaluating what kind of subsidy is needed, if any, a state is inclined to give the maximum allowed, whether or not it is truly needed. Additionally, few firms refuse subsidies, especially capital-intensive firms that are less apt to be job creators. Another similar efficiency problem concerns private-sector accountability for public resources.

One way to minimize efficiency problems associated with economic-development programs is to target resources on industries that are (or are expected to be) at the forefront of growth (in contrast to national tax policy, which benefits declining industries). This industrial policy targeting approach, often called "picking winners" or "sunrise industries" has met with considerable skepticism, since there is little reason to believe that public officials can distinguish losers from winners before the fact (Krugman 1983).

An alternative way to reduce the economic inefficiency associated with inappropriate allocation of public resources for private purposes is to require that private-sector funds match public-sector funds. In essence, public resources are used to leverage private resources that meet both public and private objectives. Matching funds help reduce a firm's or entrepreneur's risk without jeopardizing rewards. The approach is market sensitive in that potential winners and losers are not picked or avoided. Rather, public funds are allocated to development projects that are financially sound enough to receive the bulk of support from the private sector. The appropriate level of match depends upon the participants and the activity being supported. For example, higher-match ratios should be sought from larger corporations desiring to conduct product-development work with universities, and lower matches from less wealthy entrepreneurs who want to move from a prototype stage to product commercialization. The experience of the Pennsylvania Ben Franklin Partnership program (Chapter 9) proves that greater than 3:1 private-sector-to-state matches are achievable.

An additional benefit derived from matching private to public resources is high support from political decision makers. A state legislature finds it politically acceptable to put up $10 million if, based on a 3:1 match, it can claim that those resources will establish a $40 million economic-development program. Critics may claim that private-sector money counted in the match would have been used for technological development in the absence of the public contribution. It is virtually impossible to refute this claim. But, government agencies administering technological-development programs can require private-sector accountability by demanding repayment of the public-sector grant on a prorated basis if a designated number of jobs are not created or maintained. Similarly, in the case of loan subsidies, an incentive for high performance can be for firms that create and retain more jobs than anticipated to have a prorated reduced repayment or interest rate schedule, and for firms that fail to meet job creation expectations to have the opposite.

An issue relevant to the discussion on economic efficiency of technological-development programs is distributional fairness. Certainly at the state level, and in many municipal jurisdictions as well, tensions between rural and urban, and growing and declining areas affect resource allocations. Although advanced-technology activity occurs primarily in urban areas (Chapter 4), many rural areas have a greater need for economic development. Political decision makers from rural areas want what they perceive to be their fair share of resources. Political realities are such that unless some portion of total development resources is equally distributed, political support may not be forthcoming and enduring. At the same time, policymakers must realize that all areas are not alike in their potential to nurture entrepreneurial and technological development, and that results from areas with little or no entrepreneurial climate will be less than areas already generating enterprise opportunities. To attain the most efficient use of public funds, competitive funding awards are desirable. Of course, the exact trade-off between the performance basis and equality basis is a political decision, be it in the legislative or administrative arenas.

The Critical Element of Leadership

Although leadership in political and business communities has been the topic of extensive research and discussion, little agreement exists on the characteristics that produce effective leaders. One thing that nearly all agree on, however, is that local leadership is needed to develop a local economy. The Committee for Economic Development (1982) suggests that successful public and private ventures contain five key elements: a strong sense of civic culture, a common vision, effective civic organizations, communication among key groups, and civic entrepreneurship. The agenda for local leadership seems to be a willingness to take risks to promote and shape civic values and common goals by networking with individuals and institutions who want to actively promote economic development (Duckworth et al. 1985)

Strong local support helps overcome a major constraint on effective development strategy – continuity. Citizens demand short-term results from their political leaders, but the process of creating a supportive technological and entrepreneurial development infrastructure may take years. For technological development programs to have an appreciable effect on a local or state economy may take a decade or more. For example, the development of the Research Triangle Park in North Carolina has spanned 25 years, which transcends six four-year governors and 12 two-year legislative terms. Had each governor or legislative session wanted to change the development orientation, the impact of the technology park would be much less.

The need for continuity is based on the assumption that advanced-technology economic-development programs do indeed make a difference. It is too early to tell whether or not the concepts and policies discussed in this book have a significant effect on local and state economies; the programs are young, most having begun in the 1980s. Although they are young, it is not too early to begin assessing whether early results have been achieved.

ASSESSING TECHNOLOGICAL-DEVELOPMENT PROGRAMS

To adequately evaluate advanced-technology programs, one must understand their objectives, program logic and structure, and operating environment. Intraorganizational and interorganizational contexts (Chapter 1) and the processes of change at these levels are the arenas in which technological-development infrastructure building is carried out. For intended outcomes to occur, such as a significant number of new jobs and firms created, certain changes in these arenas must occur early in the programs' lives. Because these activities and orientations occur at individual and institutional levels, multimode evaluation designs must be undertaken. The case of university-based development programs suggests some of these different evaluation approaches. Evaluators must assess whether or not faculty are knowledgeable of new arrangements and are more inclined to pursue industry support, take on entrepreneurial oriented partners, or take their own initiative to transfer research findings into commercial product and process applications. In the interorganizational realm, evaluators can assess whether or not new arrangements exist to span barriers that have prevented greater industry/university collaboration, and if these new arrangements are being used. In university-based programs, if faculty do not perceive greater flexibility and institutional support for development activity (as opposed to basic and applied research) and if arrangements are not in place to assist those who want to pursue such activity, the eventual outcomes of new jobs and firms are unlikely ever to occur.

Evaluations that go beyond the early-stage changes brought about by technological-development programs will be complex and difficult. One important reason is similar to the challenge discussed earlier concerning subsidies. Would the desired economic activity have occurred anyway? In the interdependent world of complex economies, it will not be easy to untangle causes from effects or endogenous from indigenous variables. Perhaps the acid test of whether or not these programs really make a difference is to look at the laboratories themselves. Are state and local economies creating opportunities that keep pace with national developments, and more important, has the quality of life in those areas moved in the same direction with similar magnitude as national and international trends?

CONCLUSION: NURTURING ENTREPRENEURIAL SPIRIT

The rather recent and widespread transition in economic-development thinking has left state and local policy at a crossroads. Some tried and true approaches are retained, while others not appropriate for technological and entrepreneurial development are falling rapidly by the wayside. The desire to close the gap between appropriate new approaches and outmoded old approaches has created a rush by policymakers and development officials to jump on the advanced-technology economic development bandwagon. New approaches are not panaceas; they beget new tensions and occasionally fan the flames of old tensions. State and local governments that, at a minimum, choose not to investigate the potential for technological development may find themselves having to play the difficult game of catch-up as they move into the twenty-first century.

Breaking into entrepreneurial and technological development is not easy. The most important actor in homegrown development – the entrepreneur – is someone who is generally independent, inaccessible, and thinks government involvement means government interference. Many entrepreneurs are technologically competent people who have good enterprise ideas and a desire to strike out on their own. At the same time, many of these individuals lack the knowledge or experience necessary to successfully transform an idea into a start-up and turn that initiative into a stable or growing small business. This is where state and local governments can play an important role. They can provide (or help broker) financial, technical, and management assistance to reduce early-stage development costs, arrange help that can fill knowledge gaps, and establish a supportive entrepreneurial infrastructure. As new economic-development programs such as the ones discussed in this book become a standard fixture in homegrown business settings, a new era of technology-based small-business activity will likely evolve. The experience of the last decade indicates that technological and entrepreneurial development is an important component of economic growth. Catalytic government involvement to support such forces can lead to even greater economic prosperity.

NOTES

1.   Although the attraction-approach era is slowly declining, the competition for large facilities occasionally becomes supercharged when a large plum, such as the General Motors Saturn project, is announced to the public. Often the least attractive areas for industrial development compensate for their unattractiveness by offering the greatest amount of incentives. These areas can gain considerably if the industrial facility remains in the area and creates jobs. These areas also have the most to lose, that is, the up-front incentives offered, if the stay is short.

Appendix

Institute of Public Administration
The Pennsylvania State University
205 Burrowes Building
University Park, PA 16802

SURVEY OF ADVANCED TECHNOLOGY
FIRMS IN PENNSYLVANIA

SECTION I — Background Information

1. Is your facility a:
   (1) _____ single plant operation or
   (2) _____ the headquarters for a multiplant operation?
   (3) _____ other (specify) _____

2. How many years has your firm been in operation? _____ yrs
   How many years has your firm been in Pennsylvania? _____ yrs
   How many years has it been at its present location? _____ yrs

3. Where is your business located? County _____
   Municipality (city, borough or township) _____

4. Is this the correct Standard Industrial Classification (SIC) of your principal product?
   _____ (SIC) (1) _____ yes (2) _____ no

5. If this is not the correct SIC or no longer represents your major category of product or service, fill in the correct SIC or identify the major product or service.
   (SIC) _____ or product _____

6. What percentage of your current sales are made in each of the following geographic areas?

   (1) within Pennsylvania _____%   (3) within remainder of U.S. _____%
   (2) within Mid-Atlantic/Northeastern region (4) internationally _____%
       (exclusive of Pennsylvania) _____ %

7. What percent of your gross sales revenue is devoted to research and development? _____%

8. What is the present employment of your firm in Pennsylvania, _____
   and the total employment of the firm? _____

9. Indicate the percentage increase or decrease in employment of your firm, for the past two years.

   Pennsylvania: + _____% or – _____%
   Total: + _____% or – _____%

   In the next two years, do you plan to increase the total employment of your firm? (Check all that apply)

   (1) _____ no plans for increasing employment
   (2) _____ increase at present site by _____ employees
   (3) _____ increase at another site in Pennsylvania by _____ employees
   (4) _____ increase in another state (specify) _____ by _____ employees
   (5) _____ expansion outside the U.S. (country) _____ by _____ employees

10. What percentage of your firm is owned by current managers?

    (1) _____ 25% or less   (3) _____ 51% to 75%
    (2) _____ 26% to 50%   (4) _____ 76% or more

11. What is your present title/position? _____

SECTION II — Attractiveness of Present Location

12. We want to know how you feel about factors that affect business operations at your current location. Please rate the attractiveness of each item listed on a scale ranging from 0 to 9. Circle the single value that best represents your belief. A 0 value indicates that the item is not applicable to your firm or its location. Values from 1 to 3 represent gradations of low attractiveness, values 4 to 6 represent moderate attractiveness and values 7 to 9 represent high attractiveness.

	NA	Current Attractiveness of Present Location	
Item			
Labor			
1. Availability of labor	0	1 2 3 4 5 6 7 8 9	___ 6
2. Skill level of labor	0	1 2 3 4 5 6 7 8 9	___ 7
3. Wage and salary levels	0	1 2 3 4 5 6 7 8 9	___ 8
4. Labor productivity	0	1 2 3 4 5 6 7 8 9	___ 9
Government			
5. Taxes on business income and property	0	1 2 3 4 5 6 7 8 9	___10
6. Taxes on personal income and property	0	1 2 3 4 5 6 7 8 9	___11
7. Local regulations (zoning, building codes, etc.)	0	1 2 3 4 5 6 7 8 9	___12
8. State regulations (environmental, business, etc.)	0	1 2 3 4 5 6 7 8 9	___13
9. Local government attitude toward business	0	1 2 3 4 5 6 7 8 9	___14
10. State government attitude toward business	0	1 2 3 4 5 6 7 8 9	___15
Business Operations			
			___16
11. Proximity to markets	0	1 2 3 4 5 6 7 8 9	___17
12. Cost /availability of energy	0	1 2 3 4 5 6 7 8 9	___18
13. Cost of industrial or commercial property	0	1 2 3 4 5 6 7 8 9	___19
14. Capital availability	0	1 2 3 4 5 6 7 8 9	
15. Developed local infrastructure (roads, utilities, sewer, etc.)	0	1 2 3 4 5 6 7 8 9	___20
16. Regional surface transportation network	0	1 2 3 4 5 6 7 8 9	___21
17. Proximity to major research universities	0	1 2 3 4 5 6 7 8 9	___22
18. Proximity to large commercial airport	0	1 2 3 4 5 6 7 8 9	___23
19. Availability of business services	0	1 2 3 4 5 6 7 8 9	___24
20. Availability of land for expansion	0	1 2 3 4 5 6 7 8 9	___25
21. Interaction with firms in area	0	1 2 3 4 5 6 7 8 9	___26
Living Arrangements			
22. Good schools for children	0	1 2 3 4 5 6 7 8 9	___27
23. Availability of recreational activities	0	1 2 3 4 5 6 7 8 9	___28
24. Availability of cultural activities	0	1 2 3 4 5 6 7 8 9	___29
25. Proximity to family and/or friends	0	1 2 3 4 5 6 7 8 9	___30
26. Cost of living	0	1 2 3 4 5 6 7 8 9	___31
27. Adequate mid-priced housing	0	1 2 3 4 5 6 7 8 9	___32
28. Crime rate	0	1 2 3 4 5 6 7 8 9	___33
29. Reasonable commuting distance	0	1 2 3 4 5 6 7 8 9	___34
30. Meteorological climate	0	1 2 3 4 5 6 7 8 9	___35
31. Environmental quality	0	1 2 3 4 5 6 7 8 9	___36

13. From the preceding list of 31 items and others not included on the list, in the left column rank in descending order the top five items that influenced the decision to locate at your present site. Using the same list of 31 items or others not included on the list, in the right column rank in descending order the top five items that would affect a future decision to expand at your present site or another nearby site.

Initial Location	Possible Expansion	
1st _____	1st _____	___37 ___38
2nd _____	2nd _____	___39 ___40
3rd _____	3rd _____	___41 ___42
4th _____	4th _____	___43 ___44
5th _____	5th _____	___45 ___46
		___47 ___48
		___49 ___50
		___51 ___52
		___53 ___54
		___55 ___56

236

SECTION III — Education and Training

In this section, we are interested in training and the role of educational institutions. If you are uncertain regarding the definitions of terms used in this section, see the back of the cover letter.

14. Indicate the percentage makeup of your present work force for each of the following four categories:

- 1. _____ % unskilled
- 2. _____ % skilled
- 3. _____ % technical
- 4. _____ % professional

```
57    58
59    60
61    62
63    64
```

15. Rate the difficulty you have in recruiting qualified potential employees from your local area. Circle the single value that best represents your belief. A 0 represents not applicable. Values 1 to 3 represent little difficulty in locating candidates, values 4 to 6 represent moderate difficulty and values 7 to 9 represent considerable difficulty.

	NA	Difficulty of Recruitment	
1. unskilled	0	1 2 3 4 5 6 7 8 9	65
2. skilled	0	1 2 3 4 5 6 7 8 9	66
3. technical	0	1 2 3 4 5 6 7 8 9	67
4. professional	0	1 2 3 4 5 6 7 8 9	68

16. For each of the four categories of skills, please indicate the predominant mode of entry level training. Circle one value for each labor category.

	No Training	Modes			
		Predominantly Within Firm	Predominantly Outside Firm	Combination Strategy	
1. unskilled	0	1	2	3	73 74
2. skilled	0	1	2	3	75 76
3. technical	0	1	2	3	77 78
4. professional	0	1	2	3	79 80

```
69
70
71
72
```

17. Rate the importance of the following roles that universities and colleges in Pennsylvania play in your business activities. Circle the single value that best represents your belief. Values 1 to 3 represent a minor role, values 4 to 6 represent a moderate role and values 7 to 9 represent a major role.

```
    1
2    3
4    5
```

	NA	Role of Universities in Business Activities	
1. Degree program for employees	0	1 2 3 4 5 6 7 8 9	6
2. Faculty research activity	0	1 2 3 4 5 6 7 8 9	7
3. Faculty consultants	0	1 2 3 4 5 6 7 8 9	8
4. Access to laboratories	0	1 2 3 4 5 6 7 8 9	9
5. Access to libraries and information systems	0	1 2 3 4 5 6 7 8 9	10
6. College graduates	0	1 2 3 4 5 6 7 8 9	11
7. Cultural activities	0	1 2 3 4 5 6 7 8 9	12
8. Part-time teaching opportunities for employees	0	1 2 3 4 5 6 7 8 9	13
9. Joint research efforts	0	1 2 3 4 5 6 7 8 9	14
10. Other (specify) _____	0	1 2 3 4 5 6 7 8 9	15

SECTION IV — Sources of Financing

In this section, we are interested in some of the financial arrangements and considerations that may affect your firm. This information is important to us to determine how advanced technology financial needs can be better served.

18. For the purposes of this study, venture capital is defined as capital necessary to allow a business to start up and/or grow through early stages of development, excluding personal resources of the firm's principals. Have you ever obtained, or tried to obtain, venture capital financing:

(a) from Pennsylvania sources?

    (1) _____ no (go to question 18b)

    (2) _____ yes Were you successful? (1) ___ No (2) ___ Yes (3) ___ Mixed Success

```
16
17
```

(b) from out-of-state sources?

    (1) _____ no (go to question 19)

    (2) _____ yes Were you successful? (1) ___ No (2) ___ Yes (3) ___ Mixed Success

```
18
19
```

19. Rate the availibility of venture capital for business startups in Pennsylvania, on a scale of 0 to 9. Circle the single value that best represents your belief. A 0 value indicates no knowledge of venture capital financing. Values 1 to 3 represent low accessibility, values 4 to 6 represent moderate accessibility and values 7 to 9 represent high accessibility.

NK   Accessibility of Venture Capital
0   1   2   3   4   5   6   7   8   9   ____ 20

20. What are your current sources of financial support? Please indicate in the appropriate column the approximate percentage of current capitalization from each source. In the other column, rate the difficulty of obtaining capital from each source listed. Circle the single value that represents your belief. A 0 value represents no knowledge of the source or it is not applicable to your firm. Values 1 and 2 represent little difficulty, 3 represents some difficulty and 4 and 5 represent considerable difficulty.

	Percentage of Current Capitalization	Difficulty of Obtaining Capital		

Equity Financing

1. Personal resources of firm/s principals _____ %   0 1 2 3 4 5   ____ 21 ____ 22
2. Private placement of stock to individuals _____ %   0 1 2 3 4 5   ____ 23 ____ 24
3. Private placement of stock to corporation which is
   not principally a financial institute _____ %   0 1 2 3 4 5   ____ 25 ____ 26
                                                                                  ____ 27
4. Private placement of stock to professional venture
   capital firm _____ %   0 1 2 3 4 5   ____ 28 ____ 29
5. Public sale of stock _____ %   0 1 2 3 4 5   ____ 30
6. Other (specify) _____ _____ %   0 1 2 3 4 5   ____ 31 ____ 32
                                                                                  ____ 33 ____ 34
Debt Financing   ____ 35 ____ 36

7. Commercial bank _____ %   0 1 2 3 4 5   ____ 37 ____ 38
8. Insurance company _____ %   0 1 2 3 4 5   ____ 39 ____ 40
9. Commercial finance company _____ %   0 1 2 3 4 5   ____ 41 ____ 42
10. Private placement to individuals _____ %   0 1 2 3 4 5   ____ 43 ____ 44
11. Public sale of taxable bonds _____ %   0 1 2 3 4 5   ____ 45 ____ 46
12. Tax-exempt industrial revenue bonds _____ %   0 1 2 3 4 5   ____ 47 ____ 48
13. Government-sponsored loan program
    (specify) _____ _____ %   0 1 2 3 4 5   ____ 49 ____ 50
14. Other (specify) _____ _____ %   0 1 2 3 4 5   ____ 51 ____ 52

The total for all items should be   100   %   ____ 53 ____ 54
                                                                                  ____ 55 ____ 56
21. Does your company stock trade publicly?   ____ 57 ____ 58

(1) _____ no   ____ 59 ____ 60
(2) _____ yes   On what exchange? _____   ____ 61 ____ 62

SECTION V — General Issues   ____ 63 ____ 64

Please mark the response that best matches your belief about each statement.

22. The business climate in Pennsylvania is favorable for advanced technology industries.
    strongly   strongly
    (1) ____ agree   (2) ____ agree   (3) ____ neutral   (4) ____ disagree   (5) ____ disagree   ____ 65

23. Generally, private financial institutions in Pennsylvania do not understand your company's product, market or risk position.
    strongly   strongly
    (1) ____ agree   (2) ____ agree   (3) ____ neutral   (4) ____ disagree·   (5) ____ disagree   ____ 66

24. Colleges and universities in Pennsylvania could be much more responsive in developing working relationships with advanced technology firms.
    strongly   strongly
    (1) ____ agree   (2) ____ agree   (3) ____ neutral   (4) ____ disagree   (5) ____ disagree   ____ 67

25. If you are interested in receiving information on state business assistance programs check the appropriate categories below.

(1) _____ financial programs   (3) _____ technical assistance   ____ 68 ____ 69
(2) _____ market development   (4) _____ work force training programs   ____ 70 ____ 71
                                                                                    ____ 72
26. Would you like to receive a free copy of the final report?   (1) _____ yes   (2) _____ no   ____ 73 ____ 74
                                                                                    ____ 75 ____ 76
Issues concerning advanced technology development are more complex than have been addressed in this survey. On an additional sheet, please make any comments or observations about critical concerns that may have been overlooked in this survey. Thank you for your assistance with this survey.   ____ 77 ____ 78
                                                                                    ____ 79 ____ 80

Bibliography

Abernathy, William J., and Richard S. Rosenbloom. 1982. "The Institutional Climate for Innovation in Industry: The Role of Management Attitudes and Practices." *Research Policy* 11:209-225.

Adcock, George, 1984. "Incentives for High Tech." *Industrial Development,* Site Selection Handbook, 153:546-550, 555.

Advisory Commission on Intergovernmental Relations. 1985. *The Question of State Government Capability.* Washington, D.C.: Government Printing Office.

Ady, Robert M. 1983. "High-Technology Plants: Different Criteria for the Best Location." *Economic Development Commentary* 7:8-11.

Ady, Robert M. 1981. "Shifting Factors in Plant Location." *Industrial Development* 150:13-18.

AFL-CIO. 1983. "The Future of Work." Report by the Committee on the Evolution of Work, AFL-CIO, Washington, D.C., August, 1983.

Alexander Grant and Co. 1984. "General Manufacturing Business Climates: 1983." Chicago: Alexander Grant and Co.

Allen, David N. 1985. *Small Business Incubators and Enterprise Development.* A Report for the U.S. Department of Commerce. Washington, D.C.: Economic Development Administration.

Allen, David N., Judith E. Ginsburg, and Susan Marx. 1984. *Home-Grown Entrepreneurship: Pennsylvania's Small Business Incubators.* University Park, PA: Institute of Public Administration.

Allen, David N., and Greg E. Robertson. 1983. *Silicon, Sensors and Software: Listening to Advanced Technology Enterprises in Pennsylvania.* University Park, PA: Institute of Public Administration and the Pennsylvania MILRITE Council.

Allen, Gerald L. 1984. *Colorado High Technology Industry Survey.* Business Research Division, Graduate School of Business Administration. Boulder, CO: University of Colorado.

American Bankers Association. 1982. "Commercial Banks." In *Investing in America,* edited by Renee A. Burger, Kristen S. Moy, Neal R. Pierce, and Carol Steinbach, pp. 11-34. Washington, D.C.: The President's Task Force on Private Sector Initiatives.

American Electronics Association. 1983. "Technical Employment Projections, 1983-1987." In *Workplace Perspective on Education and Training,* edited by P. E. Doeringer, pp. 1-184. Boston, MA: Martinus Nijoff.

Andrews, Victor L., and Peter C. Eiseman. 1981. *Who Finances Small Business Circa 1980?* Washington, D.C.: Interagency Task Force on Small Business Finance.

Armington, Catherine, and Marjorie Odle. 1982. "Small Business – How Many Jobs?" *The Brookings Review,* Winter, pp. 14-17.

Armington, Catherine, Candee Harris, and Marjorie Odle. 1984. "Formation and Growth in High-Technology Firms: A Regional Assessment." In *Technology, Innovation and Regional Economic Development,* pp. 108-144. U.S. Congress. Washington, D.C.: Office of Technology Assessment.

Arthur Anderson & Co. 1983. *San Francisco's Strategic Plan: Making a Great City Greater.* San Francisco, CA: Arthur Anderson.

Ayers, Robert U. 1983. *Robotics: Applications and Social Implications.* Cambridge, MA: Ballinger.

Bates, Timothy. 1983. "A Review of the Small Business Administration's Major Loan Programs." In *Small Business Finance,* edited by Paul M. Horitz and R. Richardson Pettit, pp. 211-239. Greenwich, CT: JAI Press.

Bates, Timothy, and William Bradford. 1979. *Financing Black Economic Development.* New York: Academic Press.

Batra, Reveendra, and Gerald Scully. 1972. "Technical Progress, Economic Growth, and the North-South Wage Differential." *Journal of Regional Science* 12:375-386.

Battelle Memorial Institute. 1982a. "The Development of Research and Science Parks: Problems and Potentials." Special Report III prepared for the New York State Science and Technology Foundation. Columbus, OH: Battelle-Columbus Laboratories.

Battelle Memorial Institute. 1982b. "The Higher Education System in New York and Its Potential." Prepared by the New York State Science and Technology Foundation. Columbus, Ohio: Battelle-Columbus Laboratories.

Becker, Gary S. 1975. *Human Capital.* 2nd ed. New York: Columbia University Press.

Ben Franklin Partnership Fund Board. 1985. "30 Month Progress Report: Ben Franklin Partnership Challenge Grant Program for Technological Innovation." Harrisburg, PA: Pennsylvania Department of Commerce.

Bendick, Marc, Jr. 1983. "The Role of Public Programs and Private Markets in Reemploying Displaced Workers." *Policy Studies Review* 2:715-733.

Birch, David L. 1985. "Matters of Fact." *Inc.* 7:31-42.

Birch, David L. 1984. "The Changing Rules of the Game: Finding a Niche in the Thoughtware Economy." *Economic Development Commentary* 8:12-16.

Birch, David L. 1979. *The Job Generation Process.* Cambridge, MA: MIT Program on Neighborhood and Regional Change.

Birley, Susan. 1984. "Finding the New Firm." In *Academy of Management Proceedings 1984,* edited by John A. Pearce and Richard Robinson, Jr., Academy of Management, pp. 64-68.

Birley, Susan. 1985. "The Role of Networks in the Entrepreneurial Process." *Journal of Business Venturing* 1:107-111.

Blalock, Hubert M. 1972. *Social Statistics.* New York: McGraw-Hill.

Bloch, Erich. 1983. "The Corporate Mission in Research and Development." In *Partners in the Research Enterprise,* edited by Thomas Hangfitt, Sheldon Hackney, Alfred Fishman, and Albert Glowsky, pp. 99-108. Pittsburgh, PA: University of Pennsylvania Press.

Bluestone, Barry, and Harrison Bennett. 1982. *The Deindustrialization of America.* New York: Basic Books.

Booth, Douglas E., and Louis C. Fortis. 1984. "Building a Cooperative Economy: A Strategy for Community Based Economic Development." *Review of Social Economy* 43:339-359.

Brennan, Peter J. 1983. "Advanced Technology Centers: Strategies for Corporate Growth." *Scientific American* 248:E3-E16.

Brevard, Cornelius. 1980. "Partnership Interaction and Effectiveness." In *Private Management and Public Policy: Reciprocal Impacts,* edited by Benton Lewis, pp. 19-39. Lexington, MA: Lexington Books.

Bridges, Benjamin. 1965. "State and Local Inducement for Industry." *National Tax Journal* 18:1-15.

Brockhaus, Robert H. 1982. "The Psychology of the Entrepreneur." In *Encyclopedia of Entrepreneurship,* edited by Calvin A. Kent, Donald L. Sexton, and Karl H. Vesper, pp. 39-55. Englewood Cliffs, NJ: Prentice Hall.

Brockhaus, Robert H. 1980. "Risk Taking Propensity of Entrepreneurs." *Academy of Management Journal* 23:509-520.

Brody, Herb. 1985. "States Vie for a Slice of the Pie." *High Technology* 5:16-28.

Brooks, Harvey, 1983. "Technology, Competition, and Employment." *American Academy of Political and Social Science* 470:115-122.

Brown, Wayne S. 1985. "A Proposed Mechanism for Commercializing University Technology." *Technovation* 3:19-25.

Browne, Lynn E. 1983. "High Technology and Business Services." *New England Economics Review*, July/August, pp. 5-17.

Bruno, Albert V., and Tyzoon T. Tyebjee. 1982. "The Environment for Entrepreneurship." In *Encyclopedia of Entrepreneurship*, edited by Calvin A. Kent, Donald L. Sexton, and Karl H. Vesper, pp. 288-315. Englewood Cliffs, NJ: Prentice Hall.

Brunn, Michael O. 1980. "Technology Transfer and Entrepreneurship." In *Research Development and Technological Innovation*, edited by Devendra Sahal, pp. 203-214. Lexington, MA: D. C. Heath.

Buck, M. Allison, Daryl J. Hobbs, Donald D. Myers, and Nancy C. Munshaw. 1984. "Feasibility of High-Tech Company Incubation in Rural University Settings." Rolla, MO: Missouri IncuTech, Inc.

Burgraf, Shirley P. 1983. "Overview and Critique of Revitalization Issues." *Policy Studies Review* 2:666-676.

Burrows, James C., Charles Metcalf, and John B. Kaler. 1971. *Industrial Location in the United States*. Lexington, MA: D. C. Heath.

Business-Higher Education Forum. 1983. "America's Competitive Challenge." Report to the President of the United States. Washington, D.C.: Business-Higher Education Forum.

Business Week. 1985. "Americas High-Tech Crisis." *Business Week*, March 11, 1985, pp. 56-60, 62, 67.

Business Week. 1984a. "A 'Yale Connection' Brings New Hope to an Old City." *Business Week*, October 29, 1984, pp. 32D, 32H.

Business Week. 1984b. "Will Money Managers Wreck the Economy?" *Business Week*, August 13, 1984, pp. 86-93.

Business Week, 1984c. "The Myth of the Vanishing Middle Class." *Business Week*, July 9, 1984, pp. 83, 86.

Business Week. 1984d. "The Revival of Productivity: The U.S. Is Poised for a Strong, Sustained Surge in Worker Efficiency." *Business Week*, February 13, 1984, pp. 92-100.

Business Week. 1983. "Industrial Policy: Is It the Answer?" *Business Week*, July 4, 1983, pp. 54-62.

Campbell, Alan K. 1958. "Taxes and Industrial Location in the New York Metropolitan Region." *National Tax Journal* 11:195-218.

Carland, James W., Frank Hoy, William Boulton, and JoAnn C. Carland. 1984. "Differentiating Entrepreneurs from Small Business Owners: A Conceptualization." *Academy of Management Review* 9:354-359.

Carlberg, Michael. 1981. "A Neoclassical Model of Interregional Economic Growth." *Regional Science and Urban Economics* 11:191-203.

Charpie, Robert et al. 1967. *Technological Innovation: Its Environment and Management*. U.S. Department of Commerce. Washington, D.C.: Government Printing Office.

Chase Econometrics. 1984. *Long Term Regional Forecasts*. Bala Cynwyd, PA: Chase Econometrics.

Choate, Pat. 1982. "Retooling the American Work Force." In *Workplace Perspective on Education and Training*, edited by Peter E. Doeringer, pp. 1-49. Boston, MA: Martinus Nijoff.

Churchill, Neil C., and Virginia L. Lewis. 1983. "The Five Stages of Small Business Growth." *Harvard Business Review* 61:30-50.

Committee for Economic Development. 1982. *Public-Private Partnership: An Opportunity for Urban Communities*. Washington, D.C.: Committee for Economic Development.

Congressional Budget Office. 1985. *Federal Financial Support for High-Technology Industries*. U.S. Congress. Washington, D.C.: Government Printing Office.

Congressional Budget Office. 1981. *Small Issue Industrial Revenue Bonds*. U.S. Congress. Washington, D.C.: Government Printing Office.

Conway Data Inc. 1984. "The Fifth Legislative Climates." *Industrial Development* 153: 4-13.

Conway, McKinley. 1985. "The Megatech Industries: What Determines Their Location?" *Industrial Development*, Site Selection Handbook 154:626-635.

Cooper, Arnold C. 1982. "The Entrepreneurship – Small Business Interface." In *Encyclopedia of Entrepreneurship,* edited by Calvin A. Kent, Donald L. Sexton, and Karl Vesper, pp. 193-207. Englewood Cliffs, NJ: Prentice Hall.

Cooper, Arnold C. 1979. "Strategic Management: New Ventures and Small Business." In *Strategic Management,* edited by Dan E. Schendel and Charles W. Hofer, pp. 316-327. Boston, MA: Little, Brown.

Cooper, Arnold C. 1971. *The Founding of Technologically-Based Firms.* Milwaukee, WI: Center for Venture Management.

Cooper, Arnold C., William C. Dunkelberg, and Stanley Furta. 1985. "Incubator Organization Background and Founding Characteristics." In *Frontiers of Entrepreneurship Research,* edited by John A. Hornaday, Edward B. Shils, Jeffery A. Timmons, and Karl H. Vesper, pp. 61-79. Wellesley, MA: Center for Entrepreneurial Studies.

Cooper, Arnold C., Gary E. Willard, and Carolyn Woo. 1984. "Strategies of High Performing New and Small Firms: A Re-Examination of the Niche Concept." Paper presented at the fourth annual Strategic Management Society Conference. Philadelphia, PA: Wharton School.

Cooper, Arnold C., and Arthur Riggs, II. 1975. "Non-Traditional Approaches to Technology Utilization." *Journal of the Society of Research Administrators,* Winter, pp. 12-19.

Council for Northeast Economic Action. 1982. *How Banks Participate in Local Economic Development: Five Models.* Boston, MA: Council for Northeast Economic Action.

Council of State Planning Agencies. 1980. "State and Local Investment Strategies." Washington, D.C.: Council of State Planning Agencies.

Coy, Robert W. 1984. *The Pennsylvania Economy: Past, Present and Future.* Harrisburg, PA: The Pennsylvania MILRITE Council.

Coy, Robert W. 1982. *Human and R&D Resources for Advanced Technology in Pennsylvania.* Harrisburg, PA: The Pennsylvania MILRITE Council.

Daniels, Belden, and Nancy Barbe. 1981. *Development Finance: The New England Experience Reconsidered.* Cambridge, MA: Council for Community Development.

Davies, Stephen. 1980. "Diffusion, Innovation and Market Structure." In *Research, Development, and Technological Innovation,* edited by Devendra Sahal, pp. 153-170. Lexington, MA: D. C. Heath.

DeJong, Gordon R. 1983. "Demographic Forces Reshaping Pennsylvania's Economy in the 1980s." *What's Ahead for Pennsylvania's Economy?* A Report from a conference on Pennsylvania's economic future, April 19, Camp Hill, Pennsylvania.

Demuth, Jerry. 1984. "What Can Incubators Offer?" *Venture* 6:78-84.

Denison, Edward F. 1979. *Accounting for Slower Economic Growth: The United States in the 1970's.* Washington, D.C.: The Brookings Institution.

Denison, Edward F. 1974. *Accounting for United States Economic Growth 1929-1969.* Washington, D.C.: The Brookings Institution.

Denison, Edward F. 1962. *The Sources of Economic Growth in the U.S. and the Alternatives Before Us.* New York: Committee for Economic Development.

Disman, Allan M. 1983. "State Capital Formation and Small Business Needs." *Governmental Finance* 12:13-22.

Doeringer, Peter, and Patricia Pannell. 1982. "Manpower Strategies for New England's High Technology Sector." In *New England's Vital Resource: The Labor Force,* edited by John Hoy and Melvin Bernstein, pp. 11-35. Washington, D.C.: American Council on Education.

Doody, Eugene, and Betsy Munzer. 1981. *High Technology Employment: Massachusetts and Selected States.* Boston, MA: Massachusetts Division of Employment Security.

Downs, Anthony. 1967. *Inside Bureaucracy.* Boston, MA: Little, Brown.

Doyle, Peter H., and Candice Brisson. 1985. *Partners in Growth: Business-Higher Education Development Strategies.* Washington, D.C.: Northeast-Midwest Institute, The Center for Regional Policy.

Drucker, Peter. 1985. *Innovation and Entrepreneurship: Practice and Principals.* New York: Harper & Row.

Duckworth, Robert P., John M. Simmons, and Robert H. McNulty. 1985. *The Entrepreneurial American City.* Washington, D.C.: Partners for Livable Places.

Dye, Thomas R. 1980. *The Determinants of Public Policy.* Lexington, MA: Lexington Books.

Education Commission of the States. 1983. Task Force on Education for Economic Growth. Denver, CO: Education Commission of the States.

Employee Benefit Research Institute. 1982. "Pension Funds." In *Investing in America,* edited by Renee A. Berger, Kristen S. Moy, Neal R. Pierce, and Carol Steinbach, pp. 69-79. Washington, D.C.: The President's Task Force on Private Sector Initiatives.

Epping, G. Michael. 1982. "Important Factors in Plant Location in 1980." *Growth and Change* 13:47-51.

Ehrbar, A. F. 1983. "Grasping the New Unemployment." *Fortune* 107:106-126.

Erickson, Rodney, James H. Miller, and Michael J. Wasylenko. 1983. "The Competitive Position of Pennsylvania Businesses." Report of the Business Council of Pennsylvania, Harrisburg, PA.

Erickson, Rodney. 1972. "The 'Lead Firm' Concept: An Analysis of Theoretical Elements." *Tijdschrift voor Economische en Sociale Geografie* 63:426-437.

Etzioni, Amitai. 1983. "Reindustrialization of America." *Policy Studies Review* 2:677-694.

Ewers, H. J., and R. W. Wettman. 1980. "Innovation-Oriented Regional Policy." *Regional Studies* 14:161-179.

Farrel, Kevin. 1984. "The Trick to Selling a Small Deal." *Venture* 6:56, 58, 60.

Feller, Irwin. 1984. "Political and Administrative Aspects of High Technology Programs." *Policy Studies Review* 3:460-466.

Feller, Irwin. 1981. "Three Coigns on Diffusion Research." In *The Knowledge Cycle,* edited by Robert Rich, pp. 81-97. Beverly Hills, CA: Sage.

Feller, Irwin. 1974. "Innovation, Diffusion and Industrial Location." *Locational Dynamics of Manufacturing Activity,* edited by I. Collins and D. Walker, pp. 83-107. New York: Wiley.

Fischel, William A. 1975. "Fiscal and Environmental Considerations in the Location of Firms in Suburban Communities." In *Fiscal Zoning and Land Use Controls,* edited by E. S. Mills and W. E. Oats, pp. 119-173. Lexington, MA: D. C. Heath.

Fisher, Peter S. 1983. "The Role of the Public Sector in Local Development Finance." *Journal of Economic Issues* 17:133-153.

Fortune. 1984. "Good News Ahead for Productivity." *Fortune* 110:40-52.

Friedman, Robert. 1983. "Reducing Unemployment Through Enterprise Development." *Economic Development and Law Center Report,* July/August, pp. 11-17.

Friedman, Stephen B. 1981. "Assessing Public Incentives for Private Development." *Management Information Services Reports* 13. Washington, D.C.: International City Management Association.

Fuchs, Victor R. 1962. *Changes in the Location of Manufacturing in the United States Since 1929*. New Haven, CT: Yale University Press.

Furst, Al. 1984. "Incubators Hatch More Than Chickens." *High Technology* 4:70-71.

Fusfeld, Herbert I. 1983. "Overview of University-Industry Research Interactions." In *Partners in the Research Enterprise,* edited by Thomas Hangfitt and Sheldon Hackney, pp. 10-20. Philadelphia, PA: University of Pennsylvania Press.

Ganz, Carole. 1981. "Linkages Between Knowledge, Creation, Diffusion and Utilization." In *The Knowledge Cycle,* edited by Robert Rich, pp. 185-206. Beverly Hills, CA: Sage.

Gasse, Yvon. 1982. "Elaborates on the Psychology of the Entrepreneur." In *Encyclopedia of Entrepreneurship,* edited by Calvin A. Kent, Donald L. Sexton, and Karl Vesper, pp. 57-66. Englewood Cliffs, NJ: Prentice Hall.

Gill, Michael D., Jr. 1984. "A Status Report on Selected Segments of the Venture Capital Industry." *Technology Venturing: American Innovation and Risk Taking.* Austin, TX: The Institute for Constructive Capitalism.

Glasmeier, Amy K. 1984. "High Technology Industries in the Mid-1970s: The Distribution of Industries and Employment." Institute of Urban and Regional Development. Berkeley, CA: University of California.

Glasmeier, Amy K., Peter G. Hall, and Ann R. Markusen. 1984. "Recent Evidence on High-Technology Industries' Spatial Tendencies: A Preliminary Investigation." *Technology, Innovation and Regional Economic Development.* U.S. Congress. Washington, D.C.: Office of Technology Assessment. Appendix C, pp. 145-167.

Gold, Bela. 1981. "Technological Diffusion in Industry: Research Needs and Shortcoming." *Journal of Industrial Economics* 29:247-269.

Gottlieb, Daniel. 1983. "High Technology Surges." *High Technology* 3:70-73.

Governor's High Tech Cabinet Council. 1985. *High Tech in Colorado: Maintaining Our Competitive Edge.* First Year Report and Executive Summary of High Technology Strategic Plan. Denver, CO: Governor's High Tech Cabinet Council.

Greenhut, Melvin. 1956. *Plant Location in Theory and Practice.* Chapel Hill: University of North Carolina Press.

Gregerman, Alan S. 1984. *Competitive Advantage: Framing a Strategy to Support High Growth Firms.* Washington, D.C.: National Council for Economic Development.

Grossman, Ilene K. 1984. *Initiatives in State Economic Development.* Chicago: Business Development Task Force of the Midwestern Conference of the Council of State Governments.

Grubb, W. Norton. 1984. "The Bandwagon Once More: Vocational Preparation for High-Tech Occupations." Program Report No. 84-B6, May, Institute for Research on Educational Finance and Governance. Palo Alto, CA: Stanford University.

Gunn, Thomas G. 1982. "The Mechanization of Design and Manufacturing." *Scientific American* 247 (September 1983):115-144.

Hall, Peter, Ann Markusen, Richard Osborn, and Barbara Wachsman. 1983. "The Computer Software Industry: Prospects and Policy Issues." Working Paper No. 410, Institute of Urban and Regional Development. Berkeley, CA: University of California.

Hall, Richard H. 1972. *Organizations: Structure and Process.* Englewood Cliffs, NJ: Prentice Hall.

Hall, William K. 1980. "Survival Strategies in a Hostile Environment." *Harvard Business Review* 58:75-85.

Hambrecht, William R. 1984. "Venture Capital and the Growth of Silicon Valley." *California Management Review* 24:74-82.

Hangfitt, Thomas W., Sheldon Hackney, Alfred P. Fishman, and Albert V. Glowsky, eds. 1983. "Government, Industry and Academia: A Burmuda Triangle?" In *Partners in the Research Enterprise.* Pittsburgh, PA: University of Pennsylvania Press.

Hansen, Derek. 1981. *Banking and Small Business.* Washington, D.C.: The Council of State Planning Agencies.

Harding, Charles F. 1983. "Local Initiatives." *Technology, Innovation and Regional Economic Development: Encouraging High Technology Development,* Paper no. 2, pp. 39-49, Office of Technology Assessment. Washington, D.C.: Government Printing Office.

Hayes, Thomas C. 1983. "Brainpower: A New National Concern." *New York Times,* March 27, 1983, p. 5.

Heller International Corporation. 1984. *A Small Business Agenda for the 1980s.* Chicago: Institute for Small Business.

Hill, Christopher T., and James M. Utterback. 1980. "The Dynamics of Product and Process Innovation." *Management Review* 69:14-20.

Hill, Christopher T., and James M. Utterback. 1979. *Technological Innovation for a Dynamic Economy*. New York: Pergamon.

Hise, Robert T., Charles Futrell, and Donald Snyder. 1980. "University Research Centers as a New Product Development Resource." *Research Management* 23: 25-28.

Hoffman, Eric, and Paul M. Roman. 1984. "The Effect of Organizational Emphases Upon the Diffusion of Information About Innovations." *Journal of Management* 10:277-292.

Holland, Robert C. 1982. "Public-Private Partnerships: Key Options for America's Cities." *The Journal of the Institute for Socioeconomic Studies* 7:36-47.

Hoover, Edgar M. 1948. *The Location of Economic Activity*. New York: McGraw Hill.

Hoover, Edgar M., and R. Vernon. 1959. *Anatomy of a Metropolis*. Cambridge, MA: Harvard University Press.

Howell, James M. 1982. "States as Economic Laboratories." *Society* 19:58-62.

Hoy, John C., and Melvin H. Burnstein. 1981. *Business and Academia: Partners in New England's Economic Renewal*. Hanover, NH: University Press of New England.

Hrebiniak, I. G. 1978. *Complex Organizations*. St. Paul, MN: West.

Hula, Richard C. 1985. "Marketing Strategies as Policy Tools: The Search for Alternative Approaches to Urban Revitalization." *Journal of Public Policy* 4:181-207.

Institute for Research on Educational Finance and Governance. 1983. "Education and Work." *IFG Policy Notes* 4:1-8.

Ioannou, Lori. 1985. "States Move to Stake Entrepreneurs." *Venture* 7:60-62, 69.

Institute for Small Business. 1984. *The Nine Prime Issues: A Small Business Agenda for the 1980's*. Chicago: Heller International Corporation.

Jackman, Thomas. 1983. "A Field with Something for Every Body." *New York Times High Technology Supplement*, March 27, 1983, pp. 36-37.

Jacobs, Jerry. 1979. *Bidding for Business: Corporate Auctions and the 50 Disunited States*. Washington, D.C.: Public Interest Research Group.

Jarboe, Kenan P. 1984. "High Technology Firms in the Ann Arbor Area: A Survey of Location Decision Factors." Ann Arbor: Michigan Technology Council.

Johnson, P. S., and D. G. Cathcart. 1979. "The Founders of New Manufacturing Firms: A Note on the Size of Their 'Incubator' Plants." *The Journal of Industrial Economics* 28:219-224.

Katz, Daniel, and Robert Kahn. 1978. *The Social Psychology of Organizations*. New York: Wiley.

Kelton, Christina M. L. 1983. *Trends in the Relocation of U.S. Manufacturing*. Ann Arbor, MI: UMI Research Press.

Kennedy, Charles, and A. P. Thirwall. 1972. "Technical Progress: A Survey." *Economic Journal* 82:11-72.

Kent, Calvin A. 1982. "Entrepreneurship in Economic Development." In *Encyclopedia of Entrepreneurship*, edited by Calvin A. Kent, Donald L. Sexton, and Karl H. Vesper, pp. 237-256. Englewood Cliffs, NJ: Prentice Hall.

Kieschnick, Michael. 1981. *Taxes and Growth: Business Incentives and Economic Development*. Washington, D.C.: The Council of State Planning Agencies.

Kilby, Peter. 1971. *Entrepreneurship and Economic Development*. New York: The Free Press.

Kleinfield, N. R. 1984. "A Few Clouds Over Route 128." *New York Times*, July 18, 1984, pp. D1, D17.

Knack, Ruth, James J. Bellus, and Patricia Adell. 1984. "Setting Up Shop for Economic Development." In *Shaping the Local Economy: Current Perspectives on Economic Development*, edited by Cheryl Farr, pp. 41-49. Washington, D.C.: International City Management Association.

Kravitz, Lee. 1984a. "The Venture Capital 100." *Venture* 6:60-68.

Kravitz, Lee. 1984b. "Why SBIC's Want to Break from the SBA." *Venture* 6:64.

Krugman, Paul R. 1983. "Targeted Industrial Policies: Theory and Evidence." *Industrial Change and Public Policy*, pp. 123-126. Kansas City, KS: Federal Reserve Bank of Kansas City.

Kuttner, Robert. 1983. "The Declining Middle." *Atlantic Monthly*, July, 1983, pp. 60-72.

Kysiak, Ronald C. 1983. "City Entrepreneurship: Institutionalizing the Process." *Economic Development Commentary* 7 (Winter, 1983):20-23.

Landau, Martin, and Russel Stout. 1979. "To Manage Is Not to Control: Or the Folly of Type 2 Errors." *Public Administration Review* 39:148-156.

Lawrence, Paul R., and Davis Dyer. 1983. *Renewing American Industry*. New York: The Free Press.

Ledebur, Larry C., and David W. Rasmussen. 1984. "Economic Development in the Post-Federal Era: State Industrial Incentives." Paper presented at the annual meeting of the American Society for Public Administration, Denver, CO.

Levin, Henry M. 1984. "State Planning for Higher Education and Jobs in an Age of High Technology." Policy Paper No. 84-C1. Palo Alto, CA: Stanford University, School of Education.

Levin, Henry M., and Russell W. Rumberger. 1983. "The Educational Implications of High Technology." Institute for Research on Educational Finance and Governance. Palo Alto, CA: Stanford University.

Levy, John M. 1981. *Economic Development Programs for Cities, Counties and Towns*. New York: Praeger.

Liles, Patrick R. 1974. *New Business Ventures and the Entrepreneur*. Homewood, IL: Irwin.

Litvak, Lawrence. 1981. *Pensions Funds and Economics Renewal*. Studies in Development Policy 12. Washington, D.C.: The Council of State Planning Agencies.

Litvak, Lawrence, and Belden Daniels. 1979. *Innovations in Development Finance*. Studies in Development Policy 3. Washington, D.C.: The Council of State Planning Agencies.

Lloyd, Peter E., and Peter Dicken. 1977. *Location in Space: A Theoretical Approach to Economic Geography*. New York: Harper & Row.

Losch, August. 1954. *The Economics of Location*. New Haven, CT: Yale University Press.

Lund, Leonard. 1984. "Factors in Corporate Location Decisions." In *Crisis and Constraint in Municipal Finance*, edited by James H. Carr, pp. 267-288. Piscataway, NJ: Center for Urban Policy Research.

Malecki, Edward J. 1984. "High Technology and Local Economic Development." *Journal of the American Planning Association* 50:262-269.

Malecki, Edward J. 1983. "Technology and Regional Development: A Survey." *International Regional Science Review* 8:89-125.

Malecki, Edward J. 1981. "Science, Technology and Regional Economic Development: Review and Prospects." *Research Policy* 10:312-334.

Mansfield, Edwin. 1980. "Technology and Productivity in the United States." In *The American Economy in Transition*, edited by Martin Feldstein, pp. 563-616. Chicago, IL: University of Chicago Press.

Mansfield, Edwin. 1968. *Industrial Research and Technological Innovation*. New York: Norton.

Mansfield, Edwin, John Rapaport, Anthony Romeo, Edmond Villani, Samuel Wagner, and Frank Husic. 1977. *The Production and Application of New Industrial Technology*. New York: Norton.

Marcus, Bruce W. 1982. "Regional Economic Development and Public Development Banking." In *Mobilizing Capital*, edited by Peter J. Bearse, pp. 449-463. New York: Elsevier.

Markusen, Ann R. 1983. "High Tech Jobs, Markets and Economic Development Prospects." Working Paper No. 403. Institute of Urban and Regional Development. Berkeley, CA: University of California.

Marver, James D., and Carl V. Patton. 1976. "The Correlates of Consultation: American Academics in 'The Real World'." *Higher Education* 5:319-335.

Mazzoitti, Donald F., and John W. Savich. 1984. "State Advanced Technology Programs: New Initiatives for Cities." *Economic Development Commentary* 8:7-10.

McCaleb, Thomas S. 1983. "Tax Policy and Small Business Finance." In *Small Business Finance*, edited by Paul M. Horitz and R. Richardson Pettit, pp. 187-238. Greenwich, CT: JAI Press.

McCarthney, Iaton. 1983. "Academia, Inc." *Datamation*, March, 1983, pp. 1-5.

McCombie, J. S. L. 1982. "How Important is the Spatial Diffusion of Innovations in Explaining Regional Growth Rate Disparities?" *Urban Studies* 19:377-382.

McGowan, William. 1983. "Can High-Tech Retraining Cure the Terminally Unemployed?" *Business and Society Review*, Summer, 1983, pp. 52-56.

Mendell, Stefanie, and Daniel M. Ennis. 1985. "Looking at Innovation Strategies." *Research Management* 28:33-40.

Merrifield, D. Bruce. 1984. "Research and Development Limited Partnerships: The Need for Cooperative Research." In *Economic Development Commentary* 8:9-11.

Mescon, Timothy S., and Sheila A. Adams. 1980. "Incubating New Business Development: The Texas Connection." *Southwest Business and Economic Review* 18:1-12.

Meyers, Marlee S. 1984. "Innovative Techniques for Research and Development Financing." In *Proceedings of the International Congress on Technology and Technology Exchange,* pp. 519-520. Pittsburgh, PA: International Technology Institute.

Mincer, Jacob. 1974. *Schooling, Experience and Earnings.* New York: Columbia University Press.

Moore, Barbara H. 1983. *The Entrepreneur in Local Government.* Washington, D.C.: International City Management Association.

Moore, William L., and Michael Tushman. 1982. "Managing Innovations Over the Product Life Cycle." In *Readings in the Management of Innovation,* edited by Michael Tushman and William Moore, pp. 131-150. Boston, MA: Pitman.

Moriarty, Barry M. 1978. "A Note on Unexplained Residuals in North-South Wage Differential Models." *Journal of Regional Science* 18:105-108.

Morrison, Edward F. 1985. "Small Business: A Strategic Perspective." *Economic Development Commentary* 9:7-11.

Mulkey, David, and B. L. Dillman. 1976. "Location and the Effects of State and Local Development Subsidies." *Growth and Change* 7:71-80.

Naisbitt, John. 1982. *Megatrends.* New York: Warner Books.

National Association of Small Business Investment Companies. 1982. "Venture Capital." In *Investing in America: Initiatives for Community and Economic Development,* pp. 81-95. Washington, D.C.: President's Task Force on Private Sector Initiatives.

National Governors Association. 1983. *Technology and Growth: State Initiatives in Technological Innovation.* Task Force on Technological Innovation. Washington, D.C.: National Governors Association.

National Science Board. 1982. "University-Industry Research Relationships: Myths, Realities, and Potentials." Fourteenth Annual Report. Washington, D.C.: National Science Foundation.

National Science Foundation. 1983a. "Trends to 1982 in Industrial Support of Basic Research." Special Report 83-302. Washington, D.C.: National Science Foundation.

National Science Foundation. 1983b. "Academic Employment of Scientists and Engineers Continued to Grow in 1982, but Slower than in Other Economic Sectors." *Science Resource Studies*, July 29, 1983, pp. 1-4.

National Science Foundation. 1982. *Academic Science R&D Funds: Fiscal Year 1980*. Washington, D.C.: Government Printing Office.

National Science Foundation. 1981a. "Problems of Small High Technology Firms." Special Report 81-305. Washington, D.C.: National Science Foundation.

National Science Foundation. 1981b. "The Process of Technological Innovations: Reviewing the Literature." In *Workplace Perspectives on Education and Training*, edited by P. E. Doeringer, pp. 46-59. Boston, MA: Martinus Nijoff.

National Science Foundation. 1980a. Unpublished data on scientists and engineers in the United States. Washington, D.C.

National Science Foundation. 1980b. *Research and Development in Industry, 1979*. Washington, D.C.: Government Printing Office.

Nelson, Richard R. 1981. "Research on Productivity Growth and Productivity Differences: Dead Ends and New Departures." *Journal of Economic Literature* 19:1029-1064.

Nelson, Richard R., Merton J. Peck, and Edward D. Kalachek. 1967. *Technology, Economic Growth and Public Policy*. Washington, D.C.: The Brookings Institution.

New York Times. 1985. "Saturn Bidders Swamp G.M." *New York Times*, March 22, 1985, p. D3.

New York Times. 1983. "Poverty Rate is Held Likely to Stay High Several Years." *New York Times*, October 19, 1983, p. 22.

North Carolina Board of Science and Technology. 1984. *New Challenges for a New Era*. Volume 2, Economic Revitalization Through Technological Innovation. Raleigh, NC: Office of the Governor.

Norton, R. D., and John Rees. 1979. "The Product Cycle and Spatial Decentralization of American Manufacturing." *Regional Studies* 13:141-151.

Oakey, Raymond P. 1981. *High Technology Industry and Industrial Location*. Aldershot, England: Gower.

Office of Technology Assessment. 1984a. *Technology, Innovation and Regional Economic Development.* Background Paper 2. Washington, D.C.: Government Printing Office.

Office of Technology Assessment. 1984b. *Technology, Innovation and Regional Economic Development.* Washington, D.C.: Government Printing Office.

Office of Technology Assessment. 1982. *Informational Technology and Its Impact on American Education.* Washington, D.C.: Government Printing Office.

Osborne, Alfred E. 1980. "Financing Small High Risk Enterprises." In *Cities and Firms,* edited by Bryce Herrington, pp. 133-158. Lexington, MA: Lexington Books.

O'Toole, James. 1983. "Getting Ready for the Next Industrial Revolution." *Phi Kappa Phi Journal* 63:16-18.

Pascarella, Thomas A., and Richard D. Raymond. 1982. "Buying Bonds for Business." *Urban Affairs Quarterly* 18:73-89.

Pavitt, Keith, ed. 1981. *Innovation and British Economic Performance.* London: MacMillan.

Pennsylvania Business Council. 1985. *1985 Update: The Competitive Position of Pennsylvania Businesses.* Harrisburg, PA: Pennsylvania Business Council.

Pennsylvania State Planning Board. 1981. *Choices for Pennsylvanians.* Harrisburg, PA: Commonwealth of Pennsylvania.

Perroux, Francois. 1973. "Multinational Investments and the Analysis of Development and Integration Poles." *Economies et Societes* 24:831-868.

Perroux, Francois. 1956. "Note sur la Notion de Pole de Croissance." *Economie Appliquee* 7:307-20. Tr. in *Economic Policy for Development,* edited by I. Livingstone, pp. 278-289. Baltimore: Penguin, 1971.

Peters, Lois S., and Herbert I. Fusfeld. 1983. "Current U.S. University/Industry Research Connections." *University-Industry Research Relationships.* National Science Board. Washington, D.C.: Government Printing Office.

Phillips, Robyn S., and Avis C. Vidal. 1983. "The Growth and Restructuring of Metropolitan Economies." *Journal of the American Planning Association* 49:219-306.

Pierce, Neal. 1984. "Congress Curbs Free Lunch IRB's." *Public Administration Times* 7:2.

Pierce, Neal R., and Jerry Hagstrom. 1983. "America's Power Axis." *National Journal* 15:1107-1112.

Pierce, Neal R., Jerry Hagstrom, and Carol Steinbach. 1979. *Economic Development: The Challenge of the 1980s.* Studies in Development Policy, vol. 1. Washington, D.C.: The Council of State Planning Agencies.

Ping, Charles J. 1981. "Bigger Stake for Business in Higher Education." *Harvard Business Review* 59:122-129.

Plosila, Walter H., and David N. Allen. 1985. "Small Business Incubators and Public Policy: Implications for State and Local Development Strategies." *Policy Studies Journal* 13:729-734.

Plosila, Walter H., F. Roger Tellefsen, and William J. Cook. 1984. "Pennsylvania's Advanced Technology Program – The Ben Franklin Partnership." In the Proceedings of the International Congress on Technology and Technology Exchange, October, 1984, Pittsburgh, PA, pp. 247-249.

Pollack, Andrew. 1983. "Engineers: A Dropout Problem for the U.S." *New York Times High Technology Supplement*, March 27, 1983, p. 1.

Posner, Bruce G. 1984. "Report on the States." *Inc.* 6 (October 1984):108-129.

Powell, James D., and Charles F. Bimmerle. 1980. "A Model of Entrepreneurship: Moving Toward Precision and Complexity." *Journal of Small Business Management* 18:33-36.

Premus, Robert. 1982. *Location of High Technology Firms and Regional Economic Development.* U.S. Congress, Joint Economic Committee. Washington, D.C.: Government Printing Office.

Pressman, Jeffrey L., and Aaron Wildavsky. 1973. *Implementation*, 2nd ed. Berkeley, CA: University of California Press.

Price, Robert S. 1981. *ABC's of Industrial Development Bonds.* Philadelphia: Packard Press.

Quinn, James B. 1978. "Strategic Change: 'Logical Incrementalism'." *Sloan Management Review* 20:7-21.

Quinn, James B. 1979. "Technological Innovation, Entrepreneurship and Strategy." *Sloan Management Review* 20:19-30.

Rasmussen, David W., Marc Bendick, and Larry C. Ledebur. 1982. "The Cost Effectiveness of Economic Development Incentives." Washington, D.C.: The Urban Institute.

Rasmussen, Wayne D. 1982. "The Mechanization of Agriculture." *Scientific American* 247:77-89.

Rees, John, and Howard Stafford. 1984. "High-Technology Location and Regional Economic Development: The Theoretical Base." In *Technology, Innovation and Regional Economic Development*, U.S. Congress, Appendix A, pp. 97-107. Washington, D.C.: Office of Technology Assessment.

Reich, Robert B. 1983. *The Next American Frontier*. New York: Times Books.

Reinshuttle, Robert J. 1983, *Economic Development: A Survey of State Activities*. Lexington, KY: The Council of State Governments.

Ressler, Ralph. 1983. "Manpower Training in Site Selection." *Industrial Development* 152:21.

Reynolds, Paul D., and Steven West. 1985. *New Firms in Minnesota: Their Contributions to Employment and Exports, Their Startup Problems and Current Status*. Minneapolis, MN: Center for Urban and Regional Affairs.

Richards, Judith W. 1983. *Fundamentals of Development Finance*. New York: Praeger.

Riche, Richard E., Daniel E. Heckler, and John V. Burgen. 1983. "High Technology Today and Tomorrow: A Small Slice of the Employment Pie." *Monthly Labor Review* 106 (November 1983):51-58.

Richardson, Harry W. 1978. "The State of Regional Economics: A Survey Article." *International Regional Science Review* 3:1-48.

Ripley, Randall, and Grace A. Franklin. 1983. "The Private Sector in Public Employment and Training Programs." *Policy Studies Review* 2:695-714.

Rivchun, Carol. 1985. "Assisting Entrepreneurs: Building Management Skills of Small Business Owners." *Economic Development Commentary* 9:3-6.

Roberts, Edward B. 1969. "Entrepreneurship and Technology." In *Factors in the Transfer of Technology*, edited by W. H. Gruber and D. Marguis, pp. 219-237. Cambridge, MA: MIT Press.

Rogers, Everett M., and Judith K. Larsen. 1984. *Silicon Valley Fever: Growth of High-Technology Culture*. New York: Basic Books.

Roniger, George P. 1983. "Economic Development in a Footloose World." *New York Affairs* 7:20-25.

Rosseau, Denise M. 1979. "Assessment of Technology in Organizations: Open Versus Closed System Approaches." *Academy of Management Review* 4:531-542.

Rothwell, Roy, and Walter Zegveld. 1981. *Industrial Innovation and Public Policy.* Westport, CT: Greenwood Press.

Roy, Rustum, and Deborah Shapley. 1985. *Lost at the Frontier: U.S. Science and Technology Policy Addressed.* Philadelphia, PA: ISI Press.

Rumberger, Russell W. 1984. "High Technology and Job Loss." Palo Alto, CA: Institute for Research on Educational Finance and Governance, School of Education, Stanford University.

Sahal, Devendra. 1981. *Patterns of Technological Innovation.* Reading, MA: Addison-Wesley.

Schmenner, Roger W. 1982. *Making Business Location Decisions.* Englewood Cliffs, NJ: Prentice Hall.

Schmenner, Roger W. 1981. "Location Decisions of Large Firms: Implications for Public Policy." *Economic Development Commentary* 5:3-8.

Schmidt, W. E. 1984. "Rural Southern Towns Find Manufacturing Boom Fading." *New York Times,* March 21, 1984, p. 1.

Schumpeter, Joseph A. 1934. *The Theory of Economic Development.* Cambridge, MA: Harvard University Press.

Schuon, Marshall. 1983. "It's Tune Up Time for Auto Mechanics." *New York Times High Technology Supplement,* March 27, 1983, pp. 51-52.

Schwartz, Garfield. 1983. "Challenges to Pennsylvania: An Overview of Economic Prospects." Washington, D.C.: Garfield Schwartz Associates.

Scott, Allen J. 1982. "Locational Patterns and Dynamics of Industrial Activity in the Modern Metropolis." *Urban Studies* 19:111-142.

Shaffer, Richard A. 1984. "Venture Capital Firms Are Hit by Slower Growth in Financing." *Wall Street Journal,* August 17, 1981, p. 15.

Shapero, Albert. 1982. "Investors and Entrepreneurs: Their Roles in Innovation." From conference proceedings, "The Restructuring Economy: Implications for Smaller Firms," Small Business Research Conference, pp. 494-499, Bentley College, Waltham, MA.

Smilor, Raymond W., and Michael Gill, Jr. 1984. "The New Business Incubator: Linking Talent, Technology, Capital and Know-How." Austin, TX: The Institute for Constructive Capitalism.

Sorkin, Donna L., Nancy B. Ferris, and James Hudak. 1984. *Strategies for Cities and Counties: A Strategic Planning Guide*. Washington, D.C.: Public Technologies, Inc.

Speigelman, Robert G. 1964. "A Study of Industry Location Using Multiple Regression Techniques." Washington, D.C.: Economic Research Service, U.S. Department of Agriculture.

Stafford, Howard A. 1980. *Principles of Industrial Facility Location*. Atlanta: Conway.

Stanford Research Institute International. 1984. *The Employment/Economic Development Connection: New Tools, New Roles, New Directions*. Washington, D.C.: The National Alliance of Business.

Steinnes, Donald N. 1982. "Do 'People Follow Jobs or Do Jobs Follow People?' A Causality Issue in Urban Economics." *Urban Studies* 19:187-192.

Stengel, Geoffrey, and Walter H. Plosila. 1982. *Advanced Technological Policies for the Commonwealth of Pennsylvania*. Harrisburg, PA: Pennsylvania Department of Commerce.

Stoll, Hans R. 1983. "Small Firms Access to Public Equity Financing." In *Small Business Finance*, edited by Paul M. Horvitz and R. Richardson, pp. 173-186. Greenwich, CT: JAI Press.

Temali, Mihaila, and Candace Campbell. 1984, *Business Incubator Profiles: A National Survey*. Minneapolis, MN: Hubert H. Humphrey Institute, University of Minnesota.

Teitz, Michael B., Amy Glasmeier, and Douglas Svensson. 1981. *Small Business and Employment Growth in California*. Working Paper No. 348, Institute of Urban and Regional Development. Berkeley, CA: University of California.

Thirwall, A. P. 1980. "Regional Problems are 'Balance-of-Payments' Problems." *Regional Studies* 14:419-425.

Thompson, Wilbur R. 1965. *A Preface to Urban Economics*. Baltimore, MD: Johns Hopkins University Press.

Thornburg, Dick. 1982. "Partners in the Research Enterprise." National Conference on University-Corporate Relations. *Science and Technology*, December 15, 1982, pp. 1-4.

Thurow, Lester C. 1984. "The Disappearance of the Middle Class." *New York Times*, February 5, 1984, pp. 1-3.

Tornatzky, Louis G., J. D. Eveland, Myles G. Boylan, William A. Hetzner, Elmina C. Johnson, David Roitman, and Janet Schneider. 1983. *The Process of Technological Innovation: Reviewing the Literature.* Washington, D.C.: National Science Foundation.

Tornatzky, Louis G., William A. Hetzner, J. D. Eveland, A. Schwarzkopf, and R. Colton. 1982. *Industry-University Cooperative Research Centers.* Washington, D.C.: National Science Foundation.

U.S., Bureau of the Census. 1984. *Statistical Abstracts of the United States.* Washington, D.C.: Government Printing Office.

U.S., Bureau of the Census. 1983. *Provisional Projections of the Population of States by Age and Sex: 1980 to 2000.* Washington, D.C.: Government Printing Office.

U.S., Bureau of the Census. 1982. *County Business Patterns: Pennsylvania and the United States, 1982.* Washington, D.C.: Government Printing Office.

U.S., Department of Commerce. 1981. *1977 Census of Manufacturing.* Washington, D.C.: Government Printing Office.

U.S., General Accounting Office. 1984. *Estimated Employment Effects of Federal Economic Development Programs.* Washington, D.C.: Government Printing Office.

U.S., General Accounting Office. 1983a. *SBA's 7(a) Loan Guarantee Program: An Assessment of Its Role in the Financial Market.* Washington, D.C.: Government Printing Office.

U.S., General Accounting Office. 1983b. *The Federal Role in Fostering University-Industry Cooperation.* Washington, D.C.: Government Printing Office.

U.S., General Accounting Office. 1982. "Advances in Automation Prompt Concern Over Increased U.S. Unemployment." Washington, D.C.: Government Printing Office.

U.S., General Accounting Office. 1981. "New Strategy Required for Aiding Distressed Steel Industry." *Report to the Congress of the United States.* Washington, D.C.: Government Printing Office.

U.S., General Accounting Office. 1981. "Small Businesses Are More Active as Inventors than as Innovators in the Innovation Process." *Report to the Chairman, Committee on Small Business, United States House of Representatives.* Washington, D.C.: Government Printing Office.

U.S., General Accounting Office. 1980. "More Can Be Done to Ensure That Industrial Parks Create More Jobs." *Report to the Congress of the United States.* Washington, D.C.: Government Printing Office.

U.S., Small Business Administration. 1985. *The State of Small Business: A Report of the President*. Washington, D.C.: Government Printing Office.

U.S., Small Business Administration. 1984. *State Activities in Venture Capital, Early-Stage Financing, and Secondary Markets*. Washington, D.C.: Government Printing Office.

U.S., Small Business Administration. 1982. *The States and Small Business*. Washington, D.C.: Government Printing Office.

U.S., Small Business Administration. 1977. *Task Force Report on Venture and Equity Capital for Small Business*. Washington, D.C.: Government Printing Office.

Urban Institute. 1983. *Directory of Incentives for Business Investment and Development in the United States*. Washington, D.C.: The Urban Institute Press.

Useem, Elizabeth. 1981. "Education and High Technology Industry: The Case of Silicon Valley." Amherst, MA: University of Massachusetts, Department of Sociology.

Vaughan, Roger J., Robert Pollard, and Barbara Dyer. 1985. *The Wealth of States: The Political Economy of State Development*. Washington, D.C.: Council of State Planning Agencies.

Vaughan, Roger J. 1980. "Capital Needs of the Business Sector and the Future Economy of the City." In *Cities and Firms* by Herrington J. Boyce, pp. 109-131. Lexington, MA: Lexington Books.

Vaughan, Roger J. 1983. *Small and New Business Development: An Action Guide for State Governments*. Coalition of Northeast Governors, Policy Research Center.

Vaughan, Roger J., and June A. Sekera. 1983. "Investing in People." *Policy Studies Review* 2:733-749.

Vesper, Karl. 1983. *Entrepreneurship and National Policy*. Walter Heller International Institute for Small Business Policy Papers, sponsored by Carnegie-Mellon Graduate School of Industrial Administration.

Von Hipple, Erick. 1976. "The Dominant Role of Users in the Scientific Instrument Innovation Process." *Research Policy* 5:212-239.

Vozkis, George, and William F. Flueck. 1980. "Small Business Problems and Stages of Development." In *Academy of Management Proceedings*, edited by R. Huseman, pp. 373-378.

Wall Street Journal. 1983, "Robots . . . Computer Retailer – A Chip's Progress." *Wall Street Journal*, September 23, 1983, pp. 1-3.

Wenk, Edward, and Thomas J. Kuehn. 1977. "Interinstitutional Networks in Technological Delivery Systems." *Science and Technology Policy*, edited by Joseph Haberer, pp. 153-165. Lexington, MA: Lexington Books.

Wetzel, William E. 1983. "Angels and Informal Risk Capital." *Sloan Management Review* 24:23-34.

Wharton Applied Research Center. 1979. *Factors Influencing the Economic Development of Pennsylvania*. Philadelphia: University of Pennsylvania.

Wholey, Joseph S. 1983. *Evaluation and Effective Public Management.* Boston, MA: Little, Brown.

Wiewel, Wim, James S. DeBettencourt, and Robert Mier. 1984. "Planners, Technology and Economic Growth." *Journal of the American Planning Association* 50:290-296.

Wingate, Ann, and H. Craig Leroy. 1981. *High Technology Industries and Future Jobs in Connecticut*. Hartford, CT: Business and Industry Association.

Wolman, Harold, and Larry Ledebur. 1984. "Concepts of Public-Private Cooperation." In *Shaping the Local Economy: Current Perspectives on Economic Development*, edited by Cheryl Farr, pp. 25-32. Washington, D.C.: International City Management Association.

Zock, Richard. 1983. "Small Business Access to Capital Markets Through Pension Funds." In *Small Business Finance*, edited by Paul M. Horitz and R. Richardson Pettet, pp. 137-154. Greenwich, CT: JAI Press.

Zupnick, Jan W., and Stacy Katz. 1981. "Profiles in New Enterprise and Economic Development Initiatives." In *Expanding the Opportunity to Produce: Revitalizing the American Economy Through New Enterprise Development*, edited by Robert Friedman and William Schweke, pp. 494-520. Washington, D.C.: The Corporation for Enterprise Development.

Index

About the Authors

David N. Allen (Ph.D., Indiana University) is an Assistant Professor of Public Administration at the Institute of Public Administration, The Pennsylvania State University, University Park, PA. He has written journal articles, reports, and papers on the topics of technological and entrepreneurial development. Support for his research has been provided by the U.S. Department of Commerce, Economic Development Administration and cooperative research endeavors with Pennsylvania's Department of Commerce and MILRITE Council. He is a principal in TEC-NEC, a firm that provides consulting services to government, university, and private sector clients. He is the Secretary of the National Business Incubation Association and serves on the Editorial Board of *The Economic Development Quarterly*. His primary teaching responsibilities are graduate classes in research methodology and applied statistics, public management, and economic development.

Victor Levine (Ph.D., Columbia University) is a visiting professor of Education at the University of Zimbabwe. Previously he was an Assistant Professor of Education at The Pennsylvania State University. He has published primarily in the areas of educational policy and job-related public policy. He has served as staff economist for the U.S. Department of Agriculture, Food and Nutrition Service, Office of Policy, Planning and Evaluation; Research Associate at the Human Resources Center, The Wharton School; and Research Economist at the Educational Testing Service. He teaches courses on the economics of education and economic-development policy.